W9-BPL-093

AHMADINEJAD

Kasra Naji, who moved to London shortly after completing this book, has worked as a journalist in Tehran for many years. He has reported for CNN, the BBC, the *Financial Times*, the *Guardian*, the *Los Angeles Times*, *The Economist* and ABC.

KASRA NAJI

AHMADINEJAD

THE SECRET HISTORY OF
IRAN'S RADICAL LEADER

University of California Press

Berkeley   Los Angeles

955.061
Naj
1/10 g

University of California Press, one of the most distinguished university presses in the United States, enriches lives around the world by advancing scholarship in the humanities, social sciences, and natural sciences. Its activities are supported by the UC Press Foundation and by philanthropic contributions from individuals and institutions. For more information, visit www.ucpress.edu.

University of California Press
Berkeley and Los Angeles, California

© 2008 by Kasra Naji

First published by I.B.Tauris & Co. Ltd in the United Kingdom

Library of Congress Cataloging-in-Publication Data

Naji, Kasra, 1952–.
  Ahmadinejad : the secret history of Iran's radical leader / Kasra Naji.
    p.   cm.
  Includes bibliographical references and index.
  ISBN 978-0-520-25663-7 (cloth : alk. paper)
  1. Ahmadinejad, Mahmoud. 2. Presidents—Iran—Biography. 3. Iran—Politics and government—21st century. I. Title.

DS318.84.A36N35   2008
955.06'1092—dc22   2007044590

Typeset in Goudy Old Style by A. & D. Worthington, Newmarket, Suffolk
Manufactured in the United Kingdom

17 16 15 14 13 12 11 10 09 08
10 9 8 7 6 5 4 3 2 1

CONTENTS

FOREWORD

The election of Mahmoud Ahmadinejad to the presidency of the Islamic Republic of Iran in 2005 catapulted a hitherto obscure radical politician on to the international stage. Since then, he has rarely been off it. Exploiting the surprise which his dramatic election victory engendered among observers of Iranian politics, Ahmadinejad has shown tremendous energy in maintaining the momentum of his dramatis persona. Nearly a century ago, the American banker Morgan Shuster, similarly bewildered by the political activity he had encountered, commented that Iranian politics could perhaps best be described as an *opera bouffe*, a comic opera in which players enter and exit the stage with alarming speed and often change their political clothes in the process. Whether one agrees with Shuster's observation or not, there can be little doubt that the image of a vast political theatre is one that commends itself well to the Iranian environment. And Iran's politicians, for all their seriousness, have long been renowned for showmanship. Dr Mohammad Mosaddeq regularly invited both awe and ridicule for his emotional outbursts, and Mahmoud Ahmadinejad has likewise been known for shedding the occasional tear at moments of high 'national' emotion. But if foreign observers tended to try and deconstruct Mosaddeq, and perhaps pierce the myth he had developed among his supporters and constituents, in the case of Ahmadinejad the reverse is arguably the case. In stark contrast to his illustrious predecessor – with whom Ahmadinejad has sought to compare himself – the international community has not only bought into the image Iran's diminutive if energetic president has invented for himself, but has in many ways surpassed it. In the two years since his election, foreign representations of Ahmadinejad have tended to portray him as a villain of extraordinary proportions and existential consequences, complete with forked tail and horns: the personification of evil. Unfortunately for someone of Ahmadinejad's worldview, such a characterization from the 'Great Satan' is not only to be expected but is to be welcomed as a sign that he must be doing something right!

In this excellent biography, Kasra Naji seeks to restore some balance to the narrative of Ahmadinejad's ascent to power. Naji comes to his subject as an Iranian who has witnessed the process from within. Exaggeration, from wherever it originates, be it the pen of foreign opponents seeking a mighty foe or the propagandists in the Iranian presidential office, is swiftly laid to rest as the author lays bare Ahmadinejad's life and ideas. In this task he has been ably assisted by access to a range of sources, both documentary and personal, through interviews with key players, which have hitherto been ignored or indeed in many cases suppressed, to shed light on Ahmadinejad's early political career and, significantly, his much touted war record. What emerges is a man of firm and distinct conviction, reinforced by the ridicule his ideas have attracted from many of his compatriots, and further convinced, as a consequence, that his political emergence is a direct result of providential favour. Drawing strength from the contempt which surrounded him, Ahmadinejad's 2005 election, flawed as it was, provided him with the last laugh, which he has been enjoying at the expense of his political rivals ever since. Time will tell whether Ahmadinejad will fall victim to the image that he has created for himself, but early indications are that he has too easily succumbed to the intoxication of power. A recent book by a supporter describes him as the 'miracle of the third millennium'. Iranians are apt to note (with a wry smile) that such a characterization is open to a wide variety of interpretations.

Ali M. Ansari
University of St Andrews

ACKNOWLEDGEMENTS

This book would not have been possible without the government of the Islamic Republic of Iran. Had I not been denied the right to work for so long, I would never have had the time to embark on such a long project – even being refused a press card to work as a journalist can have a silver lining.

I must also thank my wife, Frances Harrison, whose idea it was to write a biography of President Ahmadinejad. Her advice throughout was invaluable.

But I dedicate the book to my son, Cyrus Naji. He showed great patience for a six-year-old in tolerating my long periods in front of the computer writing this book, always showing a sense of humour about it. At one point he suggested the book's title should be 'Ahmadinejad – or why my hair went white'!

I would like to thank all those in Iran who talked to me on and off the record at a time when speaking to international journalists was not exactly encouraged by the authorities. Many cannot be named for their own well being but will surely recognize their contributions. Like so many journalists and politicians in Iran, they thought the story should be told so that the outside world would understand the complexities of their country. I salute the courage of my journalist colleagues in Iran who continue to tell the story there under great pressure, and thank them all for their hospitality, kindness and cooperation.

Thanks go also to my agent in New York, Diana Finch, and my editor in London, Abigail Fielding-Smith, for their advice, and to Iraj Bagherzadeh of I.B.Tauris for taking on such a project and for his many suggestions that improved the book immensely.

Kasra Naji
November 2007

INTRODUCTION

DID YOU HEAR THE ONE ABOUT AHMADINEJAD?

Soon after mayor of Tehran Mahmoud Ahmadinejad was elected president in June 2005, anxiety replaced election fever among many Iranians. They wondered what to make of the scruffy, austere, Islamic fundamentalist, the son of a blacksmith, who had confounded experts and non-experts alike to win a landslide victory.

To let off steam, it seemed many had new jokes to tell about the man whom they feared would ban short-sleeved shirts for men, force women to wear the all-enveloping *chador*, segregate men and women in all public areas, keep on and on about Islamic martyrs, and generally make life more difficult for Iranians by imposing an even stricter interpretation of Islam than that which already prevailed.

Some joked that they had stopped shaving and washing to fit in better with the new Iran. One joke had the authorities tracing the source of an outbreak of cholera to Ahmadinejad washing his underwear in Tehran's biggest water reservoir. Another said that Ahmadinejad parted his hair to segregate the male and female lice. Almost all the jokes were hugely unsympathetic to the small man whom many regarded as an uncultured peasant.

One particular joke pointed to fears for the future. It involved him and his election rival, the stalwart of the Islamic Revolution and twice former president, Ali Akbar Hashemi Rafsanjani. 'Did you hear about Rafsanjani's choice of name for the new northern expressway?' it asked. 'Martyr Ahmadinejad!' came the reply. Everyone knew that whatever happened with Ahmadinejad, Iran was in for a period of upheaval.

Insiders recognized that Ahmadinejad's victory heralded a sea-change in the politics of Iran. Ahmadinejad represented the successful power grab of militarists in the Islamic regime, made up of a loose alliance of powerful sections of the country's ideological army, the Revolutionary Guard, the most hardline section of the clergymen and a crop of Islamic neo-conservatives – the younger generation in the right-wing Islamist camp. Ahmadinejad's victory brought to power an entirely new set of people who until then had been kept at bay on the margins of power because of their extreme views. After 27 years of post-revolutionary upheaval in Iran, the Revolution had been wrested from the grip of the old guard who wanted to put it behind them and build a successful Islamic nation.

The rise to power of the militarists did not bode well for the future of Iran, which was already locked in a serious dispute with the international community over its nuclear and missile programmes. The new rulers believed that Iran had to be militarily powerful and that the survival of the Revolution at home depended on it spreading its tentacles abroad. They believed that power rightly belonged to those who had sacrificed the most in defending the country in the eight-year war with Iraq in the 1980s. They were of the opinion that the reforms of the previous eight years under President Khatami amounted to a serious deviation that should never be allowed to happen again – the reforms had to be rolled back, and democracy was a Western import alien to their vision of Islam.

Half-way into Ahmadinejad's four-year term of office, Iran found itself on the brink of a war with the US over its meddling in Iraq, under increasing international sanctions because of its nuclear programme, and in turmoil at home as changes swept the country. Ahmadinejad and the militarists around him spread their ideology while hardening their grip on power.

When I met him in the summer of 2007, to let him know that I was writing this book, the president seemed elated at the thought. Any publicity was good publicity as far as he was concerned. I found him still basking in the attention he was getting both at home and abroad. He was awestruck by his own ascent to power. Two years earlier he would have found it difficult to believe that he would be the president. Like a fish out of water, Ahmadinejad displayed a restlessness that seemed to flow from a constant rush of adrenaline. His aides have said that he works 20 hours a day. Beneath his calm and jocular exterior, Ahmadinejad is obviously seething with emotional intensity. On several occasions he has quietly shed tears in public – for example, when a singer on the stage in front of him sang about Iran reaching the summit of nuclear expertise. His erratic policy making – dramatic cuts in interest rates out of the blue, the surprise sacking of the entire management of the country's biggest state insurance company, his announcement and later withdrawal of an order to change banking hours, his unfathomable refusal to allow winter-time adjustment of the clocks – all these showed symptoms of a reckless temperament.

When I met him he had just ended a press conference with a group of journalists from Islamic countries. Some of the journalists had praised him for speaking out against 'the bullying' US and Western countries and against 'the unjust' system of the United Nations, dominated by the five big powers. Ahmadinejad saw the praises of the journalists from the poorer countries as a confirmation, in his mind, that he was on the right path to lead a revolution of the world under-class. They had stirred his emotions. And being deeply religious, he believed he was doing it all for the satisfaction of God, for the greater good. His heart was in the right place – he wanted to help the poor and the underprivileged.

He already knew of my book project. He had heard about it from his spokesman, Gholam Hussein Elham, whom I had approached several weeks earlier. When I handed Elham a letter of request for an interview with the president, he immediately read it and then looked into the distance with a knowing smile on his face, as if this confirmed the popularity of his master. But when Ahmadinejad promised me that he would consider the request for an interview to fill in the gaps in my book, I did not hold my breath. In spite of a good deal of research, there are periods in Ahmadinejad's past that remain mysteriously unaccounted for.

I had seen him in action from close quarters several times in press conferences and other presidential functions. When in April 2007 he had just seen off 15 British sailors after their two-week captivity in Iran, he told me earnestly that the sailors had enjoyed their stay. And when I exuded deep scepticism, he insisted, with a slight laugh, that for the sailors their time in Iran was a welcome break from their arduous daily routine of patrolling the waters off southern Iraq. His manner was relaxed and good natured – ready to share a joke. At official functions and in his frequent speeches, he has shown a great deal of self-confidence and a total absence of doubt, even though others might have raised their eyebrows in astonishment. In Persian, he is articulate, with an easygoing simple language that is part of the daily discourse of the average Iranian. He is at complete ease when speaking to ordinary people in remote parts of the country, but radiates an awkward reserve when speaking to others about whose loyalty he is uncertain. It is also clear that he makes up for his lack of experience in affairs of government or international relations with a blind belief in Islam as an encyclopaedic religion that has an answer for every question.

The story of how Ahmadinejad, a relatively unknown figure, came to be the public face of the new regime is, however, less clear. Where he has come from is a mystery even to many in the corridors of power in Tehran. He seemed to have been thrust into leadership by one of those quirks of history that from time to time throw up unlikely leaders on unsuspecting nations. Ahmadinejad has certainly come a long way from the sun-baked dusty village on the edge of the salt desert in central Iran.

CHAPTER 1

FROM THE DESERT
TO THE PALACE

I was born to a poor family in a remote village at a time when affluence meant dignity, and living in a city was the height of sophistication.[1]

The son of a blacksmith

There were scenes of chaos as a devastated President Ahmadinejad wearing a black shirt – the sign of mourning – took off his shoes and socks and stepped into the dusty grave.

The noisy crowd of about 200 that had gathered around the freshly dug grave seemed restless under the baking sun and wanted to push their way closer to the front. The crowd included family members, officials, security men and mourners. Women wearing black *chadors*, the all-enveloping veil worn by devout women in Iran, stood to one side on the edge of the grave. Some were weeping. The stampede had kicked up a small cloud of dust in section 48 of Tehran's biggest cemetery, known as Beshesht-e-Zahara, on the southern edge of the sprawling city.

As the crowd watched, Ahmadinejad, with his feet wide apart on the edges of the narrow grave, rolled up his sleeves. He was handed the light, bony body of his father, wrapped in a white shroud, and slowly lowered it into the grave. He was mindful of the Islamic tradition that the dead should be buried with their heads facing Mecca. His father had died the previous day at dawn in a Tehran hospital after a long coronary illness. He was 82.

1

For Ahmadinejad the day had begun at the township on the north-eastern edge of the capital where his father lived. The Martyr Mahalati Township had been built for the personnel of the Revolutionary Guard and their families. The men among the relatives and neighbours had carried the coffin of his father wrapped in Iran's tricolour flag a short distance from the mosque to a junction down the road where the body was to be put on an ambulance for transfer to the cemetery. Hundreds of friends and supporters had joined the short procession which had developed into a chaotic scramble as people and photographers jostled to get closer to Ahmadinejad and get a glimpse of him in mourning. Ahmadinejad had tried to impose some order amid the chaos, giving instructions to his officials and bodyguards, but to no avail. In the chaos, the Chief Justice, Ayatollah Hashemi Shahrudi, said an impromptu prayer over the coffin that had been momentarily placed on the street. A white ambulance belonging to the cemetery then took the coffin to the burial ground where the body was washed according to Muslim tradition and wrapped in a white shroud ready for burial.

Inside the grave, standing over his father's body, Ahmadinejad said a few words of prayer in the cool loneliness of the grave, and opened the shroud around the face of the body, as Islamic tradition requires. When he finally climbed out, he was covered in dust. With bloodshot eyes and fighting to hold back his emotions, he grabbed hold of his youngest son, Ali Reza, and gave him a passionate hug as both burst into tears. Next to them, sobbing uncontrollably, was Ahmadinejad's mother, known as Syedeh Khanum, meaning literally a lady descendent of the Prophet. As they watched, a few men, including one of his loyal security guards, shovelled earth into the grave.

A large framed colour photograph of Ahmad Ahmadinejad was placed on the top of his grave. It showed a simple, frail, skinny old man with white hair and a white inch-long beard, wearing a pair of old-fashioned black-rimmed glasses, an oversized, white bottom-up shirt and a grey jacket with wide lapels – the fashion that was popular in Iran in the 1950s. His had been a life of ups and downs, but he had remained deeply religious and a die-hard supporter of the Islamic Revolution.

Standing on the edge of the grave and still covered in dust, Ahmadinejad gathered himself together and took hold of the microphone to thank those who had come to his father's burial. He then paid his own tribute. 'His life was devoted to the Imam [Khomeini] and the Velayat [the concept of the Supreme Leadership, currently embodied in the person of Ayatollah Ali Khamenei]. This selfless, religious and revolutionary father was proud of being just a simple servant of Imam Hussein,' he said emotionally, referring to the grandson of the Prophet Mohammad whom Shiites revere as their Third Imam.

Many Iranians are obsessed with poetry, and Ahmadinejad's father was no exception, although he could barely read and write. 'Although in the old days he had not stayed at school beyond the fifth grade, he had a knack and love for poetry. He had written verses and poems for the Imam and the Leader, and had read out some of them in the presence of the Leader,' Ahmadinejad said, his voice occasionally breaking, painting a profile of a simple man deeply devoted to the Islamic Revolution.

State television had broadcast images of the burial ceremony in its news bulletins. The pictures showed Ahmadinejad getting his hands and clothes dirty doing what many ordinary middle-aged men had done before him – burying his father. They struck a deep chord with the Iranian public. For Ahmadinejad, the burial of his father was a moment to reflect on the previous 50 years and on his father's role in his upbringing as a God-fearing man. Many in the crowd were relatives from the village of Aradan in central Iran where he was born.

On the edge of the salt desert

The small sleepy town of Aradan on the northern edge of the salt desert of central Iran has not grown much in the half-century since Ahmadinejad was born there on 28 October 1956, the fourth of seven children. 'Life was difficult for our family and my birth made it more difficult,' Ahmadinejad wrote many years later in his presidential weblog.

Aradan is two hours' drive southeast of Tehran and not far from the foot of large barren hills that fence the desert from the north. Large billboard photographs of 338 martyrs of the district adorn the lamp posts on both sides of the road that leads to the town. Aradan, like many other towns and villages in Iran, gave up many of its sons to the war with Iraq in the 1980s.

The centrepiece of the town is a short stretch of the old bazaar that has survived the developers' attention. Lined with shops, the bazaar is covered by a brick-and-mud arched ceiling that provides shelter from the intense heat of the long summers and the frequent sandstorms common to deserts. The bazaar opens on to a square that locals say used to be a caravanserai for merchants travelling by camel or mule between Tehran and Mashhad. Today the square provides one of the few green spaces in the town for the elderly to sit in and chat.

The local mosque is an unremarkable converted two-storey house. Covered with black banners of different sizes and shapes pronouncing the edicts of the leaders of the Revolution, it also serves as the symbol of the central government's authority.

Ahmadinejad's first childhood home, a rented, modest two-storey mud-and-brick house, is today a derelict building in the back alleys of Aradan. Neighbours use it today to rear their chickens.

Not far from the bazaar, Haji Ali Agha Sabaghian, a cousin of Ahmadinejad, owns an old-fashioned grocery shop that does not look as if it has changed much since 1957, when Ahmadinejad's father moved his family to Tehran. A short, slender old man with a slight white beard and black sheepskin hat, Ali Agha says that Ahmadinejad's family were deeply religious, and known in the neighbourhood for their Koran-reading classes. 'Although he [Ahmadinejad's father] could not read and write well, he knew the Koran very well. Every year during the month of Ramadhan he would run Koran-reading classes.' Ali Agha's shop is lined with sacks of rice, sugar and lentils and large cans of cooking oil. Old folk come and sit on the sacks and chat as he serves customers. He says that since the Ahmadinejads left Aradan, they have only returned for short visits on big family occasions like births, deaths and weddings. Ahmadinejad's father had a grocery very much like Ali Agha's, before he changed profession and opened a barber's shop. 'They left when Mahmoud was only a baby,' Ali Agha says, handing over a bag of sugar across the counter to an elderly woman customer.[2]

Ahmadinejad's surname used to be Sabaghian – meaning 'dye-masters', the men that dyed woollen threads for hand-woven carpets and kelims. But according to Ali Agha, the president's father changed the family name to Ahmadinejad – meaning 'of the Ahmadi race', or better 'of the Ahmadi ilk'. Ahmadi, coming from Ahmad, is a popular Muslim name that derives from Hamd – 'the praise of God'. At the time the registry office did not allow a totally free hand in choosing one's surname, and it is likely that they suggested the name, which appealed to Ahmad's religious fervour. 'Many people, would change their names to something that would not betray their village background. I know people who, when they left for the city, changed their name from Kaffash [cobbler] to Pezeshkpour [of the family of medical practitioners],' said another distant relation.[3]

Moving away from the poverty of village life was common in those days, when land largely belonged to feudal landlords and villagers were tenants living mostly in squalor, lacking basic amenities and sometimes days away from the nearest hospital. Work outside farming was simply not available.

'Although my father had never fallen for the material attractions of the city life, the pressures of life forced him to leave for Tehran just a year after I was born,' says Ahmadinejad in his weblog, giving the impression that he left because of the ill effects of the Shah's land reforms. In fact the family moved to Tehran several years before that.[4]

In the aftermath of World War II, many villagers migrated to towns and cities in search of work and a better life, just as Iran was recovering from the impact of the war and experiencing a very modest economic upturn. The young Shah, having replaced his autocratic father, Reza Shah, whom the British had ousted in 1941, was still consolidating his grip on power. Oil prices were modest and Iran remained extremely poor. Religion had stayed out of politics for the most part, and even the deeply religious young Ahmad had no quarrel with the secular Shah. 'Politics those days was the forte of those who could afford a decent meal,' said a relative of Ahmadinejad, adding that Ahmad was too poor to bother with politics.[5]

In his blog, Ahmadinejad writes proudly of his poor village background, fostering his image as a common working man: 'I was born to a poor family in a remote village at a time when affluence meant dignity, and living in a city was the height of sophistication.'

Today, although the feudal landowners have gone, the migrations have not stopped. Few young people stay in Aradan. Unemployment is a major problem, and the young in search of work leave for Tehran.

Those who have stayed in Aradan work on small farms which still have access to water. Desertification has eroded farmland, as a result of which Aradan has stopped producing its particularly sweet watermelons. Drinking water is available only in cans and bottles.

Almost all the town voted for Ahmadinejad when he was pitted against Rafsanjani in the presidential election run-off in 2005. They saw him as one of their own. And when he won, they strung the main street with colourful lights and celebrated late into the night. They were looking forward to a change in fortune for their little town. Poverty and unemployment would end. Massoumeh Sabaghian, a cousin of Ahmadinejad, captured the mood of the town. 'We are looking forward to him establishing justice, saving the poor and cutting off the hands of thieves,' she said, speaking figuratively about ending corruption. 'If anyone can bring justice, it's Ahmadinejad, who has close links to the Revolutionary Guard and the Basij.'[6]

Well into his presidency there is widespread frustration with Ahmadinejad among the constituency he is supposed to represent. Even in his birthplace, there are no longer posters of him in shops. 'What has he done for us?' asks a man in the tailor's shop. 'He promised to bring the oil money to our dinner table.' He pauses. 'Where is it? What happened to his promises?' He is full of anger about Ahmadinejad's foreign policy too. 'Whatever he does is all wrong. His tongue is too sharp. We have to be more measured. He cannot go around saying we are a train with no brakes,' he says, referring to Ahmadinejad's description of Iran's quest for nuclear capability as a runaway train with no brakes and no reverse gear.[7]

In Aradan they are still waiting for piped drinking water. The hospital, whose building was donated by a local philanthropist, remains an empty shell. The townspeople have petitioned the president through his brother, Davoud, who is a senior official in his government, to help build the hospital, but he could not or would not help. He said the government had other priorities throughout the country, and building a hospital in Aradan with a population of fewer than 10,000 did not make economic sense.

The rapid rise in the price of basic foodstuffs in 2006 and 2007 has also turned many people away from Ahmadinejad. Back at the grocery shop, Ali Agha puts on a brave face on the lack of any improvements since Ahmadinejad came to power. 'We don't want anything for ourselves in Aradan. There are many people in the country who are a lot worse off than we are,' he says. But reflecting on the president's attitude to planning, he remembers the day Ahmadinejad's father, Ahmad, came to see him. 'Ahmad wanted to go on pilgrimage to Mecca one year and could not decide whether he should do it, since he did not have much money and could not afford it. But one day he came in and said that he had decided he would take the plunge, come what may,' says Ali Agha. 'He was prone to taking risks, like his son, believing in divine help.'

Ahmad's biggest risk was to abandon his barber's shop in Aradan and move to Tehran – jobless and penniless with wife and four children, including baby Mahmoud, in tow. He moved to Narmak, an undeveloped area on the eastern outskirts of Tehran. Apart from a dirt road that was the main street, a small number of scattered houses and shops and lots of stray dogs, Narmak was then essentially a patch of desert.

East Tehran

A frail old man, Hassan Rabi'ee, stands outside what used to be his shop and points across the road to the pleasant boulevard lined with trees and well-to-do shops. 'All this used to be desert when we moved here,' he says with a tinge of nostalgia.

Together with Ahmadinejad's father and another relative, he had moved to Narmak from Aradan in about 1958 in search of work and a better life. 'There was no work and no money in Aradan.' Together they started in an iron-works shop – the same shop that was now being refurbished to become a coffee shop. 'I was a blacksmith, as was my father and my father's father. But Ahmadinejad's father did not know the first thing about this profession; he had a grocery shop in Aradan,' says Rabi'ee, fiddling with the worry beads in his hands.[8] Nonetheless they set out to make iron doors and window frames for the new houses that were being rapidly built in the area.

Around the time the government brought in French town planners to draw up a blueprint for a pleasant district that would combine short roads, affordable two-storey houses and many small squares which would double up as small parks.

Narmak today is an up-and-coming, modestly middle-class

neighbourhood in eastern Tehran with wide tree-lined main avenues boasting modern-looking shops selling fashionable clothes and other goods to the relatively well-to-do residents. The trees have grown and the small parks every 500 yards or so are a pleasant and welcome escape from the otherwise traffic-choked concrete jungle that is Tehran. The small parks also provide quiet places where young couples can sit on benches and hold hands, particularly in the summer evenings, away from the dreaded moral police patrol cars that occasionally drive up and down the main streets. On the high street, there are well-turned-out fashionable young women in dark glasses and tight clothes, showing the fringe of their hair under their colourful scarves. They display a far less strict attitude to Islam than the authorities would like to see.

The scene today is a world away from the Narmak to which the Ahmadinejad family moved in 1958. At that time Ahmad and the whole family lived in one room on the top floor of the house which they shared with Ahmad's sister and her family, who lived down-stairs.

Hard work as a blacksmith paid off and enabled Ahmadinejad's father to save enough money 15 years later to buy a modest two-storey brick house not far from the shop. By then Narmak was already a developing neighbourhood on the eastern edge of the city.

Ahmadinejad's schooling began in the Narmak of the early 1960s, around the same time as tension between the state and the Shiite clergymen in the holy city of Qom began to surface. It was the political events of this period that would eventually lead in 1979 to the Islamic Revolution, which a generation later would propel Ahmadinejad into the presidency of his country.

In 1963, Ayatollah Ruhollah Khomeini, a relatively obscure religious scholar based in Qom, led a revolt in the city against the Shah's modernization drive under the so-called White Revolution. Intended to reorder Iran's social and economic structure, the White Revolution included land reform, a plan that sought to buy land from feudal landlords and distribute it in small plots to peasants. This aroused hostility among the clergy because landlords were paying hefty taxes to the religious establishment in Qom, and Qom was against any disruption of this arrangement. Another measure of the White Revolution that the Qom clergymen opposed was the plan to enfranchise women.

With the scene set for confrontation between the Shah's regime in Tehran and the clergy in Qom, Khomeini emerged as the militant voice of resistance to the state.

January 1963 was a date that proved fateful in Iran's history, and marked the beginning of the struggle of the religious establishment against the Shah – something that 16 years later led to the Islamic Revolution. In that month the army entered Qom and forcefully quelled anti-Shah riots. But far from calming Khomeini, the army's intervention in Qom fired him up to preach ever more challenging sermons. The position was exacerbated by the government's decision to grant legal immunity to the growing number of American advisors in Iran for any crime committed on Iranian soil. This brought Khomeini's blood to the boil. He saw this as a 'capitulation' to the US and stepped up his attacks. In June 1963, on the occasion of Ashura, the holiest day in the Shiite calendar, he delivered a strongly worded speech in a seminary in Qom. He warned the Shah that he would be forced to flee the country if he continued with his policies. Two days later, army officers arrested him. This led to riots in Tehran and a number of big cities across the country, which were put down by the army. Hundreds of demonstrators, and by some accounts thousands, were killed in the ensuing clashes. Martial law was imposed in several cities, and calm only returned after several days. Khomeini himself was bundled out of the country, first briefly to Turkey. Eventually his exile was established in the holy city of Najaf in neighbouring Iraq.

It was against this dramatic backdrop that Mahmoud began his education. His first school, named after Iran's thirteenth-century classic poet Sa'adi, was a government-run primary on the main road, a few hundred yards from his father's shop. His fellow school children remember a small quiet boy with a dark complexion. His first teacher was a young woman named Najmeh Gholipour, whom Ahmadinejad remembered many years later when as president he met with a group of 'model teachers'. When she walked on to the podium to receive her plaque of recognition, an emotional Ahmadinejad, against all his doctrinaire Islamic upbringing, took the hand of the elderly teacher, bowed and kissed it. The event had been choreographed in advance and the lady had been made to wear long black gloves to ensure no direct contact between her and the president's kiss. But his ever watchful colleagues on the extreme wing of his supporters were quick to pounce. They considered the kiss 'a painful act' and warned that 'this government, it is worth mentioning, came to power with Islamic slogans and promises with the votes of the religious and fundamentalists, and today it is acting against all it stood for'.[9]

As Ahmad's fortunes improved, his son Mahmoud moved from the government primary school to a private high school in Narmak called Daneshmand (the Scientist), which was regarded as the best private school in the area, with fees to match. Already Mahmoud knew how to read selected parts of the Koran in Arabic with ease, and he was keen to show off his skill to other children. Friends and relatives remember Mahmoud constantly playing football in the street. His father used to wake him up at dawn every day for early morning prayers, and then he would work with Mahmoud on his Koran reading, according to childhood friends. As Ahmadinejad himself later put in his blog: 'To keep us away from the so-called modern atmosphere of those days under the Shah that had robbed the country of its identity, my father introduced us to the mosque and the Manbar [an Islamic pulpit – i.e. to the world of preachers and sermons].'

'He was a studious boy; he would use the couple of hours after dawn prayer to study, and then he would leave for school. The rest of the day was devoted to playing football and playing with the rest of us,' says Saeed Hadian, a businessman and childhood friend of Ahmadinejad.[10] During his high-school years, Ahmadinejad was apolitical but deeply steeped in his father's religious teachings. In his six years at the high school, he came top of his class, according to Saeed Hadian.

But Ahmadinejad was also keen to have fun. In his later years at high school, he was particularly proud of a white racing bicycle with turned-down handlebars that his father had bought him. Along with his friends he would hang around the girls' school down the road to see the girls coming out and be seen by them. He and his friends would make day trips to the countryside outside Tehran, where they would go mountain climbing, or just walking and picnicking. Occasionally they would go to see graphic Western films. In the 1970s, even the devout would allow themselves some pleasures – they would say their prayers five times a day, according to Islamic requirements, and then in the evening go out and drink beer or vodka, says one school friend of Ahmadinejad.[11] There is, however, no evidence that Ahmadinejad himself ever indulged in alcohol.

Photographs of Ahmadinejad during one of these trips show a young man caught up in the times, sporting slightly long hair and sideburns and wearing tight flared jeans, though his clothes do betray a poorer background than those of his closest friends.

The Revolution

Ahmadinejad's political days began when he entered university in 1975 – four years before the Revolution. He had passed the university entrance examination with distinction, coming 132nd out of some 200,000 students vying for about 10,000 university places. While his performance at the exams meant that he could go to the top universities like Tehran or Aryamehr (later named Sharif), he chose to read development engineering at a polytechnic in Narmak that later became the University of Elm-o-Sanat – the University of Science and Technology. His friends say he chose Elm-o-Sanat because it was situated in Narmak.

These were times of increasing unrest in universities, where underground left-wing and Islamic opposition to the Shah was spreading. Thanks to the tripling of oil prices in 1973, Iran could now afford to put poverty behind it. The Shah had embarked on an ambitious plan to develop Iran into a modern industrial country. But as development projects surged ahead, political development lagged behind. No opposition was tolerated. Political oppression stood in contrast to the rapidly developing economy. The Shah had gone on the record as saying that those who did not like his rule could leave the country. Social permissiveness – allowing alcoholic drinks to be sold openly in shops, women to wear miniskirts and cinemas to show graphic Western films – had become the bane of the clergymen in Qom and other cities.

At university, Ahmadinejad was introduced to the writings and lectures of Dr Ali Shariati, a left-wing Islamic philosopher who had laid down the intellectual ground for the young university students of a religious background who wanted change. Shariati had been arrested and thrown into jail for activities that the Shah's secret service, SAVAK, deemed subversive. But his books and writings quietly and secretly changed hands among students who were eager to read anything that would teach them about a fair and equitable society but which also respected Muslim traditions. Ahmadinejad was no exception.

'Together [with Ahmadinejad] we drove to Amol [five hours' drive to the north of Tehran on the shores of the Caspian Sea] one day with a great deal of secrecy to borrow a copy of Shariati's book, *Islamology*. I had built a secret hiding place in the dashboard,' said Saeed Hadian. *Islamology* was one of the most important works of Shariati, in which he had expounded on the idea of Islam as a political ideology rather than just a religion.

At home, gradually and very cautiously, Ahmadinejad turned the Koran-reading classes into a little more than just an occasion for religious education. He would invite friends and university students to his home to listen to a mullah whom he would invite from Qom, three hours' drive south of Tehran to discuss the Koran and politics. At the same time, Ayatollah Khomeini's theses laying out the contours of an Islamic republic ruled by a top religious leader, or 'faghih', were secretly changing hands and being photocopied.

Ahmadinejad was also active in the Narmak Jam'e mosque where every Ashura, he would help organize neighbourhood street processions. These were part of the Shiite tradition to mourn the 'martyrdom' of Imam Hussein, the Third Imam of the Shiites. In these processions on and around Ashura, local men would walk through the neighbourhood a few times a day, either beating their chests or flagellating themselves with chains, to the rhythm of a sombre drum beat. During this period, Ahmadinejad would also help organize the food at the mosque for the needy and others – another Ashura ritual. Ahmadinejad was still living at his father's house, sharing a room upstairs with his two brothers. His four sisters shared a separate room downstairs.

By his third year at university and on the eve of the Revolution, Ahmadinejad was a supporter of Ayatollah Khomeini, whose speeches in exile he would help print clandestinely and distribute with the help of a few of his trusted friends. His brothers were now involved in Islamic politics too.

The Shah's secret service had marked the family as one of potential dissidents. They had been suspected of printing opposition flyers and tracts at home. So when the police came to their door one day before the Revolution, the brothers fled, hiding in a relative's house. They later drove to the provincial town of Gorgan and stayed with other family members. Disappointed, the police set fire to the entrance of their house before they left. Ahmadinejad only returned home when the dust had settled.

'I remember just before the Revolution, we used to receive one-page newsletters which we would then print out in large numbers on a makeshift printing device, and distribute in Narmak,' said an old friend of Ahmadinejad, adding that the news-sheets were often summaries of the latest Khomeini speeches or edicts.

Back at home, Mahmoud's father changed his occupation. Now he put everything he had into a grocery shop in the same area of Tehran. What precipitated the change was the constant bickering between his wife and her brother's wife that made continued partnership at the blacksmith's shop untenable, said one relative.[12]

Meanwhile the Revolution disrupted Ahmadinejad's studies at the university. There were daily demonstrations in almost all cities and towns, with demonstrators calling for the Shah's overthrow. The year 1978 represented a relentless cycle of escalation in which demonstrations, violence and deaths were followed by more demonstrations, violence and deaths.

In the early months of the troubles, neighbourhoods such as Narmak were generally quiet. In Tehran, men and women who were engaged in active opposition would go to the central areas of the city near the University of Tehran campus and the surrounding streets to demonstrate. Running battles with soldiers who were armed with powerful Belgian-made G3 rifles had become a daily occurrence. The Shah now was reluctant to give the army the order to shoot to kill, fearing unrest. But this made the demonstrators even more daring in their running battles with the army. Unrest spread even further, engulfing even remote towns and villages. An epic revolution was under way.

Ayatollah Khomeini, who by now had moved from his exile in Najaf to Neauphle-le-Château, a village not far from Paris where he held court, orchestrated the whole process from exile, promising freedom and an elected government. When the workers in the oil industry went on strike and stopped oil exports, the Shah's regime suffered a major blow. Western countries dependent on Iranian oil urged the Shah to come to an arrangement with the opposition to allow oil exports to flow again. This further weakened the Shah, who by now had lost his ability to make decisions. Ayatollah Khomeini was adamant that there would be no negotiations. He wanted the Shah to go. And when the Shah decided to go into exile, supposedly for a short while to calm the situation, he knew he would not return.

The Shah's chosen prime minister, Shapour Bakhtiar, was no match for the revolutionary tide that was sweeping the country. On 11 February 1979, after a tumultuous few days in which demonstrators ransacked several army bases and took away arms, the monarchy finally fell. The demonstrators took charge of all the centres of power and declared the victory of the Revolution. Ayatollah Khomeini, who had come back ten days earlier from exile, quickly appointed a government. Many of the top civilian and military leaders of the Shah's regime were quickly executed, to send out the message that there was to be no going back. An Islamic republic was proclaimed, replacing more than 2,500 years of monarchy in Iran.

In Narmak the Ahmadinejad brothers used sand bags to erect a trench on the corner of the square near their house, and set up a neighbourhood watch. They did as many had done in all neighbourhoods throughout Tehran and other cities. The police had ceased to exist, and local youths armed with rifles stolen from army barracks took over neighbourhood policing. The youths who manned the checkpoints in the days after the Revolution were later organized under the network of Revolutionary Komitehs (Committees).

Iran had suddenly found itself in a new world. The atmosphere in the country was electric. Universities were now the hotbed of the Revolution. Leftists and Muslim groups were putting forward ideas for the future that many felt were liberating. They were vying for support from among the young by holding daily rallies inside campuses, which were open to all. In 1979, socialist and Marxist ideology still had strong appeal for university students, and supporters of Ayatollah Khomeini found themselves at a disadvantage. Clashes occurred frequently inside and outside universities and in other parts of Tehran and other cities. Many young people were now armed with automatic rifles that had been ransacked from military bases. Thus occasionally shooting would break out between different factions. By this time, Ayatollah Khomeini and senior clergymen around him were seriously concerned that a lifetime's chance for Shiite clergymen to take over the reins of power and implement Khomeini's idea of 'the rule of clergyman' might be lost forever. They also feared that Marxists and other left-wing groups and parties, of which there were many, might push Islam to a position more isolated than that which prevailed under the Shah. Iran had entered a phase of its revolution akin to a civil war. Violence took centre stage. The mosques became centres for mobilizing religious forces, which took over neighbourhood policing Komitehs by professing to be only loyal to Ayatollah Khomeini, who was still vastly popular and respected.

Soon after the Revolution and the transfer of power to the new regime Ahmadinejad, according to himself, set up the Islamic Society of Students at his university. Former students dispute this and say that the Islamic Society existed in an underground form well before the Revolution. In reality, Ahmadinejad at this time was inclined towards the shadowy Islamic sect of Hojatieh, which was devoted to revering Shia Islam's missing Twelfth Imam, the Mahdi, whom they believed would return one day to establish peace and justice.[13]

Ahmadinejad's involvement with the Hojatieh created an intellectual dilemma for him. As revolutionary fervour swept the country, student politics was thrown to the forefront of change in Iran. But the Hojatieh believed that Islamic activists had no business getting involved in politics and in establishing an Islamic society. It was the prerogative of the Mahdi to create an Islamic society when he chose to return. So for a student like Ahmadinejad, caught up in the excitement of the Revolution, to be inhibited by Hojatieh teaching must have proved difficult. He rationalized his devotion to the Hojatieh and his commitment to an Islamic society by following the path of Khomeini who, despite his marked involvement in politics, was greatly revered as representing purist Islam. So when in 1983 Khomeini, long involved in politics himself, banned the sect as a deviant aberration – four years after the Revolution – the problem for Ahmadinejad was solved. In fact such was the power of Khomeini that, on hearing his edict, the Hojatieh ended its activities and declared itself dissolved, although rumours continued to suggest that some members were quietly active.

Ahmadinejad gradually emerged as a leading student activist supporting the pro-Khomeini Islamists at his university. The general political atmosphere in his university was right wing – meaning in this context doctrinally traditionalist and committed to leadership by clerics – whereas in other universities left-wing politics was dominant. The pro-Khomeini students at Ahmadinejad's university began publishing a newsletter called *Jigh-o-Daad* ('Scream and Shout') whose main characteristic was its strident anti-left tone and content. Classes had been all but abandoned, with students holding rallies in different parts of the university debating the latest issues. 'From first thing in the morning when you entered the university, there were tons of leaflets and tracts raining down on you. Small groups would gather here and there debating politics. There were rallies and speeches everywhere,' said Ahmadinejad, describing the atmosphere at the time at his university.[14]

Islamic societies had been formed in almost all universities and some government offices as core organizations of pro-Khomeini activists. Their main job was to organize supporters and counter the growing influence of the leftist groups, particularly the Marxist Fedayeen-e-Khalq and the Muslim Mujahedin-e-Khalq Organization, according to Ahmadinejad. 'They [the Islamists] had to defend the totality of the new regime and respond to its needs,' he said years before becoming president. 'For this, the students of the Islamic Society had to defend the theoretical foundations of the Revolution and the regime against Marxists and leftist and liberal Muslims. They also had to defend the integrity and the security of the regime by getting involved in institutions like the Revolutionary Guard and Reconstruction Jihad.'

Reconstruction Jihad was a movement that had been inspired by Mao's revolution in China. It started soon after the Iranian Revolution as a vehicle to take the Islamic revolutionary ideology to the rural areas. The intention was to help farmers with resources, financing and training, to eradicate poverty in the villages and in the process to bind the essentially conservative peasant community into the new order. In fact the pro-Khomeini students and others who enthusiastically headed off into remote villages in groups to lend a hand to the bewildered farmers had no idea about farming. But Iran was spared the disastrous reality of the Chinese experiment mainly because the movement was limited in scope – it simply did not attract enough volunteers.

But for the young Ahmadinejad, joining the Revolutionary Guard was an obligation. The Guard had been created as a new force parallel to the army, whose job was to avert any danger of a coup by the army, which was still in the hands of many officers whose loyalty to the Revolution was far from certain.

Back in Tehran and other big cities, Islamists felt they had to strengthen their positions at universities. In the clerical inner circle of the leaders of the Revolution, Ayatollah Mohammad Beheshti was arguably the most important figure. He was responsible for laying down the foundations for Khomeini supporters to seize exclusive power and turn what was until then a popular revolution into an Islamic revolution. He suggested the creation of a national network of Islamist students at all universities up and down the country, to coordinate and step up their activities. Soon Ahmadinejad found his way into the leadership of the Organization for Consolidating Unity (OCU), the national organization that drew on student activists whose efforts until then had been confined to their own universities. 'Ideological defence of the Revolution and organizing the Muslim forces in universities and leading them to have a presence in different arenas needed a more coherent organization than the separate and scattered Islamic societies,' was the way Ahmadinejad was to put it.

The central council of the OCU met with Ayatollah Khomeini to report on their activities and receive instructions. This was Ahmadinejad's opportunity to meet the man whom he had begun to revere, not only as a religious leader but also as his political mentor.

Ayatollah Khomeini nominated Ayatollah Khamenei and Rafsanjani as possible future interlocutors with the students. The students chose Khamenei, who had not yet attained the rank of ayatollah. It was in their dozen or so meetings while Ahmadinejad was in the OCU that Iran's future top two leaders first got to know each other.

For Ahmadinejad these were exciting times. From a humble background, he now suddenly found himself embroiled in a full-scale revolution, in touch with senior levels of Khomeini's inner circle and with an important job to perform. But Marxist and left-wing Muslim groups remained a major threat to the consolidation of Khomeini's grip on power. They had sharpened their campaign, targeting imperialism abroad and reactionaries at home. And by reactionaries they meant Khomeini and his supporters as well as the religious establishment in Qom. To counter the threat of being outflanked by the left, some of Ahmadinejad's fellow students at the central council of the OCU devised a way that would put Islamic students in a no less anti-imperialist light than the left, and would undermine the left's claim to be the sole opponents of imperialism. This, they hoped, would convey to the masses that Khomeini and his followers were progressive. Their idea was to occupy the US embassy for a few hours, or a few days at most.

The plan was introduced by some members at the central council of the OCU, but was opposed by Ahmadinejad and another right-wing member of the council. In the event, the others decided secretly to go ahead anyway, without further consulting Ahmadinejad and the other member. They did this not under the banner of OCU but under the name of 'the Student Followers of the Imam's Line'. The architects of the action invited some of the left-leaning pro-Khomeini student leaders from a number of universities to join them.

Although Ahmadinejad was kept out of the loop, he would not escape its consequences.

The Den of Spies

On 29 June 2005, only five days after his election as president, Ahmadinejad learned a lesson in the power of the Western media when he suddenly found himself accused of being a terrorist. A grainy black-and-white photograph surfaced abroad that showed a man resembling a young Ahmadinejad standing next to a blindfolded and handcuffed American hostage in the grounds of the US embassy in Tehran. A major media storm began in the West. A number of former hostages came forward to identify the president-elect of Iran as one of the hostage takers.

Still a novice in using the Western media to his benefit - some-thing he mastered later - Ahmadinejad meekly denied his involve-ment. And the CIA, which examined the photograph and its own records of the hostage taking in Tehran, reported that it was unlikely that Ahmadinejad was involved. A US official close to the investiga-tion of the photograph said that analysts had found 'serious discrep-ancies' between the figure depicted in the 1979 photograph and more recent images of the Iranian president. These included differences in facial structure and features, the official said.

The episode also served to highlight one of several unaccounted-for periods in the life of the young Islamic hardliner who had become president. Many in Iran and aboard were looking into his official biography, which did not say what he did during the hostage crisis, an important event in post-revolutionary Iran involving university students like him.

The hostage crisis had begun on the cloudy morning of 4 November 1979 when pro-Khomeini student leaders and their comrades joined an anti-American march on the redbrick US embassy building in central Tehran, which they called 'the Den of Spies'. Anti-American demonstrations were almost a daily occurrence at the time and the young student revolutionaries could easily mingle among the demonstrators who paid no heed to the tendency of the then revolutionary government, made up largely of technocrats and moderates, to find an accommodation with America. At the embassy the students suddenly broke off from the main body of the demonstrators and scaled the gate of the building in a state of frenzy, shouting 'Death to America'.

Soon the Student Followers of the Imam's Line were inside, in control of the embassy compound and more than 60 diplomats, staff and US Marine guards. It was the beginning of a hostage drama that dragged on for 444 days. It opened a new chapter in post-revolutionary Iran that Ayatollah Khomeini later described as the 'Second Revolution'. It triggered decades of estrangement and hostility, with the US cutting off relations and imposing crippling economic sanctions on Iran that continue to this day.

The occupation of the embassy and the taking of its diplomats and staff was not an expression of the genuine anti-American feelings of the students but an act of political expediency to undermine the claims of the left to be the banner holders of the struggle against imperialism. Ostensibly the students wanted to force the US to return the Shah who, wandering from one country to another in exile, had just entered the US for cancer treatment at a hospital in New York.

With Ayatollah Khomeini announcing his support for the action a few hours later, the moderate government of Prime Minister Mehdi Bazargan had no choice but to resign. It was replaced with a government of hardline Islamists. Many Iranians rallied behind the students' action and in support of Ayatollah Khomeini, strengthening his grip on power almost immediately. The resignation of Bazargan signalled the elimination of moderate, Western-oriented, or at least Western-acquiescent, figures from Iran's turbulent revolutionary politics. Outside the country, Iran took on the reputation of a pariah state, with the US and other Western countries taking hostile positions. While a number of women and black American hostages were released in the early stages of the drama, the remaining 52 hostages were kept as the on-again-off-again negotiations continued for their release. They were eventually freed after 444 days in captivity, but not before US president Jimmy Carter had attempted a humiliatingly disastrous rescue bid that never even reached Tehran and eventually saw the ignominious end of his presidency.

In June 2005, only days after Ahmadinejad's election as president, the exiled opposition, the Mujahedin-e-Khalq Organization (the People's Mujahedin), MKO,[15] posted on the Internet a photograph of two hostage takers, identifying one as Ahmadinejad. The photo showed two bearded men on either side of a blindfolded and handcuffed American hostage, thought to be Jerry Mielle, in the grounds of the US embassy compound in central Tehran. It turned out that an Associated Press photographer had taken the picture on 9 November 1979. The MKO said that the student Organization for Consolidating Unity had carried out the seizure of the embassy. 'Former OCU officials involved in the takeover of the US embassy said Ahmadinejad was in charge of security during the occupation,' said the statement.[16]

In the same statement the MKO went on to accuse Ahmadinejad of being an executioner at Tehran's notorious Evin Prison in the first months after the Revolution. 'Defectors from the clerical regime's security forces have revealed that Ahmadinejad led the firing squads that carried out many of the executions. He personally fired coup de grâce shots at the heads of prisoners after their execution and became known as *tir khalas zan*, the one who fires the final bullet in the head.'

For many years, levelling unsubstantiated accusations of this kind against the Islamic regime in Tehran had become a staple of Iranian exile groups. Misinformation had become an important tool for them to demonize the Islamic regime in Iran and help build support in the West for regime change. But the MKO had a certain credibility. Three years earlier, it had revealed that Iran had clandestinely built nuclear facilities at two different spots in central Iran. The revelations had been found to be true by independent sources. Now it was making another incredible claim and many in the media took it seriously.

The story was given further credence when the veteran BBC journalist John Simpson said that he remembered having interviewed the man in the photograph in the US embassy grounds in Tehran after the hostage crisis was over. The Associated Press photograph seemed to have jolted his memory, he said, and the man was indeed none other than Ahmadinejad.

With the photograph flashing over network television up and down the US, six former hostages came forward to confirm that they were certain that the man who had been elected Iran's president had been one of their tormentors. The photograph had jolted their memories too. Now when they saw Ahmadinejad on television or on the pages of their newspapers, they were sure he was the man. Former hostage Donald Sharer of Bedford, Indiana, told NBC television that he had been reading a state newspaper recently and saw a recent picture of the president-elect. 'All of a sudden, up pops the devil, right in front of me,' he said. Mr Sharer said he remembered the man he now identified as Ahmadinejad coming into Evin Prison to berate prisoners as pigs and dogs, making Sharer fear for his life. 'You tend not to forget people that put your life in danger,' he said. 'All I can say is I remember the fellow being very cruel-like, stern, a very narrow, beady-eyed character.'

Then another former hostage, William Daugherty, added to the furore when he told CNN that he saw Ahmadinejad's picture in the *Washington Post* and recognized it immediately. He was referring to the Associated Press photograph that by now had become the universal face of Ahmadinejad. Daugherty said the face was one he would never forget. 'When your country is being humiliated and being embarrassed, the individuals that do that really stick in your mind,' he said. 'You don't forget people who do things like that to you and your family and your country.' He continued: 'I remember so much his hatred of Americans. It just emanated from every pore of his body.' Daugherty said he saw Ahmadinejad eight to ten times in the first 19 days of captivity, before the hostages were separated.

The comments continued apace. The *Washington Times* quoted another former hostage, Charles Scott, as reacting much like Sharer and Daugherty. 'He was one of the top two or three leaders,' Scott, a retired army colonel in Jonesboro, Georgia, told the newspaper. 'The new president of Iran is a terrorist,' he said. 'There's no doubt from the way the guy moves, it's the same guy.' Kevin Hermening of Mosinee, Wisconsin, a financial planner, who was a 20-year-old Marine guard when the embassy was seized, said that Ahmadinejad was one of his interrogators the day of the takeover, and a 'higher-rank security official'. David Roeder, 66, the former deputy Air Force attaché at the embassy, said he remembered Ahmadinejad working in a supervisory role in one-third or more of the 44 interrogations he underwent. 'The interrogator and the interpreter always deferred to him, so he was clearly in charge,' he said.

Paul M. Needham, a former hostage and now a professor at the National Defense University, who lives in northern Virginia, said he did not recognize Ahmadinejad. 'I remember four specific individuals,' Mr Needham said. 'He is not one of them.' But those who did remember him are convinced. 'If they say that yes, they recognize him,' Needham said, 'there's about a 99.9 per cent probability that it is right.'

Another source that testified to Ahmadinejad's involvement in hostage taking was Mark Bowden, the author of the highly praised book *The Guests of the Ayatollah* – a detailed account of the hostage taking. He said, 'Without any doubt Ahmadinejad was one of the central players in the group that seized the embassy and held hostages.' [17]

In Tehran, meanwhile, several former hostage takers, many of whom are now reformist politicians deeply opposed to Ahmadinejad, disputed the accounts of the former hostages. Mohammad-Reza Khatami, the younger brother of the former president, Mohammad Khatami, who was also involved in the hostage taking, said he never saw Ahmadinejad at the embassy. 'I don't think he was part of it,' he said. 'I cannot remember him at all.' [18] Mohsen Mirdamadi, one of the hostage takers' leaders, told the BBC that the new president had not been there. Another reformist politician, Saeed Hajjarian, also denied the man in the picture was Ahmadinejad. Hajjarian, who was a senior intelligence officer and 'a walking memory', told the Associated Press: 'I'm opposed to Ahmadinejad's policies and thinking but he was not involved in the hostage drama.' He identified the man on the left of the hostage in the photograph as one Taqi Mohammadi, who later 'turned into a dissident and committed suicide in jail', he said. Mohammadi was arrested on charges of involvement in the 1981 bombing in Tehran that killed the country's president and prime minister at the height of the revolutionary upheavals. But one other report identified the man looking like Ahmadinejad as a man known by his surname, Ranjbaran. According to this report, Ranjbaran was later found to be an agent of the opposition MKO and was executed.[19] The man on the right of the hostage, reports agreed, was Jafar Zaker, who was killed in the Iran–Iraq War.

Abbas Abdi, a leader in the embassy operation, said Ahmadinejad was not involved, though when the embassy was occupied he wanted to be. 'He was a student at a different university,' Mr Abdi said, 'and we kept the plan secret among our own members whom we trusted. He called after the embassy was captured and wanted to join us, but we refused to let him come to the embassy or become a member of our group.'[20]

A few of Ahmadinejad's aides joined the chorus of denial. 'Those who spread these rumours have such a low IQ that they are comparing the photo with the current status of Dr Ahmadinejad,' Abolhassan Faqih, a senior Ahmadinejad campaign manager, told the Iranian student news agency ISNA. 'But if you look at a picture of Dr Ahmadinejad during his student years, you will see he did not even have a beard then.'

Most of those who did take part in the hostage taking did not hide their role, and some had even gone on to hold top government posts on the strength of their involvement. 'The seizure of "the Den of Spies" was recognized by the late Imam [Khomeini] as a cultural revolution, and therefore if Dr Ahmadinejad had been there it would not have been regarded as something bad [i.e. that he would have wanted to deny],' said Faqih.

Ahmadinejad himself did not make a statement, although when faced with a *New York Times* reporter outside his home, two days after the storm broke, he denied he was involved in the hostage taking. 'This is not true. This is just a rumour,' he said through the window of his car as he was driven away.

Nearly ten weeks later when he attended the General Assembly of the United Nations in New York, Ahmadinejad gave an interview to CNN's Christiane Amanpour in which he again denied his involvement in the hostage taking.

> Ahmadinejad: You see, I heard the same news after I was elected and, you know, frankly, I laughed at it. Either the memory had been erased and replaced anew. I don't know how they had reached such a conclusion. Back then I didn't have the beard I do now.
> Amanpour: So you were not involved?
> Ahmadinejad: No, it's not like that. I was not involved.[21]

Several sources, including the former security official Hajjarian, said Ahmadinejad believed then that the Soviet embassy, not the US embassy, should be taken. 'Ahmadinejad believed that the great Satan is the Soviet Union and that America was the smaller Satan,' Hajjarian said.

The other student leader who, along with Ahmadinejad, had opposed the takeover of the US embassy in the initial planning meeting of the student leaders was a young man known as Mohammad Ali Seyyedinejad.[22] Years later in a newspaper interview Seyyedinejad said that he and Ahmadinejad had opposed the plan on the grounds that Ayatollah Khomeini had banned lawless actions against targets that were deemed to be connected to the previous regime. 'A little earlier, the Imam had said all attacks against the offices and assets of capitalists, like hotels, had to stop. And if there had to be an expropriation [of an asset], it had to be done according to the law,' he said, almost a year before Ahmadinejad had taken over as president. 'In that meeting we told others that these kinds of actions were being carried out by groups who were in opposition to the government, and we should not act in a way that would confuse us with the opposition groups.'[23]

As for whether Ahmadinejad was in favour of storming the Soviet embassy, as had been suggested, Seyyedinejad said, 'You must have in mind that Ahmadinejad was at the Elm-o-Sanat University which was generally very right-wing and anti-left ... and anti Soviet.'

The situation is further complicated by the fact that Ahmadinejad's friends and comrades in the Islamic vigilante organization, Ansar-e-Hezbollah, proudly listed his involvement in the hostage-taking drama in their biography of him. 'Ahmadinejad had also been among the members of the Student Followers of the Imam's Line in conquering the Den of Spies [the US embassy in Tehran] as well as a founder of the Organization for Consolidating Unity [OCU],' their newspaper said.[24]

The biography was published in their weekly newspaper, *Yalesarat*, soon after Ahmadinejad was selected as the mayor of Tehran in 2003. And if as mayor in 2003 he was happy to be named as one of the student hostage takers, why would he deny his role in 2005 when he had been elected president?

There remains another possibility. Ahmadinejad could have joined the hostage-taking operation only after Ayatollah Khomeini endorsed it, and even then as a guard or later as an interrogator, rather than a student leader. He may have been a security official with access to both the embassy and Evin Prison where some of the hostages were held for a time. Abbas Abdi's account that Ahmadinejad called in after the capture of the embassy, wanting to become involved, fits in with this. The event was the biggest since the Revolution itself and it had turned into a developing drama involving pro-Khomeini university students – a drama that would go on for 15 months. It would be entirely implausible if the young Ahmadinejad, with newly developed connections to the inner circle of Ayatollah Khomeini's trusted clergymen, did not feel tempted to become involved in this drama.

Whatever the truth of the situation, the last word so far seems to be from an unlikely source: the CIA. The agency, after analysing the photograph claiming to depict the new Iranian president at the US embassy, declared definitively that the bearded figure was not Mahmoud Ahmadinejad.

As a final point, it is also clear that any links with hostage taking would pose a liability for him as president. Indeed many Iranians, including a number of the hostage takers, today view the episode as a monumental mistake that turned Iran into a pariah state in the eyes of the West and stunted its development for decades to come.

The Cultural Revolution

The sound of gunfire around Tehran University died down in the early hours of the morning of 22 April 1980 after more than 15 hours. The lights had been switched off inside the campus and in the streets surrounding it. In the dark, a deadly silence hung as hundreds of people on street corners around the campus watched in darkness the armed Revolutionary Guard and members of neighbourhood Komitehs holding their fire to see whether there were incoming shots.

The storming of Tehran University, the most prestigious in Iran, had started in the early afternoon of the previous day. Pro-Khomeini forces arrived in mid-afternoon to throw out the leftist students. The students were affiliated to the Marxist Fedayeen-e-Khalq Organization and the leftist Islamic group the Mujahedin-e-Khalq Organization. The Revolutionary Council, which was acting as the country's top decision-making body with emergency legislative powers and which was by now firmly in the hands of the Khomeini loyalists, had given the students three days to vacate their offices inside the campus or else they would be forced out 'by the people'. The students had ignored the ultimatum.

In the midst of revolutionary fervour in Iran, the occupation of the US embassy in Tehran had given the Islamists more credibility as an anti-imperialist force. But it was not enough to cement Khomeini's grip on power. More had to be done to take universities from leftist forces. Closing them all down seemed the best option for the Revolutionary Council, as the universities were at the heart of the strong secular influence in the country, forming the biggest barrier against the spread of Islam as government ideology.

At around 2 o'clock in the morning it was all over. There was no more resistance from inside the university. Throughout the 15 hours of shootings and explosions, ambulances had ferried the dead and injured to nearby hospitals. Outside these hospitals, worried relatives searched for their missing loved ones. They anxiously read the handwritten sheets attached to the hospital entrances listing the names of those who had been admitted.

Dawn brought with it the beginning of what was described as the Cultural Revolution – a term that had been quietly taken from Mao's communist revolution in China. Dozens had been killed to pave the way for the authorities to close down all universities and higher-education institutions throughout the country indefinitely, to deprive the left forces of their biggest and most effective power base. The irony that this Cultural Revolution was intended to destroy the very sort of leftists that were behind China's Cultural Revolution was lost on the Iranian regime's wordsmiths.

The universities remained closed for 30 months, during which a massive purge began of professors and students who were found to be at odds with Islamic teachings as interpreted by the pro-Khomeini revolutionaries. Ahmadinejad was in his element. He and other students at the Islamic Society were in daily clashes with left-wing students on their campus. He and his friends succeeded in closing down their own university, Elm-o-Sanat, which became the first in Tehran to shut down. In the next few days, more than 30 universities and higher-education institutions were closed down after violent clashes.

Ayatollah Khomeini supported the violent closure of the universities, declaring, 'We are not afraid of military attacks, we are afraid of colonial universities.' Earlier he had talked about the need for 'a fundamental revolution in universities throughout the country', and the need for the 'purging of professors aligned with East and West', and 'transforming the universities into calm environments for establishing higher Islamic education'.

But the violent onslaught against universities split even the pro-Khomeini students at the Organization for Consolidating Unity. Again, Ahmadinejad, who favoured the action, stood out against other student leaders who opposed it. Those who opposed the action included the leaders of the Student Followers of the Imam's Line, who were now holding 52 American diplomats hostage. They believed what had been taking place under the banner of Cultural Revolution would undermine the unity that had been forged among pro-Khomeini students by the occupation of the embassy.

Many years later, Ahmadinejad would speak about his frame of mind in those days as an ardent follower of Ayatollah Khomeini, whom he now described as 'the exalted Imam'. He spoke of the conditions at universities as he saw it, in which, he said, Marxist and leftist groups were openly in opposition to the government.

> And their supporters in universities theorized and spread their message. When these groups began their armed struggle against the government, their supporters in universities held daily rallies, made speeches and issued statements in support. They even set up tents to recruit volunteers to strengthen separatist movements in the country. They would hold memorials for the victims of separatist troubles. They would brand anyone who stood up against the government 'a people's hero.' Some groups had gradually taken arms into universities. These centres of learning had been turned into war rooms against the regime and the revolution. University education had all but stopped.[25]

During the period in which the universities remained closed, the Cultural Revolution Council purged thousands of university professors deemed to be leftist and liberal in their thinking. They were branded either as counter-revolutionaries or lackeys of the Shah's regime. Many students were also purged, while new university applicants had to pass through a strict screening process. This entailed revolutionary inspectors examining their loyalty to the Islamic Revolution by visiting their homes and neighbours to check on them and their parents. Selection committees were formed to carry out the task of screening professors and students. This task was later extended to all schools, high schools and even government departments. The clerical establishment in the holy city of Qom was enlisted to re-design humanity courses and exclude parts that were deemed fundamentally opposed to Islam.

Ahmadinejad found a job working on one of these all-powerful 'selection' committees (or 'Gozinesh' in Persian).[26] The committee would screen candidates according to their belief in fundamentalist Islam and the Islamic Revolution. Ahmadinejad was keen to get rid of communists, other leftists and secularists wherever possible. New employees, professors and students had to know the most minute teachings of Shia Islam, such as which foot should be put forward first on entering a toilet, and why.

'Ahmadinejad was of the opinion that all our problems had emanated from the universities and the Western thoughts that were taught in them,' said Mohammad Reza Jalaipour, a professor of social sciences and himself a former Islamic revolutionary. He had come to know Ahmadinejad over the years. 'He had developed an encyclopaedic view of Islam that believed Islam is an all-embracing and comprehensive religion that has the answer to every problem. He was a right-wing Islamist who believed that the West was the source of all moral corruption, and that for our administrative needs we have only to resort to Islamologists, and true Islamologists were clergymen.'[27]

As the US hostage drama dragged on inside the embassy building, and outside the debates raged on, something else happened in Ahmadinejad's life. He fell in love. He had chanced upon a fellow student at his university who he thought was the right person. A mechanical engineering student, she was even more religious than Ahmadinejad. Ahmadinejad's school friends said they were surprised when at one evening party she insisted that women eat dinner in a separate room.[28]

Always in black *chador*, Ms Farahani later attended the Teachers' Training University and found a job as a laboratory teacher at two girls' high schools in Narmak. She later went on to teach at Kharazmi University. 'She was simply dressed and very down to earth,' said a woman teacher who worked with her at a girls' high school in Narmak. 'She was a real Hezbollahi,' said the colleague, using a term that is used to describe the hardline Islamists.[29] She and Ahmadinejad married in 1980 in a simple wedding at the university. They would eventually have three children together: a daughter and two sons. The elder son, Mehdi, followed in his father's footsteps to become a development engineer. The younger son, Ali Reza, was still at high school a year into Ahmadinejad's presidency. The daughter, who, like her mother, became a mechanical engineer, is now married.

War days

In the summer of 1980, barely a year after the Revolution, Iran was in chaos. A civil war atmosphere had descended on much of the country. The closure of universities had heightened tensions. Leftist groups were in open warfare with the government. Armed clashes were common in the capital and elsewhere in the country. Those captured by pro-government forces were summarily executed. The afternoon newspapers regularly reported the names of dozens of young people who had been executed earlier in the day. By the end of the year, more than 6,000 would be executed. Ethnic minorities such as Arabs, Kurds and Turkmens were up in arms against the central government. Khomeini supporters feared a pro-Shah coup d'état. Fifty-two American diplomats and staff of the embassy were still in captivity in Iran – something that had thoroughly undermined sympathy for Iran in the world outside. In neighbouring Iraq, sensing a collapsing order in Iran, President Saddam Hussein dreamed about defeating the Persians, whom he saw as the nemesis of the Arabs.

With the closure of the universities behind him, Ayatollah Khomeini's attention focused on the ethnic unrest in western Iran. More than 4 million Sunni Kurds, suspicious of Shiite clergymen in Tehran, were fighting an ethnic war for autonomy. Their main slogan was 'Democracy for Iran; Autonomy for Kurdistan'. Almost a year earlier Khomeini had declared a jihad against Kurds who had taken up arms to achieve their aims. Iran's Kurds were spread across the three western provinces of Kermanshah, Kurdistan and West Azerbaijan. There had been incessant fighting in the Kurdish region between the Khomeini forces and Kurdish groups, including the main left-of-centre Kurdistan Democratic Party of Iran and the Marxist group Komeleh.

Like many young pro-Khomeinis, Ahmadinejad saw the Kurds as posing the greatest danger to the Islamic regime. He felt that they were about to break up the country and declare independence. Kurdistan had become a major base against the Islamic Republic. The government needed young devoted men to go to Kurdistan along with the Revolutionary Guard and put down the rebellion and prevent the break-up of the country.

The recently appointed governor of West Azerbaijan province was, like Ahmadinejad, a graduate of Elm-o-Sanat University. He needed men he could trust to help bring various towns and villages in Kurdistan under control. He had appointed Mojtaba Hashemi Samareh, another graduate of Elm-o-Sanat, as his political affairs deputy. Samareh had brought to Kurdistan a dozen or so of his fellow Elm-o-Sanat students. These included Ahmadinejad. And the move was the beginning of nearly 30 years of close friendship between the two who spent years together in Kurdistan. Samareh went on to become President Ahmadinejad's closest advisor and a deputy Interior Minister in his cabinet in charge of elections.

Back in 1980, on the invitation of Samareh, Ahmadinejad left his job on the Selection Committee in east Tehran to take up the post of District Governor of Maku, a West Azerbaijan district with a couple of small towns, several large villages and a total population of about 70,000. Situated at the bottom of a valley high up in a mountainous area not far from Iran's border with Turkey and Armenia, Maku has a population that is divided evenly between Turkic-speaking Shiite Azeris and Sunni Kurds. Before the Revolution, it also had a sizable Christian Armenian population.

In Maku, the 24-year-old Ahmadinejad had been thrown in at the deep end. The Persian-speaking young man's task was to forge an alliance with the Turkic-speaking Shiites, reassure the Kurdish-speaking Sunnis and work closely with the muscular Revolutionary Guard and security forces to drive armed Kurdish groups out of the district. It was not an easy brief in the charged political atmosphere of the time and in the midst of an armed autonomy campaign by the Kurds. He would go to Shiite mosques to tell the Shiites that the government was with them, and he would tell the suspicious Kurds in Sunni mosques that the Islamic Revolution belonged to all Iranians. But also he had to help organize the fight against armed forces of the Kurdistan Democratic Party, who, except for a few daylight hours, controlled the roads leading to the town. Intelligence was a big part of the operation, which would entail identifying sympathizers of the KDP in the area. The challenge for Ahmadinejad was to prevent a situation in which the Azeri population would feel threatened enough by armed Kurdish groups to leave town for a safer refuge. The Shiite population did not wholly trust Ahmadinejad either, as he was seen as a Fars (a Persian-speaker) out to subjugate Azeris. Life as an agent of the central government involved exposure to a good deal of danger.

As Ahmadinejad tried to settle into the job in September 1980, Saddam Hussein's forces launched a surprise assault and invaded Iran along the southern part of their joint border. Facing no organized resistance, Iraqi forces marched deep into Iran, occupying much of the province of Khuzestan where much of the population was ethnically of Arab descent. Iraqi forces began their push after an air raid on Tehran airport on 21 September 1980. Saddam Hussein had hoped that the ethnic Arab population in Khuzestan would rejoice at joining Iraq. That did not materialize, nor did any of his other aspirations. He had hoped that in the chaos of post-revolutionary Iran, he could extract concessions from Tehran and take on the role of regional policeman – a role that had been left vacant with the fall of the Shah. He also knew that beating the Persians in a war would enhance his position in the Arab world. Little did he know that the war between the two countries would last eight years – longer than anyone could have imagined. The war would leave hundreds of thousands of young men dead on both sides of the border and even more maimed and injured. And it would transform the fortunes of the two countries.

In the Kurdish region where Ahmadinejad was based, the start of the Iran-Iraq War offered Kurdish Peshmergas an opportunity to hit back at central government forces in the region. Now with Iran and Iraq at war, many Kurds on both sides of the northern sector of the border saw an enormous opportunity to realize dreams of a Greater Kurdistan, bringing Iranian and Iraqi Kurds and eventually those in southern Turkey and eastern Syria together into one independent state. But in the rest of the country, the invasion of Iran united many Iranians behind Khomeini and the government forces, which responded with a major mobilization.

Ahmadinejad was now part of a political/military campaign guarding against the spread of the Iran–Iraq War to the northern sector of the joint border of the two countries, while fighting an internal Kurdish rebellion in hostile terrain. In the summer of 1979 when Khomeini had ordered the establishment of the Islamic Revolutionary Guards Corps, Ahmadinejad had made contacts with the early founders of the Guard. These contacts came in useful in Maku where the Guard saw him as one of their own. Later, when the Guard established their Hamzeh Headquarters in Oroumieh, he was in close, almost daily, contacts with them to coordinate activities. At Hamzeh HQ, Ahmadinejad made friends with a fellow hardliner, Ismail Ahmadi Moghadam, who later moved up through the ranks to become the commander of the Basij and, later, the country's police chief. The Basij had been formed in the early days of the war with Iraq to mobilize volunteers for the front, as well as to keep an eye on the restive population. Ahmadi Moghadam was to become responsible for mobilizing the Basij and the Revolutionary Guard in support of Ahmadinejad during the 2005 presidential elections. It did not surprise many when President Ahmadinejad later appointed him as his Special Advisor.

The Kurdish rebellion was all but put down by 1983, although not before thousands of government forces and Kurds were killed or executed in the campaign. Leaders of the main political organizations of the Kurds fled across the border to Iraq, where they lived in exile as the Iran-Iraq War raged on.

Meanwhile Ahmadinejad continued in administrative work at least for another few years. After two years in Maku, he moved to the slightly bigger district of Khoy in West Azerbaijan, with a population of about 100,000, as the governor of the district, divided, like Maku, between Shiite Azeris and Sunni Kurds.

In Khoy, suspicious Kurds saw him as an agent of the Shiites with his hands covered in the blood of Kurds. They never trusted him.

And since most of the Iran–Iraq fighting was taking place in southern sectors of the Iran–Iraq border areas, in the northern sector, where Ahmadinejad was based, his job was ostensibly to guard against any moves across the border by the Iraqis. But his principal attention was devoted to putting down the Kurdish rebellion. In the process he made few friends among the Kurds, who saw his efficient and single-minded commitment to central government policy as ruthless and brutal.

After two years in Khoy, Ahmadinejad moved to Sanandaj, the centre of the province of Kurdistan, this time as an advisor to the governor general. Sanandaj was one of the main Kurdish centres in Iran. It had lost many of its sons in the fight against government forces for autonomy. By the time Ahmadinejad arrived on the scene, the rebellion in Sanandaj had been largely suppressed. However, the area remained tense, and a heavy presence of the security forces and a strong intelligence network were needed to keep Sanandaj and the rest of the province from falling to the Kurdish groups and particularly the Komeleh, the communist Kurdish group which had many followers in Kurdistan province.

While the war with Iraq raged along the southern sector of their joint border, Ahmadinejad used his spare time in the relative quiet of Sanandaj and in West Azerbaijan to resume his studies. With the re-opening of the universities after more than two years of closure, he passed his BSc in civil engineering in 1986. But he had still not undertaken his military service, which was compulsory. It seemed natural that he would choose to serve among his friends at the Ramazan Headquarters of the Revolutionary Guard, based in Kermanshah, the southern-most Kurdish province of Iran.

The Revolutionary Guard

One of the biggest and most successful operations of the Special Forces of the Revolutionary Guard based at the Ramazan Headquarters was a daring infiltration 180 km deep into Iraqi Kurdistan to set fire to Kirkuk's oil refinery and disrupt the fuel supplies to Saddam Hussein's forces.

The Ramazan Headquarters in the western city of Kermanshah was home to the Revolutionary Guard's Special Forces Brigade. It had been set up to carry out commando-style warfare and sabotage behind enemy lines. It had been inspired by a commando unit that had been set up in the early years of the war by Mostafa Chamran, one of the foremost military strategists of Ayatollah Khomeini. Chamran, who had spent years before the Revolution in south Lebanon training with the Palestinians and Shia militants, was a key player in the very early Khomeini years. His death at the front in 1981 was a heavy blow to Iran's war effort, following which his unit was reorganized and moved to the Ramazan Headquarters, named after the Muslim fasting month of Ramadhan.

The Kirkuk operation was carried out on 18 September 1987. The war had dragged on for seven years by then and Iran was running out of options. Iraq's use of chemical weapons, with Saddam Hussein's backers in the West looking the other way, had demoralized soldiers and civilians alike, tipping the balance. Tehran desperately needed to produce some victories to keep up the sagging morale at the front. And Ahmadinejad, having been trained in guerrilla warfare, was part of the support team that supplied the group collaborating with the anti-Saddam Kurdish force, the Patriotic Union of Kurdistan.

For Ahmadinejad Kirkuk was by far the most dangerous operation he had taken part in. In the two years he had spent with the Revolutionary Guard, he had worked in engineering roles such as building bridges and erecting fortifications. This was to be his most dangerous combat experience, the details of which are hazy. Years later a semi-fictional film based on this operation depicted a heroic action in which all but three of the Iranian team returned across the border in triumph. Ahmadinejad's role in the venture is unclear, but it did his reputation no harm to be associated with Kirkuk. Yet there is still some mystery surrounding his true combat status. No photographs of Ahmadinejad during the war have been published, which is surprising as Ahmadinejad ran his election campaign on a Basij ticket and on the strength of being a war veteran. He also made much of keeping the memories of the martyrs alive, glorifying the sacrifices of the dead and the maimed.

Yet many are not convinced. 'He was not the fighting type. He was a bit of a coward,' says sociologist Hamid Reza Jalaipour, who knew Ahmadinejad then. 'He spent two years with the Guard just to do his military service.' Jalaipour, who lost three of his own brothers in the war, said Ahmadinejad came through the conflict unscathed. 'He did not lose a single member of his family in the war,' he said; 'his brothers are all sound and well.'

Whatever the reality behind the war years, hero or not, for Ahmadinejad, his two years with the Guard were rewarding in other ways. He made important contacts with commanders who later became influential supporters in his bid to become president. One of the commanders at the Ramazan HQ was Mohammad Bagher Zolghadr, who later rose to become deputy commander of the Revolutionary Guard and deputy Interior Minister in Ahmadinejad's government. In the aftermath of the 2005 presidential elections, Zolghadr admitted that the Guard and the Basij had worked for Ahmadinejad's elections. Another commander at the Ramazan HQ was Mohammad Reza Naghdi, who rose to the highest levels of the Guards Corps. He now heads the directorate of the armed forces in charge of armaments.

The Ramazan HQ was also home to the Badr Brigade, which was composed mostly of exiled Shiite Iraqi dissidents, together with Iraqi officers and soldiers who had defected to Iran. It also included some Shiite Iraqi Kurds. The Badr Brigade was Iran's answer to the militant Iranian opposition, the Mujahedin-e-Khalq Organization (MKO), which had based thousands of its forces on the Iraqi side of the border with Iran. Badr regularly collaborated with the Revolutionary Guard in their operations against the Iraqi army. It later grew into a division and finally into a corps. In Iraq it was to evolve into the armed wing of the Supreme Council of the Islamic Revolution of Iraq (SCIRI) in the aftermath of the US-led invasion. SCIRI was later widely accepted as a vehicle of Iranian influence during the US/British occupation of Iraq.

Ahmadinejad's dealings with the Badr Brigade and with Iraqi Kurdish groups during his time at the Ramazan HQ brought him into contact with Iraqi figures opposed to Saddam Hussein. Many years later some of these played leading roles in post-Saddam Iraq. They included the Iraqi Shiite leader Abdelaziz Hakim, who led the Badr Brigade during the Iran–Iraq War. Abdelaziz Hakim had replaced his brother Mohammad Baqir Hakim who was assassinated in Iraq soon after the overthrow of Saddam Hussein.[30] Another of these leaders was Jalal Talabani, the leader of the Patriotic Union of Kurdistan, who was to become Iraq's first post-Saddam president.

At the very least Ahmadinejad's involvement in the Iran–Iraq War created a degree of access to individuals who would become some of Iraq's political elite and in the process provided valuable insights into the workings of Iraqi politics, all of which would prove useful after 2003. But perhaps the most important outcome of this period in Ahmadinejad's life is the network of politically muscular contacts he built up among Iran's militia groups, for whom the war proved a crucially formative experience.

The young governor general

In the winter of 1993 heavy snow in the northwestern city of Ardabil prevented Ahmadinejad's plane from landing. A 50cm-thick blanket of snow had settled on the city. A blizzard had pushed the temperature down to minus 40 degrees centigrade. Wrapped in their shawls and thick coats, dignitaries had prepared themselves to greet the new governor general at the airport. But in the event, they had to get on a bus and travel in extremely hazardous conditions to the next town, Sarab, to welcome Ahmadinejad who had by now taken the road and was expected there.

It was not an auspicious beginning. To Ahmadinejad this was a taste of things to come. The province of Ardabil that he was going to govern had only just been established as an administrative entity. He knew that being its first governor general was not going to be easy – an infrastructure had to be laid down from scratch amid high expectations.

Everyone was eager to meet the governor general but no one knew him. Local officials even went to the personal representative of the Supreme Leader, Ayatollah Khamenei, in the province to ask him about the man who had just been appointed as their top government official, but even he, who knew the political establishment in Tehran well, did not know anything about the man.

The Interior Minister, Ali Mohammad Besharati, a hardline conservative, had picked Ahmadinejad as governor general of the nascent province, and he was accompanying him. Later at a meeting with officials and dignitaries in Ardabil, Besharati introduced his man: 'I have brought for you someone who is young, and not only an engineer, but also a doctor,' Besharati said, adding light-heartedly, 'He is also evidently a mojtahed [a learned religious man].' Ahmadinejad's reputation for religious fervour, which often made him sound like a preacher, had already been well established.

Besharati hoped this would go down well in the city of Ardabil, which was a deeply religious provincial capital of nearly half a million predominantly Azeri-speaking Shiite Muslims. It was situated in the mountainous northwest of Iran. At the time the whole province had a population of little more than a million. The war with Iraq had ended nearly eight years earlier and President Rafsanjani was presiding over a period of economic liberalization and reconstruction. In Tehran, political infighting had broken out among the Islamists. Besharati was an ultra-conservative whom the right-wing Islamists in parliament had forced on President Rafsanjani, whose popularity was ebbing a year before the end of his two terms in office. Besharati was a close confidant of the parliament speaker, Ali Akbar Nategh-Nouri, who was getting ready to stand as the religious right's candidate for the next president.

One official in charge of the cultural and heritage sites of the province said Ahmadinejad evidently knew little about heritage issues. 'I felt he did not have the necessary information or technical background, at least for dealing with heritage issues,' said Bayat Jame'ee, the former director general of the Cultural Heritage Organization in Ardabil. Jame'ee was later to become a fan, sharing a sauna with Ahmadinejad and occasionally joining him at the local swimming pool. 'By his second year, he was well versed in heritage issues,' said Jame'ee, who described Ahmadinejad as a man with an extraordinary memory, determined and with an easygoing management style.

But Ahmadinejad had come with an agenda. According to one observer, he was a very political appointee. 'It was only six or seven months into his term of office when it became apparent that Ahmadinejad was working according to a factional political agenda,' Javad Zanjani, the head of Ardabil's city council, said. 'From the outset, he worked to win over the religious and influential people in town, like the clergymen, traders in the bazaar and revolutionary institutions such as the Revolutionary Guard, Basij etc,' he said.

He began placing sympathizers in key posts and strengthening his own position by building links to influential individuals and groups in Ardabil. Any development work had to be in line with his political priorities. Moreover, as it got closer to the presidential elections, getting the speaker of parliament, Nategh-Nouri, elected became the top priority. Nategh-Nouri's posters began to appear in government offices. Ahmadinejad pursued all his contacts, including the Basij and the Revolutionary Guard, to get involved in the campaign for Nategh-Nouri. He even pressed six of the seven members of parliament from the province to back Nategh-Nouri publicly. This sort of pressure inevitably created resentment. Ahmadinejad and a reformist member of parliament from Ardabil by the name of Ali Mohammad Gharibian were even reported to have come to blows. Whether this episode occurred or not is less relevant than the eagerness with which it was reported. It was at this time that Ahmadinejad also began to speak in mosques and other forums about the inevitability of Iran and the United States eventually coming to blows, saying that Iran had to prepare itself for that day.[31]

Ahmadinejad was so keen to see the religious right back in power in Tehran that he sought to help with Nategh-Nouri's campaign funding. The result would blemish his righteous image.

In line with the government of President Rafsanjani's policy of encouraging government offices to support themselves financially, provincial municipalities were encouraged to use the services of an organization whose job it was to generate income for them. Ahmadinejad used one such organization in Ardabil to sell refined petroleum to neighbouring Azerbaijan and divert the proceeds to Nategh-Nouri's election campaign. Iran imports much of its own fuel, which is distributed internally at heavily subsidized prices. Exporting the government-subsidized fuel to a neighbouring country for a profit, which was then diverted to the political funds of a presidential candidate, was highly questionable. According to Mohsen Armin, a former reformist member of parliament, roughly $1.2 million was diverted to Nategh-Nouri's campaign funds in this way. The file was still open with the judiciary even after Ahmadinejad was elected president.

However, all of Ahmadinejad's efforts came to naught. Nategh-Nouri, the candidate of the religious right, lost badly to the popular reformist candidate, Mohammad Khatami. 'Many people in the province did not vote because Ahmadinejad had created the impression that the election was a done deal, and that Nategh-Nouri would be elected,' said Javad Zanjani. Nevertheless, the experience would later help Ahmadinejad in his 2005 election as president. The 1997 election had been his first experience in electoral politics and the insights gained then would stand him in good stead.

But Ahmadinejad's connections in Ardabil, and memories of him there, would not be particularly helpful to him in his 2005 bid for the presidency. Fewer than 44 per cent of the eligible voters in the province turned out to vote in the June 2005 presidential elections, lower than the national average. And among those who did vote, few voted for Ahmadinejad. He came fifth, second to last, with little over 18,000 votes. This was a glaring reflection on his impact in one of the very few places in the whole country where people had actually heard of Ahmadinejad when he put himself forward as a candidate in the presidential race. This was someone who had been the province's governor general for more than three years. Moreover, in Khoy, where Ahmadinejad had been the district governor some years earlier, he also came fifth. And this was after he had further enhanced his position as governor after the earthquake in the province in February 1997, when huge funds were channelled to help with the reconstruction after the quake that had killed about 1,000 people, injured nearly 3,000 and demolished 40,000 homes.

One observer at the time of the election in Ardabil said that in his view the Revolutionary Guard there were a step behind the rest of the country. They had been told to vote for Ahmadinejad's rival, Mohammad Baqer Qalibaf, in the first round, and it was only in the second round that they mobilized everyone to vote for Ahmadinejad, he said.

It was while he was in Ardabil that, through his brother Davoud, Ahmadinejad bought his first home in the Tehran neighbourhood of Narmak, where he had grown up and had lived almost all his life. Ahmadinejad bought a two-bedroom house at the end of a cul-de-sac in Narmak, about a kilometre from where his father lived. He bought the house for Rls102 million – roughly $20,000 at the rate of exchange then. Since he was in Ardabil at the time, Ahmadinejad's elder brother Davoud, who was later employed at the president's office, moved in with his family.

Ahmadinejad's tenure as the governor general of Ardabil came to an abrupt end in the autumn of 1997 when the reformist government of President Mohammad Khatami replaced all governors.

Professor Ahmadinejad

For many in Iran, the 1997 election of Khatami with a massive 70 per cent majority represented an opportunity for the country to emerge from its pariah status, to establish a modus vivendi with the United States and to kick-start its economy. Political reformists looked forward to a vigorous press, open debates and robust parliamentary oversight. With the high voting turnout and Khatami's popular mandate, it seemed that the people of Iran had spoken: the Islamic Republic of Iran was a legitimate political entity, but it needed to radically rethink the way it functioned.

Replaced in Ardabil by the reformists, Ahmadinejad went back to Tehran where he found a teaching job as an assistant professor at his old university, Elm-o-Sanat. He had just completed his doctorate in transportation engineering and planning from the same university. He had been working on his thesis while he was the governor general in Ardabil. It had taken him almost 20 years to get his degree and his PhD because of the turmoil in the country and his political and administrative activities. At Elm-o-Sanat he taught traffic engineering to undergraduate as well MSc and PhD students. His pupils say he was a popular professor whose classes were fun. He was always cheerful, friendly and easygoing in the class – always ready with a joke and generous with grades. He always came prepared and was genuinely interested in his subject.[32]

Later as president, he would repeatedly describe himself as 'first and foremost a university teacher'. It was his way of saying that he had not fallen for the trappings of power and that he remained in touch with the people. When in May 2003 Ahmadinejad became mayor of Tehran, he continued his classes, and it was only his election as president in 2005 that forced him to discontinue. Teaching helped him to develop patience. This was to become evident years later in the way Ahmadinejad listened and talked with such intensity to the ordinary people who approached him during his tours around Tehran as mayor or around the country as president.[33]

Some students pointed to the classroom jokes that Ahmadinejad often came up with in interviews with the media. In one with CBS, the veteran American interviewer Mike Wallace pushed Ahmadinejad to say yes or no to a question he had asked. 'Is this a multiple choice test?' Ahmadinejad retorted with a grin. In press conferences, his words were punctuated with a school-teacherish humour. Once, he told a young journalist, who had come to the podium to ask his question wearing a jacket not unlike his, that since he had put on 'an Ahmadinejad jacket' he could ask two questions.

Political days

Although he loved to teach, Ahmadinejad in reality viewed his teaching job as a side activity to earn a living. His eyes were firmly on the political stage where his fellow right-wing religious hardliners had just suffered a humiliating defeat in the presidential election in 1997. President Khatami's more than 70 per cent of the vote now forced the hardliners to regroup. To make a comeback they had to reassess their position and make life as difficult as possible for Khatami.

Factional fighting had characterized the Islamic regime in Iran ever since the early years of the Revolution, when left, liberal and secular parties had been driven underground or out of the country. This resulted in the Islamist groups grasping full control of the country and competing with each other for power. For these Islamic parties elections were, mostly, free. In this political landscape, Ahmadinejad stood to the very right of the spectrum. While left-wing and moderate Islamists took control of the executive and the legislative branches of the government in the late 1990s, right-wing groups controlled the judiciary, the police and the security forces. More importantly, right-wing groups enjoyed the support of the Supreme Leader, Ayatollah Khamenei.

Nevertheless this was a period when a wind of change was sweeping across Iran, and fundamentalist Islam was losing its appeal. The election of President Khatami, a moderate clergyman who wanted to marry Islam and democracy, impose the rule of law and remove tension between Iran and the outside world, had drastically changed attitudes in the country. Hardline Islamic groups felt threatened like never before. They had to return to power even if it meant changing their colours to suit the times and playing down their Islamic agenda.

In this political climate, Ahmadinejad was coming up in the ranks of the right wing. He had notable revolutionary credentials. As a governor general he had emphasized the purity and supremacy of Islam in politics and society. He had forcefully campaigned for the presidential candidate of the right. He had done his time with the Revolutionary Guard during the war, and all along, since the early days of the Islamic Revolution, he had been a stormtrooper and activist for the hardline Islamists.

When the time came for the local elections in February 1999, the religious right mobilized their forces for a counter-offensive. Many candidates had registered for positions in hundreds of city councils and tens of thousands of village councils. It was Islamic Iran's first attempt to widen popular participation in political affairs. At least two rightist groups nominated Ahmadinejad as one of their candidates for the council in Tehran. The council in the capital would have 15 elected members and six reserve members. One of the groups that had nominated Ahmadinejad entered the race with pretensions of being a green party, although until then no one had heard of it. It called itself City Green Life (Zendegi-e-Sabz-e-Shahr, in Persian). A list published in newspapers of right-wing candidates in this group included a preamble that was devoid of any reference to Islam. But it claimed that it had the backing of the biggest clerical association as well as the religious conservative group Jamiat-e-Motalefeh (the Association of the Coalitionists). The Motalefeh was a secretive organization with strong links to the traders in the bazaar in Tehran, a linkage which traditionally has been an important part of the dynamics of political change in Iran. The organization had been formed underground many years earlier under the Shah's regime, with Ayatollah Khomeini as its mentor and at least one political murder, that of the Shah's one-time prime minister, Hassan Ali Mansour, in its records.

The other party that put Ahmadinejad forward as candidate was the Islamic Civilization Party, a newly established group that also soft-pedalled its Islamic credentials. The party manifesto again made no mention of Islam except in the name of the party.

In the advertisements of the two groups published in hardline newspapers, Ahmadinejad's photo showed a young man with a beard wearing a jacket and an oversized buttoned-up white shirt of the type favoured by deeply religious men in Iran. They introduced him as Dr

Ahmadinejad, with a PhD in civil engineering. Ahmadinejad knew many would find it difficult to identify with a man who had a PhD in the more obscure field of transportation.

But in the event, the reformists took the overwhelming number of seats, dealing another blow to the right-wing Islamists – their second in two years. Ahmadinejad's first electoral experience at the city level was not a happy one. With about 100,000 votes, Ahmadinejad came 23rd. While the first 15 found their way into the Tehran city council, and the next six were named as reserve members, Ahmadinejad's first bid in electoral politics ended in failure.

The results of the local council elections sent a shock wave through the Islamic establishment. They were another clear indication that Iran was in the midst of a huge change, a shift away from hardline Islamic ideas, policies and politicians. For Ahmadinejad it was a depressing development. Many years later, a staunch supporter of his described the make-up of the first elected council of Tehran as 'repulsive', adding that the council in her view had tasked itself with 'fighting Islam and removing Islamic values'.[34]

But there was no time to lose. The next parliamentary elections were only a year away, and Ahmadinejad, still teaching at Elm-o-Sanat University, had his eyes on them. By now he was quite well known in right-wing circles, and there was a real prospect that he would be selected as one of their candidates.

And he was right. Several right-wing groups and parties nominated him as one of their candidates in the run-up to the elections on 18 February 2000. These included the conservative Association of the Militant Clergymen, Isargaran (the Association of the Selfless Defenders of Islamic Revolution) and the Islamic Engineers Association. But first on the list of these groups of 30 candidates for 30 parliamentary seats from Tehran was Ahmadinejad's future rival and opponent, Ali Akbar Hashemi Rafsanjani. Having been shunned by the reformists, Rafsanjani, ever the pragmatist, was in those days content to be seen as a hardliner against what he would call 'the excesses' of the reformists. The list also included Ahmadinejad's future spokesman Gholam Hussein Elham.

The list of candidates and their photographs were published in hardline newspapers in advertisements that featured photographs of the inspirational and original leader of the Islamic Revolution,

Ayatollah Khomeini, and the present Supreme Leader, Ayatollah Khamenei, against the background of the Iranian tricolour – an appeal to the nationalistic sentiments of Iranians which never failed during elections. The advertisement introduced Ahmadinejad this time as having a doctorate in 'road and construction engineering', as a professor of Elm-o-Sanat University, a member of 'the Association of Road and Traffic Engineers of Asia and Oceania', a former cultural advisor to the Minister of Culture and Sciences, and former governor general of Ardabil.

Among the other groups that put forward Ahmadinejad was the Islamic Civilization Party, which had appeared on the political scene during the local elections a year earlier. This party described its platform as striving to 'develop' society, establish a progressive management for the country, fight to defend values (no mention of Islamic values) and work to 'invigorate' the nation.

The reformists, who wanted to initiate democratic reforms, establish the rule of law and free Iran from the web of extremism, were holding huge rallies. The atmosphere in Iran was carnival-like. Reform was the ticket for being elected, with even hardline conservatives describing themselves as reformists.

On the day, not surprisingly, Iranians voted overwhelmingly for the reformists who again won the majority of the seats in Tehran and the provinces. The conservatives were left in a state of further shock. Humiliatingly for them, their top candidate, Rafsanjani, came 29th and nearly missed being elected altogether. This was confirmation, if one was needed, that Iranians had turned their back on the kind of religious zealotry and Islamic fundamentalism that people like Ahmadinejad were advocating. The conservatives had used the Guardian Council to disqualify some 700 candidates who allegedly did not have sufficient Islamic credentials, but most reformists who did get through the Guardian Council net were elected. 'I hope they get the message,' a reformist sympathizer said, referring to the religious right.[35]

Even in the heart of the religious establishment, the holy city of Qom, the top winner was a reformist. 'The people's vote in Qom was a big no to "monopolists" who thought they could decide for the people without consulting them,' said Taha Hashemi, one of the city's incumbent MPs who lost his seat. 'The right-wing faction in the new Majlis will have to adopt more moderate positions.'[36] President Khatami could now count on the support of the legislature for his programme of reform. Iran had just experienced a revolution within a revolution.

Ahmadinejad's vote came nowhere near that of the top 30 candidates who took Tehran's 30 seats in parliament. He and his fellow conservatives had run a pathetic campaign in the run-up to the elections with a few ill-attended rallies. The impression they gave was that they had lost hope before they even began. They had certainly not moved with the times. Their defeat left them with less than a quarter of the seats in parliament.

A year later, in 2001, President Khatami was re-elected as president, rubbing plenty of salt in the deep wounds of the conservatives. Khatami's victory, and the response to it, was not as decisive and enthusiastic as that of 1997. The reformist element of the electorate were disappointed that Khatami had not effectively used his earlier mandate to push through a more radical programme. And many feared that his indecisiveness came from a reluctance to modernize the clerical caste of which he himself was a member. At the end of the day, he is nothing more than a mullah, was the oft-heard refrain. Nevertheless for the conservatives this was another defeat. All that now remained was open warfare with the reformists. The conservatives used all the levers of power at their disposal to frustrate the reform programme. They used the judiciary to close down reformist newspapers for allegedly spreading lies and undermining national security. They used the courts, dominated by conservative clerical judges, to jail reformists for allegedly insulting Islamic sanctities. They used the conservative Guardian Council, headed by the hardline clergyman Ayatollah Ahmad Jannati, to frustrate parliament by rejecting parliamentary legislation for allegedly infringing Islamic laws. They used the security forces, the Basij militiamen and vigilante groups to intimidate university students and political parties. And they used the state radio and television to keep relentless pressure on Khatami and the reformists.

With the Supreme Leader, Ayatollah Ali Khamenei, by means of the massive powers granted to him by the constitution, backing the conservatives in their campaign of force and intimidation, President Khatami had to backtrack on many of his promises. This created a feeling of gloom and disappointment among many who had voted for Khatami and the reformist parliament. The despondency among them encouraged the conservatives.

The hardliners' opposition to the government of Khatami soon reached a high point, with violence against reformers becoming routine. Ahmadinejad was now a trusted figure of the fringe of Islamic zealots who had been grouped under the title 'Ansar-e-Hezbollah', or Followers of Hezbollah. This group was known for its violent attacks against reformist rallies, university student gatherings and women they believed had not conformed to their strict code of Islamic dress. The group's members were mostly made up of the more zealous members of the Basij. They operated under a hardline clergyman with links to the chief of the Guardian Council, Ayatollah Jannati, who was also one of the several Friday prayer leaders of Tehran. They were also close to Ayatollah Mohammad Taqi Mesbah-Yazdi, the religious mentor of Ahmadinejad. There were even suspicions that the stormtroopers of Ansar had links to the office of the Supreme Leader, Ayatollah Khamenei. On many occasions, with the open backing of the security and police forces that were under the control of the hardliners, Ansar members used knives, chains and clubs to attack the rallies of reformist groups, reformist newspapers and gatherings of university students. As they stepped up their activities, Ahmadinejad seemed to get closer to them. He became a regular speaker at their secret internal gatherings.[37]

Ahmadinejad tried to frustrate the reform movement in other ways too. By now an almost full-time political activist of the religious right, he entered organizational politics when he became a spokesman for the Jamiat-e-Isargaran. As spokesman, he saw his main job as countering the reformists, and particularly President Khatami's agenda. And when Khatami, frustrated by the efforts of the right-wingers to stop his reforms, proposed a bill giving the president greater powers, Ahmadinejad opposed it. He said the bill infringed the independence of the judiciary. 'The bill for greater powers of the president is contrary to the principle of the separation of powers,' he told reporters. 'There is the concern that the executive branch which has resources, budget and power, wants to gain itself a special advantage though the bill.'[38] The irony that a hardline conservative was using the language of liberal democracy to argue for political structures that could more

easily frustrate the values of liberal democracy was not lost on observers of Iranian politics.

Ahmadinejad and the younger members of the religious right
were determined to reverse their humiliating defeats at the ballot box.
At the national convention of the Jamiat-e-Motalefeh, he said: 'This
is the time for a cultural war. We have to direct the minds of our
youth towards the basic principles, methods and the values of the
Revolution. We have to lay down Islamic guidelines for governance ...
Islamic government means a system in which all relations, inside the
family, between various people, in trade, and in all places, should take
on a true Islamic colour and scent.' [39]

For many months, Ahmadinejad and a number of younger conservatives met regularly to discuss and analyse the position of the religious right against the political developments of the country. Fired
up by their deliberations they mounted a revolt against the old-guard
conservatives who were controlling the decisions of the religious
right parties. The result of the rebellion was the creation of a neo-
conservative party by the odd name of Abadgaran (the Developers).
It drew on the mostly young members of several religious right-wing
groups with links to the Basij and other conservative revolutionary
institutions. The party came into being just before the next test at the
ballot box, the local council elections of February 2003. It described
itself as a No-Andish movement (revivalist). The rebels had come to
the conclusion that the conservative old guard which had rested on its
revolutionary laurels under Ayatollah Khomeini were stifling internal
debate through exclusive decision making. The rebels believed that
decisions had to be taken based on consensus and that party elders
should not be given the right of veto. Paternalism must be discarded
in favour of justice and meritocracy, allowing young managers with
revolutionary zeal to come forward. [40]

They felt that the second generation of conservatives had to enter
the political scene on the strength of their technocratic credentials
as well as their commitment to fundamentalist Islam. These neo-
conservatives felt that the time was ripe to forge ahead independently
of the conservative old guard, like those gathered in the Association
of the Militant Clergymen and the Jamiat-e-Motalefeh.

Ahmadinejad was one of the leaders of the rebellion. And later,
as the head of the election campaign headquarters of Abadgaran, he

presided over an early success at the polls – not because of their merit or popularity but by default.

The local elections on 28 February 2003 were held at a low point for the reformists. The previous council in Tehran, which was dominated by the reformists, had become a stage for ugly rivalries and paralysing politicking by the reformist factions, rendering the council ineffective. This had led to a good deal of disappointment among the voters. At the national level, President Khatami, the reformists around him and those in parliament made a series of misjudgements when they faced pressure from the Islamic hardliners, leaving many who had voted for them feeling dismayed and even cheated. When President Khatami failed to back university students against the violent physical attacks of the Ansar-e-Hezbollah, and when he failed to stand up for his Interior Minister, Abdullah Nouri, a champion of reform, who had been dragged to court and jailed, many finally lost faith in the president and his reform movement. Parliament had made a series of similar misjudgements.

When it came to the local elections, many stayed at home to register their dismay. On the other hand the Abadgaran succeeded in mobilizing its supporters and those of other right-wing parties to produce a big turnout. The result was the first set-back for the reformists in seven years. Hardly household names, the Abadgaran candidates, many of them second-generation conservatives, took all but one of the seats in Tehran. They claimed that 65 per cent of the 168,000 seats across the country had gone to 'revolutionary forces'. This was the first time that a quiet campaign had been conducted among members of the Basij and their families to come out in an organized way in support of the religious right candidates. This would be repeated in the next elections.

In the previous local elections, 1.4 million voters had registered their votes in Tehran, while in the latest local council elections only 0.56 million voted. At the national level only 16 million out of 41 million eligible voters turned out to vote, compared to 34 million in 1999. In Tehran the turnout figure was 12 per cent – the lowest since the Revolution. Many Iranians had disengaged from Islamic politics.

By any standard, this turnout was a national disaster, but the hardliners hailed the results as a resounding victory for them. For Ahmadinejad it was his first political success. Although he himself was not a candidate, some of his friends in Abadgaran were, and they would soon repay their debt to him.

Mayor Ahmadinejad

High above one of the busiest thoroughfares of Tehran there is a huge billboard poster of a female Palestinian suicide bomber holding an automatic rifle in one arm and clutching a small boy in the other. She is wearing military-style camouflage and a black scarf over which she is brandishing a green bandana with Arabic writing on it. The boy is holding an RPG grenade rocket. At the top of the poster is a quote from her in three languages – Persian, English and Arabic. It says, 'My children I love, but martyrdom I love more.'

It is the picture of 21-year-old Al-Aqsa Martyrs Brigade member Reem Salih Al Rayasha. On 14 January 2004 she blew herself up at an Israeli checkpoint, killing four Israeli soldiers. According to some Palestinian websites, she did this in spite of having two small children, a one-year-old baby and a four-year-old boy.

The billboard poster is one of the cultural contributions of Mahmoud Ahmadinejad to the city after he was elected mayor of the capital on 3 May 2003. Whatever else he was to do as mayor, Ahmadinejad used his civic position as a platform for the re-radicalization of Iranian politics.

The Tehran city council, whose members were, with a single exception, from the newly established hardline umbrella group of the young conservative Abadgaran, had chosen Ahmadinejad as mayor. With two abstentions, two votes against and 12 votes in favour, the council elected Ahmadinejad as the new mayor of Tehran. The council chose him from four other Islamist hardliners who had stepped forward to nominate themselves or be nominated by others in the council. The head of the council, Mehdi Chamran, an ardent supporter of Ahmadinejad, said that the council had elected him 'on the strength of his simple lifestyle, his Basij militia mentality, his skills as well as his fidelity'.[41]

But the Interior Ministry, dominated by reformists, was reluctant to approve the choice, as it was constitutionally required to do before the new mayor took office. The Ministry had picked on Ahmadinejad's 'financial corruption' when he was the governor general of Ardabil province as a reason for refusing to approve the choice. This was a reference to the export of petrol in the province to Iran's northern neighbour Azerbaijan and the diverting of the proceeds to the campaign funds of the presidential candidate of the right, Ali Akbar Nategh-Nouri. But the Ministry's reluctance smacked of sour grapes on the part of the reformists, and, under instructions from President Khatami, it finally relented.[42]

Ahmadinejad had come a long way to become a trusted figure of the young radical Islamists who credited him with turning around their fortunes after five consecutive losses at the ballot box. Some of his friends were already speaking of 'Ahmadinejad for President'.[43] He could use his position to reverse the trend of de-Islamization, as he saw it, and even grab the presidency for the right. Ahmadinejad was a mayor with a radical Islamic agenda to retake the positions that had been lost to the reformists over the previous ten years. 'What we need in practical terms is revolutionary forces who can come with the mentality of Basij members to resolve the problems of the country,' he told a group of young students in Qom.[44]

The poster of the Palestinian suicide bomber high above a busy intersection in Tehran turned out to be the first of a series of initiatives he took on behalf of the Basij and which horrified much of the public. Three months into his term of office, Ahmadinejad announced that the remains of some martyrs of the Iran–Iraq War would be buried in 72 city squares, parks and universities dotted around the capital. This was to honour the martyrs and their memories and prevent their sacrifices from being forgotten. He named Vali Asr Square, one of the busiest in the northern half of Tehran, as the first to be used. The Basij militia and sections of the Revolutionary Guard were resentful that their sacrifices in the Iran-Iraq War were being forgotten, and hardliners like Ahmadinejad were able to build on this resentment to increasingly push for the militarization of society, constantly pointing to threats from abroad and from within, all the time promising that the blood of the martyrs would not be in vain. And 15 years after the end of the war, they were still uncovering remains of dead soldiers in the old battlefields. So to bury the freshly discovered remains in highly visible public places was an ideal and constant reminder of the sacrifices of the martyrs. Not surprisingly, the suggestion provoked a reaction in the public that suspected political motives. Even the speaker of parliament, Mehdi Karroubi, himself a senior clergyman, said that Tehran must not be turned into a cemetery, and Grand Ayatollah Montazeri, one-time heir apparent to Ayatollah Khomeini, also weighed in against the plan.

Ahmadinejad soon back-tracked from using city squares as burial grounds, but universities and parks were not to be spared A riot broke out at the prestigious Sharif University when a group of Basij militiamen buried a number of martyrs in the university mosque without prior notice. In the scuffles, students smashed the car windows of the university chancellor, an appointee of Ahmadinejad and a graduate of Elm-o-Sanat University who had supported the burial of the martyrs in the university. Tombs of several martyrs were also erected in a number of parks in north Tehran that were normally the refuge of young couples.

But Ahmadinejad regarded the most ardent supporters of the Islamic Revolution, and particularly the Basij militia and their families, as his key constituency. It was on this constituency that he concentrated all his efforts. He also knew that by pursuing Islamization measures, he could gain the support of the religious right, the core of the Revolutionary Guard, some ayatollahs in the holy city of Qom, and, perhaps most importantly, the Supreme Leader, Ayatollah Ali Khamenei.

But Ahmadinejad went beyond Islamist measures to build his support base. He was a pragmatist too. He unveiled plans for building 400 sa'gha-khanehs, or drinking fountains, across the city. These were modelled on the traditional sites of previous generations where the faithful could stop and quench their thirst on hot summer days. In the old days, during Shia Islam's holy months, shops fronts would often be turned into sa'gha-khanehs. A large aluminum tank with a tap would be placed on a stool, with several copper cups chained to the tank. During religious processions in the heat of the summer months, mourners could stop at these fountains to drink water. Some of the ones that were built by Ahmadinejad were small stone monuments the size of kiosks, made with a dark green stone facade. On them were painted or etched images of neighbourhood martyrs. The political point of this social measure had, after all, to be flagged.

Ahmadinejad also began giving huge handouts to neighbourhood religious groups called 'Hei'ats' out of the municipal budget. Hei'ats were groups of people who would gather around the most religious and respected figure in the neighbourhood during the holy month of Moharram to organize religious functions and provide food to the needy. The handout was the equivalent of $2,500. It had the impact of coopting and soon corrupting these groups, as opportunists close to the Basij militia bases in the neighbourhood soon crowded them. But this did not bother Ahmadinejad, who saw the money as a back-hander for services rendered. Ahmadinejad also provided grants to mosques throughout the city, attempting to tie them into his network. He believed that during the years since the Revolution, governments had failed to support the mosques that were central to the life of neighbourhoods. He gave cash prizes to reciters and chanters of the Koran who traditionally hung around the mosques. He also helped renovate the buildings in different neighbourhoods that had become headquarters of the Basij. During the fasting month of Ramadhan, Ahmadinejad set up soup kitchens throughout the city to serve those who were fasting and who, for whatever reason, were out on the street at the time of *iftar* – the breaking of the fast.

Most of the contracts for these activities, which included the festive streetlights that went up across the metropolis on religious occasions, went of course to groups in the Tehran bazaar who were the foot soldiers of the mafia-like politico-military machinery. The loyal servants of the Revolution needed constant nourishment. This naturally accentuated a culture of 'us' and 'them' and spread corruption among those Ahmadinejad and the religious establishment regarded as reliable insiders, while deepening the alienation of those not overtly or particularly religious that formed the overwhelming majority of the country.

But as, with the help of these measures, he increased his popularity with the Basij and the Revolutionary Guard, the religious right establishment began to take Ahmadinejad more seriously. The Basij and the Revolutionary Guard gave him their full support and the religious right defended his every action. He was now carrying the banner for them in their fight against the reformists. Influential figures among the conservatives were now starting to dream about taking back the parliament from the reformists at the next elections, only a few months away.

By the late summer of 2003, Ahmadinejad's attention was now

fixed on the next parliamentary elections. Again, the right-wing Islamist groups were too divided to agree on a coherent election strategy. The return of the moderates and reformists to parliament looked like an increasingly realistic prospect. Something had to be done. The Guardian Council, that bastion of the religious right, took it upon itself to block as many of the reformists as it could. From the outset almost all reformist candidates throughout the country were disqualified as candidates in the elections. Their Islamic credentials were apparently inadequate. No amount of protest succeeded in reversing the decisions. The religious right had decided that it would take parliament by any means, no matter what. With the field now open to the hardliners, Abadgaran, which had been set up by Ahmadinejad and his young fellow right-wingers, put forward many candidates. And in the event, they swept into parliament, handing the religious right its second electoral victory. Abadgaran took all 30 seats in Tehran and many in the provinces. But it was a bittersweet victory. Nearly half of the electorate – 49 per cent – boycotted the election. In Tehran, the turnout was just 28 per cent. Ahmadinejad had used the resources of the municipality to promote the Abadgaran and their allies.[45]

He was quite happy later to claim credit for the success of the Abadgaran candidates, citing his efforts as mayor of Tehran to facilitate their election. But at the same time there was no shortage of allegations that the Revolutionary Guard and the Basij had influenced the votes.

By now Ahmadinejad was enjoying the full support of the Revolutionary Guards Corp and its top commander Yahya Rahim Safavi. A number of Guard commanders had left to join the Tehran municipality. The relationship between the Guard and the municipality was so close that it was difficult to say whether the Guard was supporting Ahmadinejad or vice versa. Many of the development projects of the city were awarded to the Revolutionary Guard, which by now had developed into a gigantic military/industrial conglomerate. In return, the Guard provided the municipality with money and other help. This included removing all barriers to the projects that had remained dormant up to then because the Guard occupied strategic plots of land with its barracks and offices that would have to be cleared to make way for new roads, highways and bridges in the city. The Guard had erected buildings in many parts of Tehran in contravention of city council rules. 'There were claims against the Guard worth billions that were outstanding under previous mayors. Once in office, Ahmadinejad waived all these claims of the municipality over night,' said Mohsen Armin, a former reformist member of parliament. 'His relationship with the Guard and the Basij was very extensive.'

The Guards' fleet of heavy earth-moving and road-building machinery was put at the disposal of the municipality. It also supplied the money for one of Ahmadinejad's pet projects: providing loans to newly married couples to help them start life together. Some 120,000 couples received the equivalent of more than $1,200 each.

'I soon realized he had a blank cheque,' says Saeed Leilaz, a political commentator who, as a representative of a car-producing company, sold thousands of buses to the municipality. Leilaz also gave a description of the mayor's office under Ahmadinejad: 'The mayor's office was a huge open-plan penthouse that Karbaschi [the former reformist mayor] used to use. But keen to display a simple lifestyle, Ahmadinejad had refused to sit in the huge luxurious environment. He had chosen the room off the main office, which used to house the secretary, as his office. When I went there I saw a whole army of young bearded men wearing white socks and slippers and with their grey shirts hanging over their grey trousers [a clothing style preferred by young members of the Basij] busy coming and going. He had signed contracts worth billions with the Basij.' Leilaz, who had dealings with Ahmadinejad, said the mayor was quick at making daring decisions without much regard for their consequences or experts' advice.

Years later, when Ahmadinejad was president, his critics in parliament tried twice to initiate an investigation into his financial dealings as the mayor of the capital. Both times Islamic conservatives blocked the inquiries into allegations that the money was spent on Ahmadinejad's election campaign. 'Given that the money spent on the president's election has been a considerable sum, and that some believe that no money has been spent on the election campaign at all, or that only little money has been spent on the elections, it would have been useful to know just how much money was spent,' said a parliamentarian, Ismaeil Gerami Moghadam. 'And if some money has been spent for special ceremonies and religious occasions ... we have to see whether the money was spent to win the trust of the people for a particular candidate, or for marking national and religious events.'[46]

There was the case of the unaccounted-for expenditure worth close to $400 million which members of Ahmadinejad's team at the municipality claimed had been spent on emergency expenses. A secret report had been prepared by Ahmadinejad's successor as mayor, Mohammad Baqer Qalibaf, detailing the case. The report, which was sent to Iran's Supreme Leader, Ayatollah Khamenei, said that the extent of the financial irregularities under Ahmadinejad was more than all the irregularities of the past several mayors put together, according to leaks in the press. Another letter from Qalibaf to Ahmadinejad, asking him to help close the case by simply confirming that the money was spent on emergencies, received a characteristically theatrical rebuke from Ahmadinejad. He wrote 'Go Eat Shit' on the side of the letter and returned it to the municipality.[47] There was also the case of the roughly $120,000 that the municipality had spent on celebrating Ahmadinejad's victory in the presidential elections. According to the municipality under Qalibaf, on that day roughly $25,000 was spent on buying sweets that were distributed across the city, another $25,000 on rewards and bonuses to various employees of the municipality, and $12,000 on hiring chairs for street parties, and more on flowers.[48]

Ahmadinejad, his comrades in Abadgaran and his supporters in the Revolutionary Guard and the Basij were now eyeing the presidential elections – only months away in June 2005. Indeed, having presided over victory in the council and parliamentary elections, Ahmadinejad felt he could pull off another success – his biggest. Some of his friends were urging him to stand. Certainly, the municipality resources were huge and could be of immense help. An enormous campaign began for the hearts and minds of those living in the poorer neighbourhoods of the capital. Suddenly a fresh push began to re-asphalt the streets of the poorer neighbourhoods with the help of the front companies of the Revolutionary Guard, while pot-holes in the richer neighbourhoods of north Tehran were ignored. Assistance to schools in the poorer areas increased too. The municipality stepped up its grants to schools to buy sports equipment. Being a traffic expert, Ahmadinejad created many U-turn points in the highways and streets of Tehran. The construction of U-turn points, which later became his legacy as the mayor of the city, facilitated the flow of heavy traffic in many corners of the capital. They made driving in the city fractionally less time consuming. This may at first glance not seem like a significant act, but in the traffic-choked atmosphere of Tehran the slightest easing of congestion was noticed, and of course Ahmadinejad was ready to take the credit.

Around the same time, Ahmadinejad fired the first shot in his election campaign, targeting the reformists by sharply criticizing President Khatami for residing in the former Shah's palace and thus being divorced from the realities of the everyday lives of ordinary people. This was a stinging attack on Khatami and it came after the president arrived late for a scheduled speech at the University of Tehran because of heavy traffic. In his speech, Khatami apologized for being late and blamed the mayor for having done so little to ease the problems for the people of the capital. Ahmadinejad rebutted Khatami's statement with a rant in which he portrayed himself as the one who had the interests of the working people at heart, and Khatami as a president who had fallen for the trappings of power, distancing himself from the people and residing in palaces. 'I think the president had to travel the long distance from Sa'dabad Palace [in north Tehran] to the university [in central Tehran] and that's why he faced some problems. I think if he had remained in the president's office [in central Tehran] he would have seen the problems the people are grappling with a lot earlier,' Ahmadinejad said. 'In Sa'dabad Palace one cannot see these problems immediately.'[49]

Ahmadinejad hesitated about running for president, as there were a number of other candidates with backgrounds in the Revolutionary Guard. These candidates, he believed, would have the votes of the Guard. Nevertheless he knew that he could count on the backing of the Basij and some of the commanders of the Guard. Despite misgivings about some conservative and hardline Islamist groups not supporting him, he toured the country, speaking at Basij gatherings and for Basij members at universities. And when he finally threw his hat in the ring, he continued the rhetoric of humility. He was, he announced, 'just a teacher and university professor who believes the government must not be indebted to any political group or party but to the people and the martyrs'.[50]

CHAPTER 2

AHMADINEJAD FOR PRESIDENT

A new push has begun. The hill we must take is Pasteur Avenue [the street where the presidential palace is situated in central Tehran]. God willing, we will take it. Victory is at hand. Either we will achieve our aim or we will become martyrs, injured or missing in action. This will happen. There is a new miracle on its way.[1]

President who?

Mahmoud Ahmadinejad was sitting cross-legged on a mat in what appeared to be an unkempt park covered with overgrown grass and weeds. He was speaking about the martyrs of the eight-year war with Iraq. 'They must not be forgotten. They did not shed their blood in vain. What we have today, we owe to the blood of the martyrs.'

His speech was interspersed with wide shots showing six or seven bearded young men, adorned in the grey loose shirts favoured by the members of the Basij volunteer militia. They were squatting on their knees behind Ahmadinejad, facing the camera and listening. Ahmadinejad continued to talk about the important Islamic values that the martyrs helped safeguard with their blood.

This poor-quality footage of the mayor of Tehran, only two years into the job, was not an underground video circulating among extreme jihadists. It was a campaign video for his candidature in the 2005 presidential elections. The content was all too familiar to anyone who had listened to the repetitive rhetoric of Iranian hardliners since the

Iran–Iraq War ended in 1988. The 267,000 dead Iranian soldiers of the bloody eight-year war had served as a political football ever since, most commonly exploited by the religious right. Religious leaders in Qom portrayed them as the fallen soldiers of Islam, not of Iran, and painted the conflict with Iraq as a battle to save the existence of an Islamic state rather than the Iranian state. Ayatollah Mohammad Taqi Mesbah-Yazdi repeatedly stressed that the country was saved not by patriotism but by Islam. This made it difficult to criticize the excesses of Iran's Islamic regime. To do so would be to trample on the ideals of the martyrs. However, the deaths had never been dwelt on during presidential election campaigns before, where even the conservative candidates tended to be aware of the watching international audience.

Iranian election laws require equal television airtime for all approved presidential candidates, regardless of their political orientation. Without this legal provision, Ahmadinejad, the establishment outsider, would have received very little television coverage at all. The video was technically poor and badly produced and, apart from the over-used clichés relating to the war dead, it offered little in the way of discernible policies or ambitions: no promises of improvements to living conditions, no vision for governance and certainly nothing in the way of warmth and charisma. If people had not been inclined to take the scruffy mayor of Tehran seriously when he first threw his hat into the ring, few would have found something in this video to make them change their minds. Even fewer would have believed he would be president of Iran in a couple of weeks.

Forty-nine-year-old Mahmoud Ahmadinejad's political profile was so low that he was little known even in Tehran where he had been the mayor for two years. Those who did know Mayor Ahmadinejad remembered him mainly for his controversial proposal to bury the remains of the martyrs of the eight-year war with Iraq in their 'rightful' places in Tehran's busy squares. So low key was Ahmadinejad's election campaign, and so unlikely seemed his chances of winning, that few local or international journalists who were covering the elections even bothered to mention him in their reports. Not a single newspaper, political party or organization supported Ahmadinejad in his bid for the top job. There were three other right-wing Islamist candidates, and all political commentators and members of the public thought any one of these stood a far greater chance of success.

Even Ahmadinejad's comrades in the Jamiat-e-Isargaran did not support him in the election campaign and opted for another Islamist candidate instead. Neither did the Islamic Engineers Association, founded by Ahmadinejad, support his candidacy. The Coordination Council, which had been formed as an umbrella organization of all the anti-reform Islamists, did not pick Ahmadinejad either. The council, headed by former presidential candidate and old friend of Ahmadinejad, Ali Akbar Nategh-Nouri, had held several sessions with Ahmadinejad and other right-wing candidates to discuss their plans for the country and the elections. It is very telling that on the hard-right extreme of Iranian politics, Ahmadinejad was still considered rather too far out. 'His plans were very cosmic,' Nategh-Nouri said of Ahmadinejad many months after the elections, explaining why the council had not supported the mayor of Tehran.[2]

Ahmadinejad did not even secure the support of his direct political allies. The conservative political organization Abadgaran, which the mayor had organized and had led to victory in the council elections in 2003, opted for a different presidential candidate. And this was in spite of the fact that Ahmadinejad had used his influence and resources in the municipality, against all rules and regulations, to help with the campaign of Abadgaran candidates in the parliamentary elections a year earlier in 2004. If all this was not enough discouragement, 50 of the very members of parliament whom Ahmadinejad had helped get elected issued a statement calling on him to withdraw from the race. For them he stood no chance of getting elected and would only divide the votes of the Islamists.[3] The ultra-conservative Jamiat-e-Motalefeh also preferred another candidate.[4]

Every Iranian newspaper – many of which are little more than sanctioned mouthpieces of various Islamic establishment groupings from across the political spectrum – had their favourite candidates. None chose Ahmadinejad. The hardline *Jomhuri Islami* (Islamic Republic) newspaper opted to support the centre-right Rafsanjani, whom it saw as a pillar of the Islamic Revolution. The other leading hardline newspaper, *Kayhan*, seemed unable to make up its mind. It spent several weeks advocating the withdrawal of some of the right-wing candidates. It implied that certain hopeless candidates could only serve to divide the hardline right-wing vote and allow an accidental reformist victory.

Although no names were named, most readers would have understood Ahmadinejad to be the hopeless one who ought to honourably withdraw for the good of the hardline movement. Just two days before the election *Kayhan* urged readers to vote for the Islamist candidate they thought had the greater chance of winning. Or in other words: don't throw away a vote on Ahmadinejad.[5] Ahmadinejad couldn't even curry favour with the high-circulation *Hamshahri*, which was actually owned by the municipality of Tehran. Unable to influence the editorial line, Ahmadinejad summarily dismissed the managing director of the newspaper, Ali Reza Sheikh Attar, for insubordination. Attar was a close friend and comrade of Ahmadinejad and had been appointed to the post soon after Ahmadinejad took office as the mayor of Tehran.[6]

On balance, Ahmadinejad was a hopeless candidate in what many considered to be an election whose outcome was a foregone conclusion. Every opinion poll agreed: the election already belonged to Ali Akbar Hashemi Rafsanjani, the experienced and wily conservative who had already served as president for two terms from 1989 to 1997. Rafsanjani was nicknamed 'the shark' for his inability to grow a proper beard (and not, as the West has understood, because of any political killer instincts). The nickname is a pun on the Persian word *kouseh*, which means both 'shark' and 'without a beard'. The 72-year-old, slightly overweight cleric always wore a white turban and buttoned-up collarless shirt and light-brown robe. With his penetrating dark eyes and small fringe of hair sticking out from under his turban, the former president conjured up an image of a cuddly bear that was only slightly ruined by the shadowy stubble he sported in lieu of proper facial hair.

In the case of Rafsanjani, absence had made the heart grow fonder. The electorate seemed prepared to overlook the terrible human rights abuses that took place under his watch and he appeared to have successfully repositioned himself as a conservative reformer, amenable to the views of the overwhelming majority of the Iranian people. His conservative credentials were strong and older members of the public would remember him as Ayatollah Khomeini's number one political fixer in the early days of the Revolution. But Rafsanjani was also shrewd and politically astute enough to have developed considerable support among younger Iranians, not least through his reputation for moderation and free enterprise. Importantly, by agreeing to an interview with CNN's Christiane Amanpour, Rafsanjani had signalled that he was open to suggestions for improving relations with the US. This was the Rafsanjani that the young people of Iran were out on the streets campaigning for, not the conservative establishment figure of the oppressive early 1990s. In Rafsanjani they saw an opportunity to revive the thwarted hopes and aspirations of 1997 and 2001 when they brought Khatami to power. Khatami had proved himself inept and spineless, as they saw it, to deliver on his promises and their dreams. Here in Rafsanjani they saw an operator who knew how to work the system. Rafsanjani might not be as sweet smelling as Khatami liked to present himself, but he had muscle, and his pragmatism had led him to recognize that Iran's longer-term interests lay in collaboration not conflict with the world. So here was a man who could deliver a measure of prosperity and stability which so many Iranians now craved.

Inheriting a considerable amount of land in Qom from his father, Rafsanjani acquired his wealth through farming and exporting pistachio nuts in the southern Kerman province. Rafsanjani's wealth brought with it a taste for luxury and comfort too. His office, as head of the constitutional arbitration Supreme Expediency Council, was in an old palace of the Shah, covered with expensive hand-made Persian carpets and gilded furniture. His taste for the good life was his weakness – and it would be adeptly exploited by Ahmadinejad in the campaign. To Islamic hardliners, his wealth and worldly trappings opened the former president to charges of decadence, corruption and deviation from the path of the Islamic Revolution. Revolutionary veterans also accused him of being divorced from the needs of the people and aloof from the sufferings of the masses. Even those prepared to support him had few illusions about his integrity.

Yet in the run-up to the election, Rafsanjani was undoubtedly flying high. The reformist news agency ISNA conducted a poll in Tehran and 12 other cities on the eight candidates which put Rafsanjani ahead with 19.1 per cent of the votes followed by hardline candidate Qalibaf at 9.5 per cent and the reformist Moin at 6 per cent. Ahmadinejad came second-to-last, with only 2.8 per cent of the vote. Even a poll by Ahmadinejad's own comrades at the hardline Jamiat-e-Isargaran did not rate his chances highly. According to their survey in 30 cities around the country, Rafsanjani was the favourite with 32 per cent of the votes, while Ahmadinejad came third from the bottom with only 4.1 per cent.

The only question for the public and political commentators was when Ahmadinejad was going to withdraw from the presidential race and allow a proper right-wing candidate to scoop up his paltry share of the vote. Up to the last day of campaigning, Ahmadinejad and his aides were forced repeatedly to deny suggestions from hardline quarters that he planned to drop out to avoid fracturing the far-right vote. One of the figures involved in the effort to bring unity to the hardliners' camp was Mariam Behruzi, who in no uncertain terms called on Ahmadinejad to withdraw. 'Given the sincerity that I see in Mr Ahmadinejad, I believe he will withdraw in favour of unity in the purist Islamic camp. He aims to serve, and serving in the municipality is an important task. God willing, he will be given a key post in the cabinet if he wants it.'[7] Even Ahmadinejad's closest comrade and the chairman of the Tehran City Council, Mehdi Chamran, was non-committal about Ahmadinejad staying in the race. 'There is widespread pressure on Ahmadinejad to withdraw. Everyone wants him to leave the race, but he himself is not prepared to go,' he said.[8] Ahmadinejad himself was becoming increasingly angered about the continual reports suggesting he was quitting. 'I have denied this, yet there are people who tell the media on a daily basis that I am withdrawing. I am going to stay to the end. The choice belongs to the people,' Ahmadinejad said. He was insistent. Not only was he going to stay in the race but he was confident he would win. He was perhaps the only person in Iran who believed this.

After his election, Ahmadinejad would portray this lack of enthusiasm from even his closest political allies as his strength, describing it as the cause of his popularity. He would argue that this demonstrated that he belonged to the people, not to the political classes. 'There is no reason for me to sacrifice the interests of the people for this group or that gang,' he said during the campaign race in response to yet another report that he was to withdraw.[9]

While it is tempting to accept this romantic image of the plucky little man of Iranian politics, swiping victory single-handedly from the big beasts of the establishment, with no help from the media, political factions or mainstream leadership, this picture is not entirely accurate.

Quietly, Ahmadinejad enjoyed the support of some of the most influential backers in Iranian politics. These included important sections of the Revolutionary Guard and the Basij, as well as the Guardian Council. He was also supported by the Imam Khomeini Education and Research Institute in Qom, which was led by his spiritual mentor, Ayatollah Mohammad Taqi Mesbah-Yazdi. Most significantly of all, it later transpired that Ahmadinejad was the preferred candidate of Supreme Leader Ayatollah Khamenei. Amazingly, the outsider and no-hoper was secretly the first choice of the ruling religious class, their institutions and militia.

Iran at the crossroads

Controversy had already surrounded the up-coming elections. Candidates outside the Islamic establishment had been barred from standing by the conservative constitutional watchdog, the Guardian Council, on the grounds of their poor Islamic credentials and for failing to meet other criteria. Of the eight hopefuls selected by the Council to run, only two were reformists. They had been allowed to run only after reformists had threatened to call for the boycott of the entire elections.

Apathy among eligible voters was high. Many saw the presidential elections as of little benefit to them. When reformists were in power they had achieved very little. They had proved incapable of fighting off the hardliners who had frustrated almost all their attempts to bring about change. While to many the hardliners were undesirable, the reformists were impotent. Why should anyone go and vote was the attitude of many.

Some Iranians outside the establishment boycotted the elections. They included the Iranian Nobel peace laureate, Shirin Ebadi, who described the whole electoral process, where candidates had to be vetted by an unelected body, as flawed. 'I have protested from the start about the electoral law. For me the only option is civil disobedience and this is the least we can do. The votes are not just, because they are not free,' Ebadi pronounced.

Iran's detractors abroad latched on to the structural faults in the electoral process as a useful tool to criticize Iran's clerical regime. US president George W. Bush weighed in on the eve of the elections.

'Today Iran is ruled by men who suppress liberty at home and spread terror across the world. Power is in the hands of an unelected few who have retained power through an electoral process that ignores the basic requirements of democracy,' he said.[10]

But the conservative Islamic establishment paid little attention. They had been here before. In the 2004 parliamentary elections, the Guardian Council had barred thousands of reformist candidates from taking part, again because of their poor Islamic credentials. It had thus handed the control of parliament to the hardliners for the first time since the 1979 Islamic Revolution. Then, as now, leaders of the hardliners had argued quietly among themselves that the credibility of the elections could be sacrificed for control of parliament with relatively few consequences. People would simply soon forget the shortcomings of the elections.[11]

The challenge for the hardliners was to ensure a high turnout to give the elections legitimacy. No one was more aware of this than Iran's Supreme Leader Ayatollah Ali Khamenei. 'The enemies will use every means to discourage people from taking part in the elections,' he warned.

Nearly 42 million people were eligible to vote in the 17 June presidential elections to find the successor to President Mohammad Khatami, the mild-mannered but ineffective champion of reform who believed Islam and democracy were compatible. It was the ninth presidential election since the Islamic Revolution, likely to be a two-stage process since no candidate was expected to achieve a 50 per cent share of the vote which would avoid a run-off.

But in spite of the widespread apathy among the voters, the elections were considered vitally important to those working in Iranian politics. After the slow but tangible reformist progress of Khatami's two presidential terms, the political direction of the nation appeared to be up for grabs. Many in the reform movement saw the presidential elections as the last chance to preserve the reforms of the previous eight years. For the reformists, the election was vital if they were to continue to steer Iran towards moderation, modernization and harmonization with the rest of the world.

At the other end of the spectrum, Ahmadinejad and the hardline candidates, who were all former Revolutionary Guard and Basij commanders, saw the presidential elections as their chance to take the executive branch, the only part of government not already within their sphere of influence. The conservative hardliners wanted to roll back some of the liberalization policies of President Khatami and to halt the processes of social permissiveness and any hint of reconciliation with the US. They believed that if they could seize the executive, they could mould Iran into their ideal society – a quasi-militaristic Islamic society that would expand its revolutionary Islamic influence way beyond Iran's borders. Without doubt, Iran stood at a political crossroads. The election results would set the nation on a political and ideological course that would see Iran redefined.

The candidates

Many young people had come out on to the streets of Tehran in the two weeks ahead of the elections – itself the result of several candidates promising more freedom, hoping to collect the votes of the young. They certainly reinforced the perception that Rafsanjani was the candidate of the urban middle classes. But their presence on the streets also carried a message: that Rafsanjani would open up the political and social atmosphere of the country.

Rafsanjani had entered the race after months of speculation about his intentions. While his supporters urged him to run, his right-wing detractors feared that if he entered the race others would stand little chance of winning, given Rafsanjani's status. As a long-time comrade of the leader of the Islamic Revolution, Ayatollah Ruhollah Khomeini, Rafsanjani had been among the few who had helped to steer the Islamic regime through the bloody and turbulent early years of the Revolution and through the eight years of devastating war with Iraq.

After the war, Rafsanjani had presided over eight years of reconstruction. He repeatedly referred to the previous 16 years under himself and Khatami as a period in which Iran gradually put behind it the hardline fervour of the early years of the Revolution. 'What we have achieved during this time is that our country, fortunately, crossed from a period of revolutionary emotionalism to a period of reason and common sense,' he said.

He now wanted to make a comeback to continue his programme for the development of Iran, building also on the years of development under Khatami, with whom he had no quarrel but whom the rank-and-file reformists distrusted as an unprincipled opportunist, quite capable of wearing the hardliners' mantle.

Rafsanjani wanted to help the private sector take on a bigger role in the economy. Indeed his biggest supporters were the traders of the bazaars and the middle classes. He also wanted to continue the international posture of Khatami, who had improved Iran's relations with much of the outside world. Western powers were hoping that Rafsanjani, with a reputation as a deal maker, might have the influence and authority to rein in the most hardline of the political forces and push through an agreement with the West on the nuclear issue. Rafsanjani had just given an interview to CNN's Christiane Amanpour – a signal that he was open to suggestions for improving relations with the US, which his young supporters would love to see.

Unlike Ahmadinejad, Rafsanjani had the backing of several newspapers, the conservative clergymen of the powerful Jameh-yi-Ruhaniyat-e-Mobarez (Militant Clergy Association) and the business community across the country. His spin masters presented him as the only candidate able to contain the radicalism of the hardliners who had entered the race. At the same time, he irritated other candidates no end when he kept repeating that he had only entered the race because there were no other worthy candidates.

The Supreme Leader, Ayatollah Khamenei, had discouraged Rafsanjani from running, telling him in a private meeting that there was no need for his involvement. But Rafsanjani, distrustful of Khamenei and his hardline ideas, felt that without him the presidential race would be effectively limited to inexperienced Islamic hardliners who, if elected, might jeopardize Iran's future and push the country to extremes.

With the possible exception of the reform-minded former speaker of parliament, Mehdi Karroubi, none of the other candidates were well known. They were four hardliners virtually indistinguishable from one another. All were former Revolutionary Guard commanders. This alarmed many members of the public, fearful of the militarization of the country and distrustful of any politician with such powerful friends in the security services.

Of the four hardliners, the most serious contender was Tehran police chief Mohammad Baqer Qalibaf. The 43-year-old was thought to be the favourite choice of Ayatollah Khamenei, and the Ayatollah's swift acceptance of Qalibaf's resignation as police chief was taken by many as an unofficial endorsement. From the outset, Qalibaf displayed a flair for the theatrics of a presidential election campaign. On the day he walked into the massive imposing building that houses the Interior Ministry to register as a presidential candidate, he abandoned his drab official clothing and wore a white suit and expensive Ray Ban glasses. He turned many heads and raised many eyebrows as he sauntered across to the Ministry looking as if he was going to a wedding on the beach of a tropical island.

Soon it became clear that he had the young voters in mind. While staying faithful to hardline ideals, he sought to appeal to the young, as well as the nationalists and reformists. Huge posters went up in Tehran and other big cities showing smiling young faces painted in the red, white and green colours of the Iranian flag. In public, he appeared clean-shaven, wearing what passes among Islamists as trendy clothes. He preferred to be known for his skills as a pilot of jumbo jets, appearing in a pilot's uniform in many of his election posters. In one of his campaign television spots, he was shown in the cockpit of a plane. Qalibaf certainly had a flair for populist presidential PR, but the greatest strength of his campaign was the widespread belief that he was the choice of the Supreme Leader Ayatollah Khamenei.

Qalibaf's detractors dubbed him Khalibaf, a Persian pun which rendered him as a blabbermouth. For many young voters it would take more than sunglasses and posters of aeroplanes to make them forget Qalibaf's role in the violent crackdown on student demonstrators in 1999 when university students came out in their biggest anti-government demonstrations to protest against the jailing of one of their professors on the charge of blasphemy. They also remembered his signature along with those of a number of other commanders of the Revolutionary Guard at the bottom of a statement threatening a coup against President Khatami. The statement was delivered in the summer of 1999 at the height of a bout of student unrest in the country. The commanders had warned President Khatami that unless he acted decisively to stop the student uprising, they would take matters into their own hands. So only those with short memories could give much credence to Qalibaf's credentials as a young popular choice. But despite – or perhaps even because of – his questionable past, Qalibaf was indisputably the hardline frontrunner.

No-chance candidate

The accepted wisdom was that Ahmadinejad had no chance. But the seemingly insurmountable odds only made the mayor of Tehran more bullish in his military rhetoric. 'A new push has begun. The hill we must take is Pasteur Avenue [which is the street where the presidential palace is situated in central Tehran]. God willing we will take it. Victory is at hand. Either we will achieve our aim or we will become martyrs, injured or missing in action. This will happen. There is a new miracle on its way,' declaimed Ahmadinejad in a campaign speech to his followers. The language of war he used was understood and appreciated by his supporters.[12]

Two years earlier, in 2003, Ahmadinejad had helped secure the victory of the neo-conservatives in the Abadgaran in the local council elections. The victory was a little hollow because voter apathy had left the field open to the hardliners, who managed a clean sweep. Ahmadinejad had also helped with the parliamentary elections in 2004 from which his friends in the Guardian Council had disqualified all the reformist candidates. Again the field was left open only to the hardliners, who managed an overwhelming majority. Now Ahmadinejad was looking for the same sort of 'miracle' that would propel him to power. And miracle it had to be, as his message to the voters was one that was hardly likely to energize a nation. His campaign motto was 'We Can', as if the nation was suffering from a chronic lack of confidence and needed to be talked up. In fact, during the past two presidential terms under Khatami, the nation had exhibited focus and direction. But the agenda had been reformist and for Ahmadinejad that was the wrong direction entirely. As a result, his speeches were an unpalatable blend of preaching and the stock promises of a candidate desperate to win votes.

The mayor of Tehran was very conscientious in covering as much of the country as possible. He travelled widely, attending rallies in places that other candidates perhaps considered unworthy of a visit. However, the rallies were hardly well-attended or inspiring affairs. According to the newspapers, who had no love for Ahmadinejad, the rallies would be attended by perhaps a few hundred people – mostly the pale-looking bearded young men of the Basij volunteer militia. They would shout slogans describing him as a Basij member and a comrade of Ayatollah Khamenei. More often than not, a man chanting mournful religious dirges about martyrs and imams – Shiite icons who had endured persecution in the early years of Islam – would open the programme. Ahmadinejad would begin his speeches with a prayer for the early return of the Missing Imam, the Mahdi – again a highly charged reference to fundamental Shiite beliefs. He would then describe his mission as laying the ground for a world Islamic movement by establishing a model Islamic government in Iran. He claimed that the establishment of such a government was the wish of the martyrs, the Prophet, imams and all Muslims and added that everyone had the duty to help institutionalize Islam in government. 'It's not like we have had a revolution and have established a government which changes hands every now and then and we will live like this for three or four hundred years. No, this revolution wants to become a world government,' he would say.

Ahmadinejad was – like any presidential hopeful – not stinting in his criticism of his rivals. Naturally, it was frontrunner Rafsanjani who was the target of much of his ire. He would berate those who, in his words, lived in palaces in spite of widespread poverty, and attacked government officials who led lives of luxury, spreading decadence and corruption and perverting the teachings of Islam. Although he never directly accused Rafsanjani, everyone knew who Ahmadinejad had in mind. He was keen to present himself as a champion of the common people against the cancer of corruption and immorality in government. Superficially he appeared to be echoing the left-wing ambitions of the 1979 revolutionaries. He would fight to bring justice, which had been compromised because of high interest rates: past monetary policies had enriched a few at the expense of the many. He promised to bring down the rate of inflation by cutting back on government expenditure. His economic model was 'an Islamic economy based on justice, whose aim is human progress'. He wanted an economy that served the people rather than helped an elite few to 'line their pockets'. He would decentralize government, sell off luxurious government buildings and offices and save money by purchasing cheaper premises. This was music to the ears of Iran's poor, who felt disenfranchised by the urban, middle-class reformist movement of the previous administrations.

The mayor of Tehran's political ideology trod a fine line between leftist empowerment and hardline Islamism. His statements were very easy to misinterpret. When he declared that he wanted to open the doors of government offices to the people to make the government more accessible and responsive, it was easy to misread him as a social democrat. But Ahmadinejad would not support the notion of democracy. Democracy, like decadence and corruption, was an evil to be defeated. It was, in his opinion, fundamentally anti-Islamic and a poisonous infection from the West. 'Some people keep saying that our revolution is aimed at establishing democracy. No. Neither in the Imam's [Khomeini's] statements nor in the message of the martyrs, nor in the words of the real pillars of the Islamic government has any such idea been considered.'[13] Ahmadinejad's intentions were clear: to establish a comprehensively Islamic system of government, free of any and every Western influence.

Another theme of Ahmadinejad's campaign was to emphasize his simple and frugal personal lifestyle. In his campaign broadcast on television, he invited the cameras into his home, revealing a modest sitting room, furnished with an inexpensive carpet and large cushions placed against the walls. There were no chairs or tables. The message was that this presidential hopeful sat on the floor in his home, just like millions of poor Iranians. How different this was from the Ray Bans of Qalibaf or the printed car stickers of Rafsanjani. Ahmadinejad even claimed that he brought his own food from home every day so as not to impose on the nation by eating at the Tehran municipal canteen. Playing the populist pauper was perhaps Ahmadinejad's strongest hand in the early stages of the campaign, but it was not contrived.

Former prime minister and president of Iran Mohammad Ali Rajaei was a key inspiration and role model for Ahmadinejad. A humble man of modest background, Rajaei was a devout follower of the Islamic Revolution of Ayatollah Khomeini and a champion of empowerment for the dispossessed. A former high-school teacher, Rajaei was president for only a few weeks in August 1981 before he was assassinated by a suitcase bomb. In his campaign, Ahmadinejad had promised to follow the ideals of Rajaei – modesty, humility, a man of the people for the people. Although Ahmadinejad's supporters welcomed this link with Rajaei, the man's widow, Ateqeh Sadiqi Rajaei, had other ideas. She said she had to come out in defence of a martyr who was not in a position to defend himself. 'In these elections, I notice with regret that, for propaganda purposes, the character of the great martyr Rajaei has been likened to Mr Ahmadinejad's, which is indeed an injustice. How can one embark on the path to justice by taking an unjust step,' Sadiqi said of Ahmadinejad in a public statement. 'I declare that Mr Ahmadinejad has no relation to the martyr Rajaei. The family of Mr Rajaei do not know Mr Ahmadinejad, nor do they have any links with him.'[14] A few years earlier, Islamic vigilantes had attacked a political meeting of a group of reformists and prevented Sadiqi from speaking. For Sadiqi, Ahmadinejad represented the unreasonable and unacceptable extreme of Islamism.

If invoking the name and reputation of Rajaei was intended as a vote winner, it was rather an odd choice. Rajaei had been in office only briefly, some 25 years earlier, and only those old enough to have followed politics in the early 1980s would remember him. Whether his name would pull the crowds was open to debate. But Rajaei, though not memorable, was a symbol of the dispossessed, and Ahmadinejad, with his crumpled clothes, worn-out shoes and quasi-leftist vocabulary, could find precious few other members of Iran's post-revolutionary elite with whom he could comfortably link his name.

Yet could Ahmadinejad, with his hardline Islamist rhetoric and disdain for secular and Western reform, really appeal to the workers and village farmers who wanted to see real improvement in this world rather than a promise of prosperity in the next? It was also rather disingenuous for the mayor to present himself as the great outsider. He was a well-established part of the Iranian governing class and had been involved in the Islamic Revolution and in the post-Revolution administration. He was an upholder of the current orthodoxy, rather than a reformer or a revolutionary, and a close friend to many of the leading figures in Iranian government. If he intended to surprise the nation and win the day, he would need something stronger than his scruffy man-of-the-people act, sincere or otherwise.

But Ahmadinejad did have something stronger. He had hundreds of thousands of members of the Basij and the Revolutionary Guard rooting for him. And they were unlikely to be passive in their support.

Hijacking an election

Polling day was 17 June 2005. The following morning, as the results were reported live on state television, something very strange happened. Six million votes appeared, vanished and then reappeared again. And these 6 million votes completely changed the outcome of the election.

On state TV, a reporter from inside the election headquarters stated that, according to the Guardian Council, more than 21 million votes had been counted and that Rafsanjani was in the lead, followed by Ahmadinejad. This was odd and certainly a surprise to many. But what happened next was even stranger. Within minutes another report was delivered repeating a statement from the Interior Ministry that 15 million votes had been counted and Rafsanjani was leading, followed by Karroubi. This result seemed to chime more closely with the findings of pre-election polls and the media understanding of the presidential race. So was the first statement a mistake?

Seconds later, the reporter was back on air. This time he confirmed that his earlier announcement was correct: 21 million votes had been counted and it was Ahmadinejad who was trailing Rafsanjani. The discrepancy was roughly 6 million votes, a not inconsiderable figure and something that could never be dismissed as a counting error. How could there be a difference of 6 million votes between the two government bodies? More importantly, why was the Guardian Council announcing the results while it had only a supervisory role? These questions gave way to accusations that this election was the most fraudulent in the history of the Islamic Republic of Iran.

The results in the early hours after the closing of the polls had shown a clear lead for Rafsanjani, and the performance of the other candidates also broadly followed the opinion polls. The general feeling was that Rafsanjani would poll the most votes, but, since he would not be able to poll more than 50 per cent, the final outcome would be decided in the second round of voting a week later. This would be a contest between Rafsanjani and whoever came second. Most believed that Rafsanjani's rival in the second round would be one of three candidates: Qalibaf, the hardline candidate who was thought to be favoured by the Supreme Leader; Moin, who was likely to get the votes of most of the reformists; or Karroubi, the popular senior cleric who had offered every Iranian over the age of 18 a cash handout of

Rls500,000 ($60). But by sunlight on Saturday 18 June, the day after the election, the results began to show an unexpected trend. A surge in votes for Ahmadinejad propelled him into second place. And by the time counting was completed, the final results of the first round of the elections shocked many. Securing close to 20 per cent of the vote, Ahmadinejad took second place with 5.7 million votes, only slightly behind Rafsanjani who had won just over 6.1 million. Karroubi came third with just over 5 million votes. The Interior Ministry said that 63 per cent of Iran's 47 million registered voters had cast their ballots. The results meant that Rafsanjani would face Ahmadinejad in the run-off elections – the first run-off since the 1979 Islamic Revolution.

Supreme Leader Ayatollah Khamenei hailed the results as a triumph for the Islamic Republic of Iran. 'With your wise participation in the elections, you have once again shown your strong will to be independent, and to defend Islamic values in an Islamic democracy,' Khamenei pronounced. At the same time, all the candidates except Ahmadinejad cried foul. Karroubi, whom the opinion polls predicted as Rafsanjani's opponent in the second round, alleged ballot rigging on a large scale. 'There has been a bizarre interference,' the senior cleric and long-serving activist of the Revolution told reporters as the results came in. Karroubi had offered an election promise of a $60 cash handout to all Iranians over the age of 18 as a means of redistributing the country's oil wealth – something many believed had significantly bolstered his chances in a country where more than 40 per cent earn less than two dollars a day. He alleged that the hardline volunteer militia force, the Basij, hand in hand with the ideological army of the Islamic Republic, the Revolutionary Guard, had stuffed the ballot boxes for Ahmadinejad. 'Interestingly, in the province of South Khorasan 298,000 votes were placed in ballot boxes from 270,000 eligible voters,' Karroubi declared.[15] Karroubi's clerical position and his standing in the Islamic Revolution gave considerable weight to his allegations. He took the rare step of publicly calling on Supreme Leader Ayatollah Khamenei to intervene and 'prevent a miscarriage of justice'.

But all Karroubi achieved was to anger the Ayatollah, who responded by admonishing him for 'poisoning the atmosphere' and aiming to create a crisis in the country. 'With the help of the Almighty, I will not allow this to happen,' he said in a verbal message sent through his aides. It was, of course, very easy to discredit any loser in an election claiming vote-rigging. Ahmadinejad dismissed Karroubi's charges as a case of sour grapes. 'It is very obvious that the one who has lost would protest,' Ahmadinejad said. 'I expect Mr Karroubi, who is a cleric and wears the sacred robes of a clergymen, to choose his words more carefully.' The Revolutionary Guards Corps issued a statement calling on Karroubi to correct himself and 'not to spoil the sweetness of this fantastic move for the people'.[16]

However, if it was no surprise that the man who lost the election should cry foul, something rather more shocking happened. Rafsanjani, the winner of the first round, expressed doubts about the validity of the election and claimed that the votes of the people had been subverted. His first reaction to the results was to privately inform the Supreme Leader that he was withdrawing from the race. But Khamenei persuaded Rafsanjani to continue with the election and remain in the running for the presidency, pointing out that his withdrawal would deal a huge blow to the credibility of the regime.[17] Rafsanjani baulked at the thought of undermining the Islamic Republic and was well aware of the political ammunition he would be handing to Iran's enemies if he boycotted the second round. But he was unable to remain completely silent, and when he announced he would stay in the race he issued a statement that spoke of 'a soiled' election and 'an organized interference' in the electoral process. His attacks did not name Ahmadinejad personally, but Rafsanjani did speak of 'those who are wearing the cloak of Islam inside out and are deceitfully engaged in defrauding the people by trying to portray their sick thoughts as original Islamic culture, and impose it on others'.[18]

Mostafa Moin, the reformist candidate who was seen as a potential threat to Rafsanjani, was even more outspoken and declared that he would not vote in the second round. He alluded to warnings of vote rigging that had circulated in the weeks prior to the election. 'When the government and political groups warned of the involvement of military personnel in the elections, their warnings should have been taken seriously,' he said. His party alleged that the Guardian Council had spent about $13 million in a campaign to mobilize 300,000 members of Basij to influence the votes. 'Take seriously the danger of fascism,' Moin said. 'Such creeping and complex attempts [at ballot rigging] will eventually lead to militarism, authoritarianism, as well as the social and political strangulation of the country.' His campaign advisors wrote an open letter to the Supreme Leader a few days after the results urging him to stop 'the coup d'état that was ... going through its last stages'.[19]

The Interior Minister, Abdul-Vahed Mousavi Lari, whose ministry was in charge of the polls, also echoed the allegations of fraud. He said that 'military organs' had accepted supervisory roles in the elections in order to influence them. A few weeks earlier, suspecting interference, he had warned the Revolutionary Guard and the Basij to stay away from polling stations.[20]

All this bickering and backbiting may have seemed unseemly to some, but to many the accusations of vote rigging were simply incredible, for to give them credence would be to think the unthinkable: the result had been rigged by persons at the highest level of Iranian government.

The plot

In fact only days before the country went to the polls, the fate of the election was decided at a high-level meeting at the residence of Iran's Supreme Leader, Ayatollah Khamenei, according to well-placed sources.[21]

At the meeting it was decided that Ahmadinejad had to be supported in preference to Qalibaf. The rationale behind this decision was a report presented to the Supreme Leader that cast doubt on Qalibaf as a suitable presidential choice. According to the report, many Revolutionary Guard commanders were critical of the lavish campaign expenditure of Qalibaf, the sources of which were either unclear or questionable. The report also alleged financial impropriety on the part of Qalibaf himself. More importantly, it argued that Qalibaf's campaign appealed to nationalist rather than Islamic sentiments. Qalibaf's overt attempts to woo the moderate, non-Islamist vote had lost him his core support. His abandonment of the Revolutionary Guard uniform in favour of a white suit and sunglasses was seen as a particularly blunt insult and a blatant move to distance himself from revolutionary values.

Perhaps Qalibaf's most foolish move was to go on record describing himself as a latter-day Reza Khan – the father of the Shah – who seized power in a British-backed military coup in 1921 to rule Iran with an iron fist for 15 years. Reza Shah – as he became after crowning himself king in 1925 – was known for a modernization programme that transformed Iran. It was this aspect of his character that Qalibaf wished to emulate. 'The country needs a Reza Khan, and I am a Hezbollahi Reza Khan,' he said a few weeks before the election, using the word 'Hezbollahi', which means an Islamic zealot in Iran.[22] This was unfortunate, as it conjured up all the wrong images in the minds of the hardliners and particularly the ultra-conservative clerics. Disdainful of Shiite clergymen, Reza Shah had driven them into silence and into the mosques, preferring a modern secular society which included – a particular anathema to the clergy – the forceful unveiling of women. With his background in the Revolutionary Guard and as a police chief, the idea of a Qalibaf with the mentality of a Reza Shah could pose a danger to the ruling clergymen. Suddenly the hardliner Qalibaf became an unattractive proposition for his hardliner support base.

His position might have been salvaged had he not trespassed on the commercial territory of the Revolutionary Guard – the smuggling of durable goods into Iran through the so-called 'unofficial' ports. These ports were run by the Revolutionary Guard to import goods which were then sold on the open market for a profit – part of a scheme that was supposed to help the Guard develop sources of income and lessen their financial reliance on the government. Speaking as Iran's police chief several months before the elections, Qalibaf had made it public knowledge that every year up to $6 billion worth of goods were being imported illegally through unofficial ports – which everyone knew only the Revolutionary Guard could have established.

By chasing the public vote, Qalibaf had merely succeeded in alienating his two powerful conservative power bases: the Revolutionary Guard and the clerics.[23] It was therefore no surprise that at a meeting in the Supreme Leader's residence a few days before the first round of the presidential election, a consensus emerged that if a homogenized hardline Islamist system of government was the aim, Qalibaf was not the most reliable vehicle to achieve it.

In order to secure the blanket conservative control of all branches of the Iranian government, the leaders had to look at where the grassroots support already lay. And here was Ahmadinejad's key strength: the Basij. Many members of the voluntary militia were already campaigning for the mayor of Tehran. This was not an organized conspiracy but simply reflected the fact that Ahmadinejad was the candidate who most closely captured their blend of fervent Islamism, conservatism and militancy. He had after all been one of their own. The Basij members campaigning for Ahmadinejad did so as individuals rather than as an organization. Three days before the elections, the Basij issued a statement emphasizing that the presence of Basij members in election activities did not mean the organizational involvement of the Basij.[24] But since the Basij commander, Mohammad Hejazi, had already told his men that they could campaign for Ahmadinejad as individuals, the signals were clear. In the last days before the election, the Basij became re-energized. In the central city of Isfahan, more than 20,000 people turned out for Ahmadinejad's last election rally. This was compared to the few hundred who attended his rallies on previous occasions. The stampede at the rally was so great that one 30-year-old campaign aide was killed – another martyr of sorts – as the crowd surged forward on the arrival of Ahmadinejad.[25]

In his post-election attacks on the Basij and the Revolutionary Guard, Karroubi pointed the finger at Mohammad Hejazi – national commander of the Basij – as one of the leading culprits in stuffing ballot boxes. 'I suggest to Mr Hejazi that if he wants to get involved in politics, he should form a political party where he can be its secretary general,' Karroubi said in his press conference on the day the results of the first round of the elections came out. 'We cannot have the Basij, funded by the taxpayer, involved in the support of a particular candidate.'[26]

Perhaps Ahmadinejad could always have counted on the support of the Basij, but the Revolutionary Guard was a different matter. They were internally divided on which candidate to throw their weight behind. The smart money was on the Revolutionary Guard backing Qalibaf. But five days before the elections, the Leader's representative in the Revolutionary Guards Corps, Ayatollah Mohammad Ali Movahedi Kermani, laid down a guideline. He issued a statement calling on the Guard to vote according to the criteria that had been set out by the Supreme Leader. These criteria included a simple lifestyle and modest campaign funds. Ayatollah Kermani mentioned no names but his message was clear: the Guard must support Ahmadinejad.[27]

After the election a top commander of the Revolutionary

Guard, Mohammad Bagher Zolghadr, virtually acknowledged that the Revolutionary Guard and the Basij had played a major role in the surprise election results. As the deputy commander of the Revolutionary Guard, Zolghadr was in a position to know. He described how the Guard had to work a 'multilayered' plan to make sure Ahmadinejad won the election. 'In the complex situation where foreign powers and avaricious forces inside the country had been plotting, and were determined to alter the election results to their own liking and prevent the establishment of an efficient, pure Islamist government, one had to act in a complex manner,' said Zolghadr, the most political of the Revolutionary Guard commanders. 'It was with the grace of God that the pure Islamist forces, by virtue of a good and multilayered plan, managed to attract the people towards the person who could serve them better and more effectively.' Zolghadr as much as admitted that the Revolutionary Guard as an institution did not stay neutral in the elections as it had repeatedly professed.

Of course, the reformists were not content to remain silent on what they saw as the theft of the election. Among the most vocal, the reformist opposition Mujahedin Enghelab Islami (MEI) was also the most precise about election fraud. 'According to the reports of the Ministries of Intelligence, Justice and the Interior, as well as the complaints of Messrs Karroubi, Moin and Rafsanjani, a military organization [presumably a combination of the Guards and the Basij] acted like a national party and implemented an operational plan that directed the votes of the people throughout the country and in particular in small towns and villages where political parties had no presence.' President Khatami also presented a secret report to the Leader detailing 'the misuse of the logistical, financial and human resources of the Guards and the Basij'.

Explanations for the unexplained magical 6 million votes that appeared out of the blue in the first round have varied. At the crudest level is the claim that each of the 300,000 Basij members throughout the country were required to produce 20 people who would vote for Ahmadinejad, thus producing 6 million ballots. Arithmetically convenient as this explanation may be, it is not likely to account for the discrepancy between the Guardian Council and the Ministry of the Interior poll figures. Former president Rafsanjani more plausibly accused the Basij and Revolutionary Guard of having used 6 million unexpired birth certificates of dead people in the elections. He told his confidants privately that as long as these birth certificates remained available, there would never be free and fair elections in Iran.

One alleged Basij member in Qom posted on the Internet the claim that he had used no fewer than eight birth certificates to vote a total of 11 times. And each vote went to Ahmadinejad. The anonymous writer said that this was done in the framework of an operation codenamed 'Nassr', or 'victory'. He explained that he and his comrades were instructed by an unknown commander based in Tehran who had travelled to Qom for this purpose. The commander told them that they were duty bound to use all means available to ensure that the right presidential candidate was successful. Everything was permitted, he was told. Trickery and cheating were justifiable weapons. For the commander and for the Basij, the election was a war, no different from the violent battles of the Iran–Iraq conflict or the Revolution itself. And in a war in defence of Islam, any action necessary was righteous. The writer explained that the Basij were told that Mostafa Moin, the reformist candidate, had been specially selected by the US. The commander detailed an international plot whereby Iranians were to have this US puppet foisted on them. In the aftermath of the election – so the claims went – millions of people were supposed to come out on the streets to celebrate. During the chaos, the revellers would call for the downfall of the Supreme Leader. At this point the US would enter dramatically and militarily, claiming to bring democracy but actually subjugating Iran and furthering its global hegemony. These notions might sound paranoid and far-fetched, but in the context of the invasion of Iraq and the international posturing of the US they captured the imagination of the Basij. Yes, they were at war with the US. Yes, the election was another, more subtle battlefront. And yes, they would do whatever was necessary to safeguard the Islamic Republic.

However, the anonymous writer made clear that it was only on the very morning of the elections that Basij members, primed with false birth certificates and charged with revolutionary zeal to protect the state, were informed of the candidate for whom they had to vote. And that name was Ahmadinejad. The writer explained that as well as managing to squeeze 11 votes from eight birth certificates, some of the different polling stations he attended were manned by other members of the Basij, who did not stamp the ballot papers. The Basij were told that the operation was top secret and that anyone divulging information about it would be treated as a traitor in wartime, according to the anonymous writer. It was indeed war.

If the rural areas of Iran were the front lines in the election war, the battle was still truly won and lost in the holy city of Qom. It was here that Ayatollah Mesbah-Yazdi, Ahmadinejad's spiritual mentor and key supporter, mobilized the students of the Imam Khomeini Institute. The seminary stopped all classes and encouraged seminarians to travel to remote corners of the country to canvass for Ahmadinejad. Ahmadinejad's supporters claimed that the junior clerics who took on the task at their own expense and without any trace of self-importance and arrogance stuck Ahmadinejad's posters on the walls and distributed his biography. Mesbah-Yazdi himself was careful to remain officially neutral in the elections. The religious establishment in Qom were keen to avoid being seen to exert overt influence over the constitutionally separate executive branch in Tehran. Mesbah-Yazdi's messages in support of Ahmadinejad were cloaked in generalities. His speeches merely described the core characteristics his followers ought to take into account when casting their votes. Not surprisingly, these characteristics added up to an obvious portrait of Ahmadinejad. Furthermore, Mesbah-Yazdi's sons Ali and Mojtaba – also clerics – issued a joint statement with other junior clerics declaring their support for Ahmadinejad and strongly advised other devotees of Islam to vote the same way.

Of course, everyone understood the Ayatollah's political preference, but the charade of political impartiality was upheld – at least during the election. Eventually, towards the end of 2006, *Parto*, the Imam Khomeini Institute's weekly newspaper, would divulge that Mesbah-Yazdi had been desperate to ensure Ahmadinejad's election. In an article, one of Mesbah-Yazdi's senior aides claimed that the Ayatollah even resorted to selling his wife's jewelry to help with Ahmadinejad's campaign funds. Not wishing to paint the president as a money-grabbing beggar, *Parto* also published a letter from a young woman and supporter who alleged 'we presented our gold ware to Mr Ahmadinejad but he did not accept them and returned them to us'.

Speaking nearly a year after the voting, Ayatollah Mesbah-Yazdi told a group of his students that their prayers had been answered.

'Because of the prayers, the wishes and the cries of the families of the martyrs, God almighty handed a victory to the families of the martyrs and the believers and brought to power people who were unknown and whom few people paid any attention to.'

The historical choice

In the second round of the presidential election, apathy was no longer an option for Iranians. What was left of their democracy seemed to be slipping away, but how could they influence events? Ordinary Iranians were in a quandary over whether to vote for the more moderate – yet still conservative and in many ways discredited – Rafsanjani to block Ahmadinejad, or to boycott the election in protest over allegations of vote rigging.

And could Rafsanjani actually block Ahmadinejad? Even if the second round were to be free of the intervention of the Basij and Revolutionary Guard and the vote were to be entirely fair, Ahmadinejad could now count on each and every hardliner to back him. He was now the candidate of the religious establishment, the choice of the Islamists and the voice of the rural and urban poor. On the other side of the political spectrum, there were plenty of reformists unable to bring themselves to support Rafsanjani, even to keep out Ahmadinejad. The religious right was unified, but the reformist and moderate opposition was disparate and disjointed.

Rafsanjani did not waste time in re-modelling himself as the champion of reform to increase his appeal. He warned of 'extremists' who, he said, had tarnished the polls with 'shocking instances of abuse and unjust organized interventions'. He decided that he needed to polarize the public, to energize any and every Iranian who opposed Ahmadinejad to vote for him. 'The Islamic Revolution is at a difficult crossroads, facing domestic and foreign threats as well as adventurism,' he said. 'I ask you to help prevent extremism with your massive participation in the second round.'

Ahmadinejad, meanwhile, in the last days of the election campaign, toured the provincial capitals. Everywhere he went, he now drew thousands and thousands of supporters. How different the response was to the lukewarm and poorly attended campaign tour of only a few weeks ago. Consistent with his approach in the first round, Ahmadinejad presented himself as a humble figure whose sole aim was to serve the people, particularly the poor, and remain true to the ideals of the Revolution. But now, this humble man had the ear of the Iranian people and the national media as never before. Newspapers reported Ahmadinejad as saying that he ran as an independent and did not have the support of any political parties or groups. As for his success in the first round, 'For me, it was not a big surprise. I know the culture of Iranians,' he said. 'I know how great the people of this country are. And I know that I have developed good relations with the people.' Either by political adroitness or sheer good luck, Ahmadinejad landed the perfect riposte to the urban moderate voices that cried election fraud: the first round results had articulated the true feelings of the ignored masses of Iran.

While Rafsanjani courted the reform vote, the mayor of Tehran was selling himself as the people's champion. He told jubilant crowds across the rural areas that if elected president he would reverse the migration trend from villages to towns by supporting farmers and helping agriculture. He promised to bring water to even the remotest villages. Sweeping though his pledges were, Ahmadinejad certainly had a sense of the desperation and fears of the Iranian rural communities. Across the nation, agricultural land had been left unattended for many years as the young had moved to towns and the old could no longer work. On his tours of the provinces, Ahmadinejad was discovering and wooing a second Iran, an Iran that cared about conservative values, an Iran that cared more about irrigation than reformist slogans on bandanas.

Suddenly Ahmadinejad had a strong, ostensibly left-wing social agenda. 'Unemployment, marriage and housing are the main priorities,' he said, capturing in one sentence the three main problems facing the youth of Iran. More than 70 per cent of the Iranian population was under the age of 30. The official unemployment figure was 15 per cent, but the true figure was significantly higher. In a society where pre-marital relationships were seriously discouraged, many young people with no prospect of jobs found it impossible to get married and start a family. The unemployed under-30s were sitting around waiting for life to begin and Ahmadinejad was offering a jump start. Even critics and opponents of Ahmadinejad accept that his man-of-the-people routine was broadly genuine. Sincere or not, he had made

a connection with the masses through simple living and simple rhetoric. 'I declared all my assets as the constitution orders. I live on a
teacher's salary and, thank God, I'm content,' Ahmadinejad said. 'My
biggest asset is huge – it is my love for serving people, and nothing
can compare to that. I take pride in being the Iranian nation's little
servant and street sweeper.'

In the final days before the run-off elections, Ahmadinejad was
invited to parliament to explain his position. The very hardliners who
had been pressing for him to drop out of the first round to avoid
splitting the vote were now keen to understand the man who was
their only election hope. They had to support Ahmadinejad now, but
they still wanted to know what they were buying into and, despite
his increasing national profile, they knew surprisingly little about
him. Speaking before parliament, Ahmadinejad launched into an
unusual and seemingly heartfelt rant that he was the victim of what
he described as a 'smear campaign'. The 290 members of parliament
were subjected to a barrage of complaints about foreign machinations
against his presidential campaign. It was a bravado performance. Here
was the no-hope candidate who had snatched a phenomenal victory,
which many thought was tainted, boldly railing about plots against
him. 'This group [of plotters] has a base inside the country too. It
started to spread the rumour that so and so is a murderer and a terrorist. No one is safe in such an atmosphere. They think with these allegations I will withdraw. But they are mistaken. I know these mafia
types and I have their home addresses and their telephone numbers,'
he said threateningly.[28]

Parliament listened, bemused. What was this strange little man
talking about? The Tehran political rumour mill was always active,
and recently reports had spread alleging that in the early years of
the Islamic Revolution Ahmadinejad had been an executioner at the
notorious Evin Prison. Many leading figures of the Shah's regime and
left-wing opponents of the new clerical rulers had been put to death
there. According to the rumours, Ahmadinejad had been in charge
of delivering the coup de grâce to those who had been felled by the
firing squads. But it was not the first time that Ahmadinejad's words
had baffled and wrong-footed his audience and it would not be the
last. Many listening in parliament on that day were uneasy about his
political judgement in making reference – and thus perhaps giving

credence – to rumours which could only damage him. And his menac-
ing claim to know his opponents' home addresses did little to dispel
allegations that he was a thug.

Among many in parliament, where the reformists and moderates
still controlled about half the seats, there were concerns that he would
roll back the reforms of the previous eight years and impose strict
interpretations of Islam that would make life a nightmare for large
sections of the population. Ahmadinejad wore his religious beliefs on
his sleeve and many were worried that he would push for even greater
Islamization of everyday life, such as further gender segregation. There
were fears that he would extend the gender divide to buses, public
transport and even the lifts in government buildings.

Ahmadinejad's performance did not impress many of the MPs.
But for hardline parliamentarians there was no other choice. They
had to live with Ahmadinejad as their candidate, but their views of
him were ambivalent. Newspapers noted that the head of the hardline
faction in parliament arrived 30 minutes late for the meeting and left
early. The hardliners in parliament had to support Ahmadinejad but,
they reasoned, they didn't have to like him and they most certainly
didn't have to listen to him. Broadly, the slim majority of parliament
members came down on the reformist side, with 150 of the 290
members issuing a statement of support for Rafsanjani. The parliament, like the nation, was split down the middle.

Outside parliament, hardline and conservative groups were all
declaring their support for Ahmadinejad, mainly to keep Rafsanjani
out of office. On the other side, the moderates and reformists – many
reluctant – threw their lot in with Rafsanjani, amid warnings of the
danger of the rise of fascism.[29]

Rafsanjani's aides pinned their hopes on a massive turnout on the
polling day. They believed that the apathetic and the abstainers in the
first-round election would pour into the polling booths to prevent
Ahmadinejad winning. Parallels were drawn with the 2002 French
presidential election when the French public, left and centre-right,
had mobilized to support conservative presidential candidate Jacques
Chirac to keep out the right-wing nationalist Jean-Marie Le Pen in
a similarly unanticipated second round run-off. Now the moderates,
after the disaster of the first round, were taking nothing for granted.
Anonymous SMS text messages were sent to millions of people warn-

ing them of 'a catastrophe' if Ahmadinejad was elected. The messages urged all to vote for Rafsanjani, regardless of their place in the political spectrum. Now was the time for unity against a common foe.

Ahmadinejad's team were optimistic. 'We will win the run-off,' close aide Nasser Qomian said. 'Iranians have felt Ahmadinejad in their hearts. Iranians are fed up with Rafsanjani, who did little to improve the life of the poor,' he added.[30] Qomian was right. The tide was turning in Ahmadinejad's favour. The man on the street reacted better to Ahmadinejad's carrots than to Rafsanjani's sticks. The moderates had manoeuvred themselves into a negative campaign whereas Ahmadinejad had surged ahead with a campaign built on promises and aspirations for a better tomorrow. Somehow, Rafsanjani and the reform agenda had been relegated to the past. Ahmadinejad was the future.

'Street sweeper' for president

On Saturday 24 June 2005, the day after the run-off election, supporters of Ahmadinejad were ecstatic. It had become clear that their man had won a stunning landslide, dealing a humiliating blow to Rafsanjani and opening a new chapter in Iran's turbulent post-revolutionary history. Members of the Basij were seen distributing traditional cakes and sweets in Tehran and other cities. Ahmadinejad and Ayatollah Khamenei had both privately and publicly urged supporters not to take to the streets for fear of provoking violent clashes with Rafsanjani voters.

When casting his vote in the poor part of south Tehran, Ahmadinejad again claimed he was the candidate of the dispossessed. 'Today is the beginning of a new political era,' he said. 'I am proud of being the Iranian nation's little servant and street sweeper,' he added, repeating his refrain of the election campaign designed to pull the votes of the poor.[31]

On the other side of Tehran, casting his vote, Rafsanjani pandered to the moderates' fears. He said he was going to form a front to prevent extremism in the country – a front that would focus on moderate tendencies in political, economic, social, cultural and foreign relations.

Even before they had started to count the votes, the hardline newspaper *Kayhan* went to press claiming a victory for Ahmadinejad. 'The nation has finished the job,' screamed the banner headline. *Kayhan* had been a vocal addition to the Ahmadinejad camp since the first-round results. The previous week, the paper had declared Ahmadinejad the victor before the country had even gone to the polls. Now it was calling the election of the mayor of Tehran while the votes were still being counted.

When his victory was confirmed, Ahmadinejad gave a speech that was surprisingly magnanimous and conciliatory. He promised to 'build up an exemplary, developed and powerful Islamic society'. In doing so, he was stretching out the hand of partnership to the moderates and reformists. 'Today, all rivalries should turn into friendship. We are part of a big family that should go hand in hand to build our proud Iran,' the 49-year-old president-elect declared, calling for reconciliation after a damaging, divisive and bitter campaign.[32] So far at least, this did not look like the 'catastrophe' predicted by the doomsayers of Rafsanjani's campaign.

Final declared results gave Ahmadinejad 17.2 million votes, or 61.69 per cent of the total, against Rafsanjani's 10 million votes, or 35.92 per cent of the total. Turnout was reported at 59.72 per cent, slightly lower than in the first round. But allegations of vote rigging again began to fly around almost immediately, as with the first-round results. In an uncharacteristically blunt public statement, 'the moderate cleric' Rafsanjani, a heavyweight of the Islamic Republic, alleged that an illegal dirty tricks campaign had been mounted. 'All the means of the regime were used in an organized and illegal way to intervene in the election,' he said. He condemned those whom he said spent hundreds of billions of rials (tens of millions of US dollars) of the people's money to defame him and his family.[33]

The eyes of the moderates were on their presidential candidate, but it seemed that Rafsanjani had lost the taste for a fight. He declared that he would not be contesting the election results. It was clear to him that the judiciary either could not or would not examine the allegations of vote rigging. His final words on the subject were unusually fatalistic and perhaps revealed an acute insight into the shape of the troubles to come: 'This I will leave to God.'

World fears

The moderates of Iran were not the only people reeling from the results. The outside world, which did not expect the election of a hardline Islamic populist amid crucial negotiations over Iran's nuclear programme, was no less stunned.

Many diplomatic missions in Tehran, including the British embassy, came under pressure from their governments for wrongly calling the elections. Their failure was understandable though. Ahmadinejad had been completely under the radar in the first-round election coverage. The British diplomats were content to admit this. 'The embassy, in its prediction of the first round of the presidential elections on 17 June, had completely failed to spot the emergence of Mahmoud Ahmadinejad,' a British Foreign Office source conceded. 'Trying to predict events in Iran is a mug's game,' the spokesman continued. When pressed on the diplomatic line to be adopted by the British government in relation to this new extreme Islamist president, the spokesman explained that the current official policy was nothing more sophisticated than 'wait and see'. He did add a worrying caveat though: 'Our analysis is this guy appears to be a throwback to the early 1980s and that cannot be a good thing.' [34]

While the British were characteristically cautious, the Americans were forthright. The US State Department delivered a very strong statement of concern. It said that the US remained sceptical that the Iranian regime was interested in addressing either the legitimate desires of its own people or the concerns of the broader international community. The US was not anticipating a friend in Ahmadinejad.

'A white coup d'état'

The second-round results were, in their own way, as baffling as those of the first round. There were only two logical explanations. Either in the space of less than a week there had been a massive sea-change in the public opinion across the whole of Iran in favour of a largely unknown Ahmadinejad, or there had been what Ahmadinejad's opponents described as a 'white coup d'état'.[35]

People wanted to understand what had happened and whom they could blame. The accusations were not long in coming. Rafsanjani's senior advisor and editor of the reformist *Shargh* newspaper,

Mohammad Atrianfar, inevitably pointed the finger at the Basij and the Revolutionary Guard. As with the first round, Atrianfar believed that the Basij had been called on to get out votes for Ahmadinejad. 'We have seen forms that were distributed among Basij members in some of the 70,000 Basij bases throughout the country that called on each member to bring out ten individuals to the polls to vote for a candidate with the characteristics of Ahmadinejad,' said Atrianfar. His analysis of the voting figures also showed the near impossibility of the results without outside interference. According to Atrianfar's analysis, approximately the same number of people voted in the run-off as in the first round. An examination of how people voted and how one might reasonably expect votes to be transferred to one of the two remaining candidates in the second round suggested to Atrianfar that something was deeply amiss. He believed that even if all those who had voted for other hardline candidates in the first round switched their votes to Ahmadinejad in the second round, Ahmadinejad would still be short of the necessary numbers to beat Rafsanjani's combined votes of the reformists and moderate conservatives.

Firmly in the reformist camp, Atrianfar's analysis could be expected to have a partisan tinge. But other observers came to similar conclusions. For Iran analyst Bill Samii, the results defied logic:

> There were 46,786,418 eligible voters, and 27,959,253 of them voted on 24 June, for a total turnout of almost 60 per cent. The previous week, 29,439,982 people voted, for a turnout of almost 63 per cent. In the second round of the election, Ahmadinejad received 17,248,782 votes, while in the first round he got 5,710,354 votes. How did he gather an additional 11.5 million votes in one week? Even if voter participation remained the same, and if Ahmadinejad received the 5,815,352 votes that went to the other hardline candidates in the first round – Ali Larijani and Mohammad Baqer Qalibaf – that would only amount to 11,525,706. It defies logic that under circumstances where there were fewer people voting, support for Ahmadinejad almost tripled. Rafsanjani received 10,046,701 votes on 24 June, while he got 6,159,453 votes the previous week. Obviously, not all Iranians who backed reformist candidates in the first round backed Rafsanjani, or he would have received their 10,409,943 votes, for 16,569,396. This would indicate that approximately 6 million voters stayed home, yet according to the official turnout figures, there were only 1.5 million fewer voters on 24 June.[36]

It seems unlikely that reform-minded voters in the first round would have cast their votes for Ahmadinejad in the second round, no matter how much they mistrusted Rafsanjani. They were more likely to simply boycott the election. And while it seemed possible that millions were energized by the dramatic choice on offer in the second round to come out and vote, not having voted in the first round, it was strange that all these new voters apparently came out for Ahmadinejad. Ahmadinejad's supporters pointed to his fervent campaigning in rural areas and the vocal Fatemeh Rajabi, wife of Ahmadinejad's spokesman, Gholam Hussein Elham, described this voting 'miracle' as 'a tsunami' which had swept away the 'Satanic' opponents, the reformists.[37]

Yet, while reformists and political commentators are correct that the figures do tell a most unusual story, there is no concrete evidence of large-scale election fraud. While the Basij may certainly have been whipping up support, dragging in friends and family members to vote for Ahmadinejad and even duplicating votes by using others' birth certificates, there is no doubt that Ahmadinejad did manage to win over a good many of the people of Iran. His frugal lifestyle and self-portrayal as a champion of the poor had done much to secure their votes. He had very successfully positioned himself as the candidate of the politically disenfranchised masses. Although in Tehran the young, upwardly mobile middle classes were calling for economic and social reform, Iran was still a nation where 40 per cent of the population survived on less than two dollars a day. Ahmadinejad's core promises to the rural classes – to reverse the migration from villages to towns, to revive the agricultural economy and to bring water to areas still reeling from years of severe drought – counted for something. By contrast, Rafsanjani's campaign was an irrelevancy for many of those outside the cities and towns. Ahmadinejad's populist campaign in which he repeatedly described himself as a humble servant of the people and 'a street sweeper' appealed to the ordinary voter who increasingly felt alienated by an elite that was preoccupied with factional politics.

But he had also managed to scoop up plenty of urban votes, not because of who he was but because of who he wasn't. Despite his obvious religious fervour, Ahmadinejad was not a cleric. And for many Iranians, this was an important and attractive quality in the person who would head the secular executive branch of government.

While outside observers saw Ahmadinejad as a throwback to the post-revolutionary excesses of the early 1980s, many Iranians actually saw him as a potential breath of fresh air in a political environment infested with clerics.

Ahmadinejad's votes came from both the religious right and the poor. The results reflected the gap between the rich and the poor, who for the previous 16 years, first under Rafsanjani and then under Khatami, had watched a small group of well-connected businessmen with links to top leaders and officials in the country lining their pockets while they were getting poorer by the year. But some blamed Rafsanjani for the victory of an upstart. Ahmadinejad, they believed, was the only choice for millions of people who had suffered under the carelessly constructed economic policies of Rafsanjani when he had been president. The silent, poor and frustrated majority, who had to keep down several jobs just to be able to make ends meet in their hand-to-mouth existence, had little to look forward to under Rafsanjani. The defeat of Rafsanjani and the reformists also showed that political and social freedoms were not high on the minds of the masses. Battling poverty and unemployment clearly was.

Yet, while he may have enjoyed presenting himself as the street-sweeper servant of the people, Ahmadinejad was a member of the political establishment through and through. Few could argue with the fact that the elections had helped centralize power in Iran. Now the hardliners were in control of the legislative, executive and the judicial branches of the government. Many observers believed that Supreme Leader Ayatollah Khamenei, rather than Ahmadinejad, was the ultimate winner. He was now able to call all the shots in domestic and foreign policies like never before. Whether the result of conspiracy and vote rigging, or through clever campaigning or through the very will of God, Ahmadinejad was now president of Iran. And that meant things were going to change.

CHAPTER 3

APOCALYPSE NOW

Let me enlighten all Christians that hardship, threats and wars will come to an end soon, and let there be no doubt that in the not-too-distant future the Prophet Jesus will rise again alongside the Mahdi to put an end to injustice in the world.[1]

He will return soon

A guard in a white navy uniform stood stiffly holding a glass of water on a silver platter. As the send-off ceremony unfolded, Iranian television showed Ahmadinejad among a group of well-wishers at the foot of the plane on the tarmac of Tehran airport. He passed three times under a Koran that had been held up by a Shiite clergyman. Then he kissed the Koran three times, each time slightly touching the book with his forehead. Finally, as he moved up the steps to board the plane his aides followed, sprinkling water.

The ritual has its roots in pre-Islamic Iran. It signals that the departing loved one will be sorely missed. In the old days, this traditional Iranian-Muslim send-off was reserved for those who were about to embark on arduous long journeys fraught with danger. But this was 13 September 2005, and Iran's combative new president was heading for New York in a jumbo jet to speak at the 60th UN General Assembly aiming to defuse the crisis over Iran's nuclear programme.

The elaborate traditional send-off shown on Iranian television symbolized a fresh attachment to traditionalism at the top. Since coming to power a month earlier, Ahmadinejad had exhibited a blend of unpredictability and attachment to tradition and religion that seemed excessive even in Islamic Iran, a country ruled by clergymen.

In the matter-of-fact world of the Iranian civil service, the new president's claim that he had been chosen by divine will to lead the nation raised many questions about the man now heading the country's executive body. For Ahmadinejad had made no secret of the fact that he believed he was destined to lead Iran only briefly before handing over the reins of power to the Missing Imam.

All three monotheistic religions share a belief in the eventual return of a messianic figure, a return that will herald an age of peace and justice on earth. For Shiite Muslims, that messiah is the Mahdi, also known as the Twelfth Imam, the Hidden Imam and the Missing Imam. His legitimacy derives from his lineage as the twelfth successor to the Prophet, following the line of Ali ibn Taleb. Born in 868 as Muhammad Ibn Hasan Ibn Ali, according to Shiite tradition he vanished at the age of six and would reveal himself again at a time when death, destruction, greed and injustice have all but engulfed the world. Most Shiite Muslims interpret the concept of the Mahdi as an abstract expectation that justice will ultimately prevail, but for others the Mahdi tradition is a literal truth. Ahmadinejad has aligned himself to this latter version of the tradition and, by extension, with its followers. During his swearing-in ceremony the newly elected president casually expressed to Supreme Leader Ayatollah Khamenei his expectation that his tenure as president was only temporary and that he would be handing power over to the Mahdi. 'What if he doesn't appear by then?' asked the amused Ayatollah. 'I assure you, I really believe this. He will come soon,' was the president's response. In an address to the nation a little later on, Ahmadinejad was very explicit: 'Our revolution's main mission is to pave the way for the reappearance of the Mahdi. Today, we should define our economic, cultural and political policies based on the Mahdi's return.' The Mahdi was suddenly on the political landscape as never before.

Ahmadinejad has been frank about his belief in the Mahdi's return. At a meeting of the foreign ministers of Islamic countries in November 2005, he stated without any awkwardness that the problems facing Iran suggested the Mahdi's return within two years.[2]

Not only does Ahmadinejad declare a belief in the Missing Imam's return, but he also asserts a particular affinity to him and claims that he regularly gets divine help in his decisions. Thus one should do everything in one's power to hasten the return of the Mahdi. 'I'm proud of this belief. It's nothing reactionary or superstitious. Indeed this is the ultimate in progressive thought. A belief in the Imam Zaman [literally 'The Imam of All Time'] is a belief in the world of tomorrow,' Ahmadinejad was proud to announce.[3]

Ahmadinejad chose many of his cabinet ministers from among devotees of his particular vision of the Mahdi. 'We have to turn Iran into a modern and divine country to be the model for all nations, and which will also serve as the basis for the return of the Twelfth Imam,' Ahmadinejad told his ministers at one of their first cabinet meetings.[4]

It is difficult to filter the truth from playful hearsay, but a popular anecdote in Tehran tells of one of Ahmadinejad's earliest cabinet meetings where planning for the return of the Mahdi featured on the agenda. Across the cabinet table a debate ensued on the need to encourage religious tourism and to publicize the culture of the Mahdi. One minister proposed that, as a matter of urgency, the government should set aside a budget for the urgent development of many new hotels. He argued that with the return of the Missing Imam in the next couple of years, there would be a rush of international pilgrims to Iran. In response, another minister argued that if and when the Missing Imam did return, there would hardly be a need for hotels, as the general public, in the spirit of justice and joy that would envelop them, would open their doors to all manner of guests, all enjoying a new epoch of peace and harmony. Ultimately the cabinet decided against building the new hotels.

Several months after his accession, Ahmadinejad was back on the subject during a tour of Kerman province. He must have felt particularly inspired, as in two consecutive speeches he divulged that world-devouring powers (code for the USA) were desperately seeking to find the Mahdi to prevent him from returning and establishing justice on earth. 'The American forces in Iraq have called in a number of esteemed clerics to question them about the whereabouts of the Hidden Imam and those who are in contact with him,' he explained. The West's vision of a New World Order was nothing other than an attempt to prevent the return of the Mahdi and the establishment of his own government. Ahmadinejad then reiterated that it was his political mission to hand Iran over to the Mahdi at the end of his tenure as president.[5] A few days later, the president gave a speech to

members of the Basij volunteer militia in the same province. The
world powers had built up a 'thick file' on the Mahdi, he revealed.
'The world-devouring powers have completed their investigations.
They are looking for his address so that they can go there and finish
him off. In our own Tehran, there are foreign elements who are asking
about the whereabouts of the Hidden Imam so as to prevent the establishment of a government of divine justice.'[6]

Iranians have been amused, bemused or confused by Ahmadinejad's
utterances – depending on their piety. But even the most fervent
believers have wondered about the president's intelligence sources
relating to Western efforts to track down the Mahdi or whether
he himself was privy to the Hidden Imam's whereabouts. And not
content with exploiting the mythology of the Hidden Imam on the
domestic scene, Ahmadinejad made a point of wheeling the Mahdi on
to the international scene as well. At a UN General Assembly session
in 2005, he warned world leaders to be ready for 'the emergence of a
perfect human being who is heir to all prophets and pious men', and
concluded his speech with a prayer that God might hasten the event.

The halo

It was to be expected that opponents of Ahmadinejad, both at home
and abroad – and especially in Washington – would leap on his utterances to portray him as either mentally unstable or extraordinarily
naive. For his part the president seemed oblivious to the ridicule he
was exposing himself to and continued to provide his opponents with
plenty of ammunition.

Days after his UN visit, Ahmadinejad reported back on the trip
to the senior clergy in Qom. There the president not only informed
the ayatollahs that divine forces were protecting him and the Islamic
Republic, but also described the 'halo-like light' that enveloped him
while he had been speaking at the UN General Assembly. Squatting
on his knees, as is traditional in Qom in the presence of revered religious leaders, the president told the conservative Ayatollah Javadi
Amoli that someone in the audience had told him that a halo had
formed around him when he started to speak and that it remained
there to the end of his speech. 'I felt it myself too,' the president said.
'I felt that all of a sudden the atmosphere changed, and for 27–28

minutes none of the leaders blinked.' Ahmadinejad continued, 'I am not exaggerating when I say they did not blink. It's not an exaggeration, because I was looking. They were astonished, as if a hand held them there and made them sit. It had opened their eyes and ears for the message of the Islamic Republic.'[7]

Ahmadinejad's visionary experiences seemed to leave the clergy of Qom cold. Ayatollah Amoli responded quite drily, simply remarking that he hoped the president would focus on implementing his election promises. Although the hardline conservative religious leaders were content to have a president who shared their politics, they were becoming wary of being usurped from their position as the moral and spiritual conscience of the nation and the supreme arbiters in matters of religion.

The Qom episode did Ahmadinejad no favours. Religious leaders felt he was crossing into their territory. Mainstream politicians thought he was indulging in superstitious claptrap and many across the social spectrum believed he was degrading Islam with ridiculous utterances.

The wishing wells

In the middle of nowhere in the deserts of central Iran there is a sprawling complex of huge turquoise domes and minarets known as the Jamkaran Mosque. Millions of pilgrims visit the mosque every year. According to the official history, one Tuesday night in 984AD the Mahdi appeared in the village of Jamkaran in the form of a 31-year-old man seated on a divan covered with a fine carpet. The Mahdi ordered Sheikh Hassan Bin Massleh Jamkarani, a learned local man, to build a mosque on a stretch of farmland on the village outskirts.[8] Thousands now converge on today's site of the mosque on Tuesday nights. One of the early decisions of Ahmadinejad's cabinet was to approve new government funds to help develop the complex and provide a rail link. Among the pilgrims who visit Jamkaran, Ahmadinejad himself can often be found sitting piously in deep concentration.

Many of the pilgrims to Jamkaran are poor and believe deeply in the return of the Mahdi – the natural constituents of Ahmadinejad. Typical of the attitude of most visitors was the response of one young man: 'Ahmadinejad's performance has been very very positive. I hope with the particular attention of the Imam Zaman [the Missing Imam] he will succeed.'

The mosque is particularly popular for its two wishing wells – one for each gender. Many thousands first visit the mosque and then move on to the wells. Requests to the Mahdi to solve their problems or grant their desires are written on paper that is then folded and dropped through the metal grids over the wells. The stories of wishes successfully fulfilled are commonplace and people continue to travel to Jamkaran looking for miracles. Mothers request cures for their sick children. Young women ask for love or a husband. Couples pray for fertility. Tales of disability, disease and despair disappear into the well on a daily basis. Yet the more devout pilgrims have one common prayer: for the quick return of the Mahdi.

'I wished for my father to regain his sight. He lost his sight some ten years ago,' says a young trendy man after dropping a message down the well. A woman in her 20s wrapped in a black *chador* whispers that she has come to wish that the man she fancies will make his move and ask for her hand in marriage. 'My patience is stretched to the limit,' she says, smiling. Another young girl, also wrapped in a black *chador*, says she has come to wish for the Imam Zaman to find her 'a husband he will approve of'. A third young woman is driven by thoughts beyond the personal and the romantic, saying that her patience is running out waiting for the reappearance of the Mahdi. 'I wish he'd come back soon. There is so much pain and injustice in the world,' she says, close to tears as her mother watches with concern. A middle-aged man living in the nearby holy city of Qom says he visits the mosque every Tuesday night. 'I don't want a mobile phone, I don't want a Pride [a small Korean-made saloon car popular in Iran], and I don't want anything. I just want him to reappear soon,' he says.

The president's well-publicized zeal for the Mahdi and his continual references to his very imminent return have done much to reinvigorate the cult of the Missing Imam. This in turn has increased the popularity of the mosque at Jamkaran. More than 1 million people were reported to have visited it on 9 September 2006, the Mahdi's birthday and a national holiday. Even allowing for exaggeration in this figure, it is clear that Ahmadinejad has elevated the Missing Imam from an undifferentiated element in Shia Islam to a clear presence in the minds of many Iranians. And all within a year of coming to office.

The 'early return of the Mahdi' has fast become an industry in Iran. Several information services were set up to keep the populace posted on the reappearance of the Missing Imam. Pre-eminent among these was the Bright Future Institute in Qom, which even had its own news agency to keep the faithful up to date with the latest developments in the Second Coming. 'There is a gap between us and the popular media,' said editor-in-chief Sayed Ali Pourtabatabaie. 'We started the idea of a saviour news agency of the Mahdi because we thought we needed a news agency to publish his news.'[9]

And in some respects the Mahdi has certainly returned. There have been several reported sightings of and interactions with the Missing Imam since Ahmadinejad brought him to the forefront of the public consciousness. Some have seen him fleetingly. Others have received proper visits. And a few lucky women claim even to have married him. A handful of believers have been arrested and jailed for claiming special connections with the Missing Imam, or for soliciting cash as a medium of communication with him. Inevitably, one or two have even claimed to be the Missing Imam himself.

The conservative newspaper *Jomhuri Islami*, which had supported Rafsanjani in the election, did not pull its punches in laying the blame for this creeping hysteria at the door of the president: 'The appearance of people claiming that they are the representatives of the Hidden Imam, or even the Hidden Imam himself, is not strange in the current disturbed situation. It is more worrying that these superstitious beliefs have found some powerful backers.'[10]

A month earlier, the paper had attacked the mythology of the Jamkaran Mosque itself, arguing that the origin of the mosque lay in the dreams of Sheikh Hassan Bin Massleh Jamkarani, who imagined an encounter with the Mahdi. The paper was uncompromising in its debunking of the cult: 'A mosque which is built on the basis of a dream can, at most, deserve to be respected just like any other mosque,' the paper's editorial said, expressing concern that Jamkaran was taking an importance on a par with some of the holiest shrines of Islam, such as the Al Aqsa Mosque in Jerusalem.[11]

Although the controversy continued to rage in the media, Jamkaran became fixed – and indeed grew in importance – as a pilgrim site, and supplications to the Mahdi continue to pour down the gender-specific wells. The mosque's own website was to boast that Jamkaran is embarking on the first phase of a development plan valued at $100 million.

The hardliners' hardliner

To understand the president's personal belief system, it is necessary to examine the influence of his key spiritual advisor, Ayatollah Mohammad Taqi Mesbah-Yazdi. This is a man who is notorious even in clerical circles for his fiercely conservative views, particularly on the issue of violence. Hard of hearing, frail looking and bespectacled beneath his white turban, he commands a significant power base within the hardline wing of the religious establishment. His uninhibited way of stating his views, his very outspokenness, yields up a very clear sense of his political and religious thinking. His opinions on the Hidden Imam and his connection with the new president are crystal clear for any political observer. From the moment of the president's election victory, Mesbah-Yazdi has repeatedly stated that Ahmadinejad's success was due to 'the special kindness of the Mahdi'.

However, it is not the Ayatollah's views on the Hidden Imam but on the use of violence that are perhaps most important to understand and be aware of, particularly in the context of his ideological influence on the Iranian president. As with Ahmadinejad, the Ayatollah is not prone to ambiguity: 'We must wipe away the shameful stain whereby some people imagine that violence has no place in Islam,' he stated in early 2006. 'We have decided and are determined to argue and prove that violence is at the heart of Islam.' [12] So close are the ideological links between Mesbah-Yazdi and Ahmadinejad and his closest aides that a study of Mesbah-Yazdi's thoughts and ideas is a study of the direction Iran may be taking under President Ahmadinejad. Mesbah-Yazdi's disciples include many of Ahmadinejad's ministers, members of parliament, senior government officials and top commanders of the Basij and the Revolutionary Guard.

But who exactly is Ayatollah Mesbah-Yazdi? The septuagenarian scholar of Islamic philosophy, born in 1934, is the director of the Imam Khomeini Education and Research Institute in Qom, the holy city 150km south of Tehran. One of the main functions of the institute is to produce missionaries to spread Shiite Islamic ideology both within and outside Iran. Not long after Ahmadinejad was elected president, Mesbah-Yazdi requested a budget increase for the institute. One of his ambitions was to train 500 Shiite clergymen to send to the USA to serve the Iranian Muslim immigrant community there – a suggestion that would have horrified the US authorities. Similarly, after visiting Indonesia, the Ayatollah reported that there were 220 million Muslims in the country, predominantly Sunni, who were thirsty for Shiite scholars.

As well as directing the institute, Mesbah-Yazdi is a senior lecturer at the Qom Seminary and a member of the so-called Experts Assembly – a body made up of dozens of senior clergymen with powers to change the constitution or choose the next Supreme Leader of the country. He was also once a director and a lecturer at the Haqqani School, a seminary in Qom which produced a stream of right-wing, hardline graduates who today occupy positions of power in Iran.

Although he provides the religious ideological framework for the current leaders of Iran, Mesbah-Yazdi has made no secret of his disdain for democracy. He has repeatedly stated that voting has no value or validity in an Islamic state, since the Supreme Leader takes his legitimacy from God and not the populace. This belief has proved highly controversial in Iran, where the founder of the Islamic Revolution, Ayatollah Khomeini, who still, even after his death, remains unquestionably the ultimate authority, time and again stressed his belief that the legitimacy of the Revolution and the Islamic Republic was drawn from the support and the votes of the people in referenda and elections.

Because Mesbah-Yazdi disdains democracy, the reform movement in Iran, as initiated by former President Mohammad Khatami, is anathema to him. His arguments and objections are religious rather than political, at least in their rhetoric. 'The prophets of God did not believe in pluralism. They believed that only one idea was right,' he said. 'What is being termed as reform today is in fact corruption. What is being promoted in the name of reforms and the path of the prophets is in fact in total conflict with the objectives of the prophets.' [13] But, as is often the case in Iranian politics, the boundary between religion and politics is seldom clear. While Khatami was in power, Mesbah-Yazdi and his disciples attacked his reform programme and labelled his government 'mercenaries of the foreigners'.[14] The most obvious group of foreign mercenaries were those elements of the press which supported Khatami's reformist agenda. For Mesbah-Yazdi these were spies and foreign agents.

The Ayatollah became popularly known as Professor Crocodile after his disciples secured the prosecution of Iranian cartoonist Nikahang Kowsar. One of Kowsar's cartoons depicted a crocodile strangling a journalist with its tail. Mesbah-Yazdi's disciples asserted that the crocodile was clearly intended to represent the Ayatollah whose name rhymes with the Persian for crocodile, *temsah*. Mesbah-Yazdi's disciples staged sit-ins at mosques in Qom, and Kowsar was eventually tried and jailed, eventually fleeing Iran to continue producing some of the finest political cartoons of Ahmadinejad and his administration abroad. The cartoon was a self-fulfilling prophecy and – whether or not this was Kowsar's original intention – Mesbah-Yazdi was certainly now the crocodile who strangled journalists with its tail.

Mesbah-Yazdi's disdain for the media did not extend to preventing the publication of an item which was to become highly controversial. *Parto* – the official weekly newspaper of the Imam Khomeini Institute of which Mesbah-Yazdi is the director – generated considerable controversy by printing advertisements for an organization known as the Headquarters for the Devotees of Martyrdom. The advertisement invited volunteers to register by posting a printed form to an anonymous PO box number. Although it did not explicitly mention suicide bombing, there was little doubt about what was meant when the advertisement described the objective of the organization as being to form divisions of martyrdom devotees in every Iranian province as part of 'an all-round preparation against the enemies of Islam and the sacred Islamic Republic government'. There was a public outcry condemning the formation of such armies at a time when Iran was being accused of supporting international terrorism. This suicide brigade was led by commander Mohammad Reza Jafary, a follower of Ayatollah Mesbah-Yazdi and supporter of Ahmadinejad. Jafary did not mince his words, telling his suicide bombers of the appropriate response to opponents of the Ayatollah: 'Anyone opposing this great man is in effect opposing Islam, and we will deal with such a person.' [15] Previously in *Parto* – which translates as 'reflections' – Jafary had eulogized Ahmadinejad when he was mayor of the capital: 'I have personally met Dr Ahmadinejad, the distinguished mayor of Tehran,' Jafary said. 'He is a Basij member and I recommend other officials to make him a role model.'[16] If a man is measured by the company he keeps, Jafary's devotion to Mesbah-Yazdi and Ahmadinejad speaks volumes.

Ahmadinejad's ambitions for a Cultural Revolution or academic purge are clearly shared by Mesbah-Yazdi. The Ayatollah advocates replacing university professors with clerical teachers from seminaries. He wants to cleanse the universities of pernicious Western influences, remove reformist and/or liberal professors from the staff and wipe Western thoughts from the humanities syllabus. 'There is a project being carried out to change and revise university books – something which involves clerics checking the books and figuring out the mistakes,' Ayatollah Mesbah-Yazdi once announced when calling for all university professors to undergo Islamic training by the clergy. 'The West is trying to weaken Iranian youth through some of the professors employed at the universities,' he said in the summer of 2006 at the same time as dozens of professors throughout Iran were summarily forced into retirement.

Compulsory retirement is not the only method of curtailing intellectual heterodoxy that Mesbah-Yazdi favours. He once energetically urged the immediate execution of Hashem Aghajari, a university professor sentenced to death by a provincial court for apostasy and jailed while on appeal. 'If this person is not executed today, there will be ten like him next year,' proclaimed Mesbah-Yazdi. Dr Aghajari was a history lecturer at Tehran University and a disabled veteran of the Iran–Iraq War. He was also a political activist and a member of the reformist Islamic opposition organization Mujahedin Enghelab Islami (the Mujahedin of the Islamic Revolution). The charge of apostasy related to comments made in a speech in November 2002, when Dr Aghajari questioned the tradition of emulation in Shia Islam, whereby laymen emulate senior clerics in their interpretation of the Koran. The question he posed was: 'Are people monkeys to emulate someone else?'

Aghajari's comments were hugely provocative. Not only was it offensive to the clerical hierarchy to suggest that they had monkeys as disciples and devotees, but, more importantly, Aghajari was undermining the very structure of traditional Shiite views of Islamic practice, namely that the path to God and the sacred lay through the mediation of the clergy. And the emulation of the senior clergy was the way in which that mediation was secured. It was therefore no wonder that a hardliner like Mesbah-Yazdi would respond robustly to any suggestion that emulation be abandoned. But to move from an angry retort to a call for quick execution had something of the impulsive trigger-happy about it – a Mesbah-Yazdi characteristic which obviously appealed to the impulsive Ahmadinejad.

Ahmadinejad does not officially acknowledge any direct connection with Mesbah-Yazdi. He was quoted on Baztab, a conservative website, stating in a private conversation with a member of parliament that 'there is no particular link between myself and Ayatollah Mesbah-Yazdi'. However, the president went on to praise Mesbah-Yazdi and to reiterate Ayatollah Khamenei's high opinion of the Ayatollah. 'I regard Ayatollah Mesbah-Yazdi as one of the great leaders of Islam and Shi'ism. The Leader [Ayatollah Ali Khamenei] has also been very kind to him and has described him as the second Motahari [Hojatoleslam Motahari, a leading Islamic theoretician who was assassinated in the early days of the Revolution]. I sincerely respect him as one of the leading scholars of Islam and the seminary.' The president concluded his tempered enthusiasm in the conversation by saying, 'My positions are based on Islam, Imam [Ayatollah Khomeini], and his Excellency, the Leader.' [17] Yet Ahmadinejad has placed several of the Ayatollah's disciples, such as Mustafa Pour Mohamadi, Gholam Ejehi and Mojtaba Samare Hashemi, in key positions of power and influence in his government. The obvious confluence of thought and commonality of objectives and ambitions suggests that the president's ideological debt to and respect for Ayatollah Mesbah-Yazdi run deep.

Serial murders in Kerman

In 2002, the southeastern city of Kerman was rocked to its core by a series of horrific murders. They captured the attention of the whole nation. After extensive investigations, six members of the volunteer Basij militia were brought to trial for the murders. Under interrogation, the gang confessed to killing three men and two women, out of the 18 victims recorded.

The casual brutality and sadism exhibited by the killers were breathtaking. The gang murdered one man by throwing him in a ditch and hitting him on the head repeatedly with a large rock before finally burying him while he was still alive. Others were drowned in a small house pool: gang members took turns to keep them under water by standing on them until they drowned. Amazingly the courts decided that only the very last person who had been standing on the victims when they took their last gasp should be charged with murder.

In court, the defendants explained that the murders were inspired by the desire to rid the earth of corrupt influences and argued that they had acted in accordance with Islamic teachings. In their eyes, the victims were 'Mahdur-ul Dam', or those whose blood can be shed because they were involved in un-Islamic activities, most commonly illicit sexual relations.[18]

The group explained that they murdered a young couple for being in a sexual relationship. 'We had been given to understand that Mohammad Reza and Shohreh were corrupt and that they had illicit sex together,' said one of the defendants in the court. 'That's why we identified them one day when they were driving in Mohammad Reza's Peugeot car. After we stopped them in the street, we took them to a large ditch full of water in the Haft Bagh district, and we drowned them both there. Afterwards we took their bodies in their car to the desert outside the city, threw them out there and set fire to the car.' The bodies of the young lovers were discovered in the desert, half-eaten by wild animals. On the night of their murder, the couple – who were formally engaged – were en route to inspect the house they intended to rent after their marriage.

Appropriate interpretation of Islamic law was central to the act of killing. Although the killers were not so interested in checking up on the facts relating to their victims, they were very keen to ensure that they killed in accordance with the Koran as they interpreted it. Hence, when they abducted a young woman by the name of Jamileh for a variety of alleged misdeeds, they were unable to kill her immediately because she was married and therefore her loose morals technically made her an adulteress. As one defendant explained, 'She was a pusher and a loose woman. Since this woman was married, we did not strangle her right away after we had abducted her. We stoned her to death after we had placed her in a pit we dug in the ground. Afterwards we took her body to the desert outside the city and threw her there to be eaten by stray animals.' Another victim, a male, was rather more fortunate. Having been picked up by the gang, a more vigorous textual exegesis suggested that killing him would be inauspicious and contrary to the teachings of the Koran. He was therefore set free.[19]

Of course, every nation and every religion has individuals with skewered perspectives and criminal and psychotic tendencies. What made the murders in Kerman exceptional was not that criminals were killing people under a deluded misinterpretation of religious law. Remarkable was the fact that the poisoned interpretation of Islam they used to justify these crimes was being espoused by a leading national religious figure – Ayatollah Mohammad Taqi Mesbah-Yazdi.

The six defendants were very clear throughout their defence that they were influenced broadly by the teachings of Mesbah-Yazdi. Indeed the ringleader, Mohammad Hamzeh, went further. He detailed how he had personally met Mesbah-Yazdi and asked him for guidance. In response, Mesbah-Yazdi had invited Hamzeh to attend a speech that he was to deliver later that evening. In the speech, Mesbah-Yazdi declared that 'the spilling of the blood of a person is allowed only if the person is given two warnings already to mend his or her ways, and they have ignored the warnings'. Hamzeh later told the court that he and his gang members had repeatedly warned those whom they later killed. Similarly, one of the other defendants made reference to a taped speech of Mesbah-Yazdi's in which the Ayatollah explained that a person is 'Mahdur-ul Dam' if he or she ignores two previous warnings. The defendant paraphrased the Ayatollah in the court, saying that whoever killed such a person would be regarded a mujahed in the path of God, and that even if society did not accept his actions and he was executed for this, God would accept him as a martyr. The implication was clear: the gang had complied with the Koran as taught by Mesbah-Yazdi and were surely innocent of murder. Even if they were to be convicted by this earthly court, the defendants seemed convinced that they had sufficient justification in Islamic law and would be exonerated and regarded as martyrs by God.[20] 'We came to the conclusion that our actions were in accordance with Islam and the law,' said the defendant. 'It was like a pain in my chest. Why should we allow a revolution for which so many martyrs paid with their blood to go to waste at the hands of such individuals?'

When the court in Kerman wrote to Mesbah-Yazdi for his explanation surrounding the claims of the defendants, he did not reply directly. Instead his office issued a statement saying that the Ayatollah had not issued a fatwa but had merely explained the views of senior clergymen on the subject. The statement also quoted the Ayatollah as saying that in this case the rule of the Supreme Jurisprudent (Vali-e-Faghih) had precedence over any court's ruling. It was his way of urging Supreme Leader Ayatollah Khamenei, with his powers over and above the constitution and the laws of the country, to intervene by ending the trial and providing Mesbah-Yazdi with a measure of cover.

This was never going to be a straightforward trial. The viciousness of the murders and the degree of public interest would see to that. But the defendants' affiliations – membership not only of the Basij but also of the Office of the Prevention of Vice and Promotion of Virtue – coupled with their argument that they had received their inspiration and theological justification from one of the leading ayatollahs gave the case a special twist. Both the political leadership in Tehran and the religious leadership in Qom brought pressure to bear on the judicial process. It was clearly not in the interests of the establishment, whether political or religious, for a whole set of theological arguments to be bandied about so publicly. But this was not a case that could be easily swept away. Kerman's chief of police made it clear that he had plenty to say on the subject, and was summarily dismissed for his pains. Eventually, despite the sensitivity of the trial and the enormous political pressures, the provincial court managed to find the six defendants guilty and sentenced them to death. In fact, the defendants were found guilty of the same charges three times because every time they were found guilty, the Supreme Court in Tehran would return the case for retrial to another court in the province. The Supreme Court argued that, given that the victims were 'Mahdur-ul Dam', the murders were not merely lawful but righteous. The Supreme Court asserted that the defendants were 'pious individuals, and their judgement that the victims should have been killed was not wrong'.

As the case ping-ponged between Tehran and Kerman, the general public grew increasingly outraged that the clerics in power were allowing, even discreetly encouraging, such acts of shocking lawlessness in the name of Islam. There was widespread anger directed in particular at the judiciary, which, instead of dispensing justice, appeared to be more concerned with getting the accused off the hook. Nemat

Ahmadi, the lawyer for the families of some of the victims, publicly acknowledged the sensitivity of the trial and the considerable vested interests at play: 'The judges in Kerman should be commended for maintaining their independence under such huge pressures.' All the while, only three of the defendants were in jail, simply because the families of the victims they had been directly responsible for killing had not, in spite of pressure, agreed to drop the charges. The others, including Hamzeh, were on bail and at liberty.

Outcry and despair at the mockery of the rule of law grew with each retrial. The English-language newspaper *Iran News* demanded that the government make it clear that people found to have taken the law into their own hands would be swiftly and severely dealt with. 'On no account should anyone who has committed an unspeakable crime such as murder be allowed to justify or explain away his or her transgression by saying that they committed the crime according to God's will or Islamic principles,' the paper declared in its editorial. Yet the message sent out by the Supreme Court's refusal to accept the guilty verdict and the deafening silence from the executive branch in Tehran was very different and was certainly not lost on other potential moral vigilantes. Serial murders continued throughout the trials, with copycat righteous murders taking place in Mashhad and Tehran.

Finally in April 2007, a fourth Kerman court delivered a verdict that the Supreme Court could accept and acquitted all six defendants. The fourth trial found the killers not guilty of murder, as they had considered their victims 'Mahdur-ul Dam'. The public response was predictable and futile. The families of the victims and their lawyers were stunned by the injustice, but public interest, ground down by the power of the religious establishment, simply waned.[21]

With the Kerman killings, a conservative hardline religious judiciary, murderous moral zealots and inflammatory violent rhetoric all combined to undermine the rule of law and to accept extra-judicial executions backed by the spurious theological rulings of President Ahmadinejad's mentor.

Ahmadinejad and the German philosopher

In a side street off Inghelab (Revolution) Avenue in central Tehran, there is a brick house that used to be the home to the controversial Iranian philosopher Ahmad Fardid. The house has now, in his memory, been turned into a foundation for research into philosophy, thanks to a generous contribution from the municipality when Ahmadinejad was mayor.

Fardid died in 1994, but his legacy looms large today on the Iran of Ahmadinejad. A proponent of violence, Fardid was a disciple of Martin Heidegger, a leading German philosopher linked to Nazi ideology. Fardid and his students have influenced many of today's top officials, including Ahmadinejad, by setting up a school of thought that synthesized Persian-Islamic philosophies with those of the West as interpreted by Heidegger.

Although an atheist before the 1979 Islamic Revolution, Fardid soon joined the tide of revolutionary Islam that was sweeping Iran in the aftermath of the Revolution, becoming one of the main advocates of government through Islamic jurisprudence (Velayat-e Faghih), as envisaged by the leader of the Revolution, Ayatollah Ruhollah Khomeini. A troubled intellectual with a sharp tongue, Fardid went even further when he became one of the staunchest advocates of the early return of the Mahdi.

The Islamic philosopher and leading thinker of Iran's reformist movement, Abdulkarim Soroush, has studied Fardid's intellectual development and his consequent impact on the political philosophy of post-revolutionary Iran. According to Soroush, Fardid and his students gradually became more well known as they began to spread their amalgamation of the ideas of Plato, Heidegger and others, on the one hand, with those of the Persian poet-philosophers Hafez and Molavi and ideas from Islam on the other. They offered their ideas to many clerics and their followers who desperately needed intellectual and philosophical support in their fight to consolidate the rule of the clergy in the political upheavals of the early days of the Islamic Revolution.[22]

In a complicated feat of philosophical reasoning, Fardid and his students elucidated the concept of the Mahdi from Heidegger's abstract notions of 'being', and set forth a series of ideas that were to guide many of Iran's policies under President Ahmadinejad. Certainly Fardid himself claimed that his political philosophy was an Islamic rendition of Heidegger's philosophy, although he and his students refused to concede that Heidegger was a leading philosopher of the

Nazis and a card-carrying member of the Nationalist Socialist Party in Germany until the end of World War II. Soroush argues that Fardid and some of his closest students theorized justifications of violence, ridiculed Western democracy, advocated anti-Semitism, denigrated and scorned human rights, condemned and rejected all of humanity's good achievements as Western decadence, dismissed tolerance as effeminate and presented all the world's organizations as conspirators against Islamic Iran.[23]

In Soroush's analysis, Fardid and his disciples took the totalitarian idea of a 'philosopher-king' from Plato, and a 'fuehrer' from Heidegger, to import a concept of 'strong leader' into Velayat-e-Faghih. From this emerged many characteristics of the hardline right-wing political philosophy that Fardid and his students propagated. Soroush explains their rejection of democracy from the fact that it relied on the actions of 'mediocre masses'. In the minds of Fardid and his followers, these masses had no business to either choose or to vote. They were there only to be led. Fardid and his colleagues interpreted liberalism as *ebahigari*, or permissiveness. They therefore rejected liberalism because it meant a permissive state of affairs leading to degeneracy, perversion and decadence. In their eyes, liberals were unethical, unreliable, immoral and corrupt beings. Fardid discarded the concept of human rights as deception rooted in the very concept of *ebahigari*, and labelled it a dirty trick used by the bourgeoisie against workers and the underprivileged.

Furthermore, Fardid and his followers propagated the European idea of anti-Semitism in a country that had no history of it. Although fiercely critical of Zionism, Iran's historical tolerance of Jews was maintained under Khomeini, who saw them as fellow 'People of the Book', protected and respected, as dictated by the Koran. But to Fardid and his disciples who were picking up Nazi idioms, Jews, and not just Zionists, were defective beings both mentally and physically, and whatever they produced was filthy and corrupt. Central to Fardid's school of thought was an all-encompassing conspiracy theory that the world had one ubiquitous master: the Zionists. He claimed that Zionists were running or manipulating foreign governments, international organizations and NGOs and quite a lot in between. To complete the paranoid fantasy, the conspiracy presupposed that Zionists and those they manipulated were lurking in every corner to subvert Iran and further their own interests.[24]

Soroush summarized Fardid's philosophy as follows:

> He used to tell them [his students] that all the things that are said in the world about justice, human rights, democracy, tolerance and freedom are lies; and that all the world's cultural and political organizations are conspirators. And that the whole world revolves around insincerity, duplicity and satanic power. Therefore, you in Iran should not concern yourselves at all with these pretty words and ideas either; you should advance your aims with violence.[25]

The parallels between Fardid's ideas and the speeches and actions of Ahmadinejad and Ayatollah Mesbah-Yazdi are very apparent. 'This whole thing bears signs of a calamitous degeneration in the course of the Revolution, especially so because Fardid's students and acquaintances are occupying senior positions and have occupied some places covertly and overtly; cultural offices abroad, cultural bodies at home, confidential bulletins, newspapers, the Cultural Ministry, *Kayhan* newspaper in particular, and so on,' continues Soroush. 'If I were to sum up his creed for you, I'd say it consisted of exactly the sort of thing that you're hearing these days from Mr Ahmadinejad and the people affiliated to Mesbah-Yazdi.'

Neither Mesbah-Yazdi nor Ahmadinejad nor any in the president's administration have explicitly allied themselves with Fardid or his philosophy. Indeed, Mesbah-Yazdi has gone on record denying any ideological crossover between himself and Fardid. Significantly, Ahmadinejad's messianism is a core part of his governing philosophy. While its moral absolutism and apocalyptic flavour are disturbing enough, it appears that the Mahdi's imminent return goes hand in hand with a paranoid aggressive hatred of global organizations and culture, a rejection of human rights and democracy and an anti-Semitism that courses through his whole worldview.

CHAPTER 4

IRAN'S NUCLEAR QUEST

*I don't agree with those who say the nuclear issue has created a crisis for the
country. What crisis? Nuclear technology is our right and no one can deprive
us of it. We have come so far, and, God willing, we will
need just one more push [to reach it].*[1]

Isfahan

With its centuries-old magnificent mosques and palaces covered with
intricate blue and white tile work and miniature paintings, Isfahan in
central Iran is known in tourist brochures for its grace and its Islamic
architecture. But few tourists come to Iran these days, and the city
is increasingly identified with Iran's modern-day preoccupation – its
controversial nuclear programme.

'As you can see the whole system is a closed system. It means that
the input and output is calculated by the IAEA, every gramme of the
yellow cake is measured,' said Iran's IAEA representative, Ali Asghar
Sultanieh, leading a host of visitors through the Uranium Conversion
Facility (UCF) on the outskirts of Isfahan.

These tourists were actually diplomats from a number of member
countries of the Non-Aligned Movement, and a group of international
journalists. They were on a rare tour of one of Iran's more sensitive
nuclear facilities. Wearing white and blue overalls, shower caps and
face masks, the visitors were shown around the facility where Iran
had been busy producing UF6 gas, which when spun in centrifuges
for long enough produces enriched uranium. The Iranians wanted to
show that the cameras of the UN nuclear watchdog, the IAEA, were
monitoring Iran's nuclear activities around the clock. The aim was to

111

convince the outside world that it needn't worry about the diversion of these peaceful activities to a weapons programme.

It was 2 February 2007, nearly four years after the IAEA chief, Mohammad ElBaradei, first visited the site and saw part of what he later called 'a sophisticated' nuclear programme that had been kept secret from the IAEA. Since ElBaradei's visit in 2003, Iran's enrichment activities had caused serious concern around the world. In many countries people found the prospect of Iran's hardline mullahs having nuclear bombs truly horrifying.

The IAEA had repeatedly called on Iran to suspend its more sensitive nuclear activities, as a means of reassuring world public opinion. Iran's defiance had led the UN Security Council to adopt two resolutions already, imposing sanctions against Tehran and threatening more if it continued to ignore the calls. But Iran had remained unmoved, saying that the suspension of its nuclear activities was not an option, that its programme was entirely peaceful and that it had no intention of building a bomb. It also reminded the international community that under the Non-Proliferation Treaty (NPT), of which it was a signatory, it not only had the right to peaceful nuclear activities but was entitled to receive nuclear technology from the IAEA and other NPT member states.

Iran's dogged determination to carry on had much to do with Mahmoud Ahmadinejad's election as president. In the 16 months since he had taken office, he had hardened Iran's position as he gradually took over the conduct of Iran's nuclear policy. He turned the issue into one of national honour, making it almost impossible for Iran to back down. His confrontational style and provocative statements worsened Iran's relations with the outside world. In due course he would liken Iran's nuclear programme to a runaway train with no brakes – a metaphor that sent shivers down the spines of Western governments.[2] The stand-off led to great tension in the region. The US sent another aircraft carrier into the waters of the Persian Gulf, with US officials saying 'all options, including military, were on the table'. Speculation was rife in the world media that military strikes against Iran's nuclear facilities to slow down its march towards nuclear capability could be imminent. In these circumstances, Ahmadinejad remained defiant, believing that the US, already bogged down in Iraq, would not attack.

The UCF facility outside Isfahan, a complex of several buildings made of brick and corrugated iron and plastic roofing, is nestled in the desert south of the city against a south-facing rocky hill. The first thing that is evident at the complex is just how vulnerable the whole facility is to an attack. Anti-aircraft gun placements that are just visible as one approaches the facility would be a feeble defence against precision-guided missiles. In the weeks before the conducted tour in early 2007, Iran had taken delivery of several anti-missile mobile defence systems from Russia, but they had not yet been deployed. The complex, if not the underground facilities, was, from a defensive point of view, a sitting duck.

Touring the main building that housed an extensive network of pipes, valves, cylinders and storage tanks, visitors saw a yellow powder that was visible from a small glass window built into the side of one huge steel cylinder. Known as 'yellow cake', the mustard-yellow powder was in fact treated uranium ore, mined in the deserts of Ardakan, not far from Isfahan. The production of yellow cake is the first step towards uranium enrichment. Visitors also saw big stainless-steel storage tanks under the watchful lenses of IAEA cameras that had been fixed high on the walls. The tanks, according to officials conducting the tour, contained UF6 – uranium hexafluoride gas. Its production is the second step towards uranium enrichment. Iran was said to have produced and stored 175 tonnes of UF6 – enough for producing enriched uranium for 20 nuclear bombs of the kind used in Hiroshima.[3]

The nuclear issue was the biggest challenge facing the government of Ahmadinejad. He had inherited a nuclear programme that was popular with the Iranian people and a terrible bone of contention on the international stage. Iran's nuclear programme had appealed to a broad cross-section of the people. Many Iranians, even those who opposed the Islamic regime in Tehran, derived a sense of pride from it. Ahmadinejad, like many Iranian leaders, felt that if one single issue were to unite the divided nation, it was this. And while some doubted the ability – militarily or politically – of the US to wage yet another campaign in the Middle East, others saw the possibility of a US attack as an opportunity to have a showdown with the demon of America, and so it might as well be over the country's nuclear capability. The feeling was: if there was going to be a war, what better issue to go to war over than the nuclear one – something that could rally the nation behind an otherwise vastly unpopular clerical leadership.

Ahmadinejad had not created this atmosphere but he took to his inheritance like a fish to water. This was the main issue on which he felt the previous administration had been too feeble. He could rally the country behind him with Iran's legitimate pursuit of nuclear knowledge and isolate his critics at the same time. He also knew that it would provide him international recognition and media exposure – something he increasingly craved.

The Shah and the bomb

Iran's nuclear programme pre-dated the Islamic Revolution of 1979. In the 1970s the Shah of Iran, with his close ties to the West and particularly the US, had embarked on an ambitious plan to build 23 nuclear power plants able to produce 23,000MW of electricity. The aim was to complete this programme by the end of the century at a total cost of $24 billion. The power plants, according to his plan, could supply electricity not only to Iran but also to other Persian Gulf countries, consolidating the nation's pre-eminence in the region. Iran had already signed the Non-Proliferation Treaty, which sought to curb the spread of nuclear arsenals. The Western countries supported the Shah's plan. They were only too keen to have another powerful ally in the Middle East as a bulwark against anti-West Arab nations. The US even encouraged Iran to expand her non-oil energy base and was prepared to sell Iran reactors and other facilities needed to set in motion an extensive nuclear programme.[4] Work soon began in the southern port city of Bushehr in the Persian Gulf, where German companies started the construction of a two-unit power plant. A French consortium was set up to provide the fuel. So clearly, Europe and the US set Iran on the path towards becoming a nuclear power.

But the Shah also had his eye on a weapons programme. Israel's possession of the bomb niggled him. Although relations were friendly, the Shah was keen to find a way of counterbalancing Israel's influence in the region. Iran was also on the southern edges of the Soviet Union. This was at the height of the Cold War and Iran had long borders with the Soviet Union, both in the Caucasus and in Turkmenistan. Most worrying was feisty next-door neighbour Iraq. The Shah viewed the Arab state as a menace to be kept in check, particularly as it had commissioned a nuclear reactor at Osirak – the one that Israel bombed in 1981. It is also necessary to view Iran's ambitions for a nuclear arsenal in the context of the Shah's obsession with his own power. He saw himself as having been appointed by the West as a regional policeman and, in his mind, allotted himself responsibility for the whole of the Middle East and the Horn of Africa. All this fitted well with the US, which was ready to help without hesitation. If there was to be a counterbalance to Israel, it was far preferable that it be a pro-Western Iran than any of the other rather unsavoury alternatives.

The US administration under President Gerald Ford offered to sell Iran a processing facility for extracting plutonium from nuclear reactor fuel – a facility whose only possible use was to produce a nuclear bomb. In fact the US was happy to enable Iran to have a complete nuclear cycle. Many years later Henry Kissinger, who was President Ford's Secretary of State, told the *Washington Post*: 'I don't think the issue of proliferation came up.' Even more interesting was that the Ford administration then included Dick Cheney, Donald Rumsfeld and Paul Wolfowitz, who 30 years later were also key figures in President George W. Bush's administration, arguing for the use of force, if need be, to stop Iran from enriching uranium.[5] But by then, yesterday's angels had turned into today's demons.

The Shah himself admitted in June 1974 to harbouring ambitions for nuclear weapons capability when he told journalists that Iran would have nuclear weapons 'without a doubt, and sooner than one would think'. The statement was later denied and the Shah corrected himself by saying that not only Iran but all other nations in the region should refrain from planning to acquire nuclear weapons.[6] There were also reports that he had set up a nuclear weapons team at the Tehran Nuclear Research Centre, and that experiments had been carried out in which plutonium was extracted from spent fuel. Many years later, the Shah's Court Minister, Asadollah Alam, confirmed in his memoirs that the Shah had envisaged Iran having nuclear weapons.[7]

The Shah's cooperation with the US reached its pinnacle when in January 1978 US President Jimmy Carter granted Iran 'most favoured nation' status for reprocessing, allowing Iran to reprocess US-origin fuel. Carter also agreed to a plan for Iran to purchase up to eight light-water nuclear reactors from the US. The West and particularly the US took the country up to the very brink of nuclear capability. In fact, the irony is that the ones to stop this march towards becoming the first Middle East nuclear power after Israel were the ayatollahs and the leaders of the Islamic Revolution.[8]

The ayatollahs and the bomb

After the Revolution, nuclear cooperation with the West was halted because of a mixture of disinterest on the part of the ayatollahs, and apprehension on the part of the West. The revolutionaries who came to power in Tehran decided that the nuclear programme was unnecessary. They theorized that the planned nuclear power plants constituted 'the continuation of dependence' on the West. They further argued that they were basically a waste of money for a country like Iran that was sitting on a sea of oil and gas. Thirty years later, nuclear power and weaponry are presented by the self-same ayatollahs and by now silver-haired Islamic revolutionaries as the symbol of Iranian independence from the West.

Iran's first post-revolutionary prime minister, Mehdi Bazargan, halted the construction of the two reactors in Bushehr – one of which was 90 per cent complete. He argued that nuclear power plants were uneconomical. This was in spite of the DM6 billion that Iran had already paid to the German contractors to build the plant.[9] All contracts for the construction of other power plants were cancelled and Iran's Atomic Energy Organization significantly cut back its activities. The Revolution had drawn a line under the policies of the Shah and the nuclear ambition was to be no exception to the rule.[10] In the post-revolutionary state, there simply were far more pressing issues than a costly and seemingly purposeless nuclear programme. Iran was in turmoil and few of the new leaders were thinking about nuclear weapons. In fact, only one of the ayatollahs exhibited interest. Ayatollah Mohammad Beheshti, arguably the most influential of Iranian leaders after Ayatollah Khomeini, was a keen advocate of Iran becoming a nuclear power. Before his assassination, along with dozens of other officials in a bomb explosion in Tehran in 1981, Beheshti managed to keep the flame of Iran's nuclear programme kindled. Before his death, he summoned a man who was one of the leading members of the Shah's nuclear programme team to tell him that he must build a bomb. The man, Dr Fereidoun Fesharaki, who now lives in the West, recalled being summoned to Beheshti's office in May 1979. He feared he would be arrested and interrogated, and possibly executed, as many top officials of the Shah's regime had been in the immediate aftermath of the Islamic Revolution. But Beheshti had other plans for him. 'It is your duty to build this bomb for the Islamic Republic,' Fesharaki recalled Beheshti telling him. Fesharaki left the country with the excuse of going abroad to identify and invite back Iranian nuclear physicists, and did not return for many years.[11]

However, the eight-year war with Iraq and its less than honourable conclusion, in which Iran reluctantly agreed to a ceasefire, changed everything. The sequence of events had been humiliating for Iran. On 16 July 1988, Ayatollah Khomeini penned a letter to all of Iran's political and military leaders. He wrote of 'a shocking' report by the commander of the Revolutionary Guard, Mohsen Rezaie, in which Rezaie had expressed utter despair at the course of the war with Iraq. The Ayatollah said that Rezaie had been unequivocal: if Iran were to come out of the war with its head held high, it would need plenty of sophisticated weapons, including nuclear ones. Rezaie's report did not perhaps have the effect he intended. Khomeini noted that the report was but one of many in the same vein and that, in light of this information, he had agreed to a ceasefire.[12] The war was over. Four days after writing the letter, on 20 July 1988, Ayatollah Khomeini publicly declared his acceptance of UN Security Council resolution 598 that called for an immediate ceasefire. He said accepting it was 'like drinking from a poisoned chalice'. He died ten months later on 3 June 1989, a broken man.

What is important about Khomeini's letter of 16 July 1988 is that it is the first evidence of the Revolutionary Guard believing in the need for Iran to have nuclear weapons. Interestingly, history has chosen to paint the Ayatollah as an opponent of nuclear weapons on religious grounds. This letter would seem to debunk that. Ultimately though, Khomeini's stated opinion, whatever his true position, would be overtaken by events. Within the year, he would be dead and replaced by Ayatollah Ali Khamenei, who was only too happy to support new president Rafsanjani in his determination to initiate a nuclear programme.

A clandestine programme began to take shape in Iran with overt and covert help from China, North Korea and a host of other sources that provided pieces of the puzzle. Iran began to give scholarships to thousands of students who went to Russia and Western countries to study in nuclear-related fields. Iranian scientists abroad were invited back to Iran for conferences and encouraged to stay.

But it was not going to be easy picking up the pieces from a decade earlier. Iran did not enjoy the friendship of the West that had come so naturally under the Shah. Under US pressure, the original German contractors of the Bushehr power plant, which the Iraqis had bombed no fewer than six times during the war, refused to resume work on the reconstruction and completion of the plant. It was not until 1995 that Iran managed to persuade Russia to take on the task.

For those who wish to associate Iran's aggressive pursuit of nuclear capacity with President Ahmadinejad, it would be worth pausing to note that it was his key rival in the 2005 election who re-established the nuclear programme. Rafsanjani also has the dubious honour of being the first Iranian president to publicly deny that Iran was after nuclear weapons. The central plank of his argument was that Iran's strict adherence to the tenets of Islam did not allow it to develop 'destructive and anti-human nuclear weapons'.[13] This was a commonly used argument by Iran throughout the 1990s and into the twenty-first century. On many occasions, Iranian leaders invoked the religious prohibition on nuclear weapons as a means of reassuring the outside world. Officials repeatedly referred to a fatwa, or religious injunction, that Supreme Leader Ayatollah Khamenei issued describing 'the production, stockpiling and the use of nuclear weapons' as an act that is not allowed in Islam. But this fatwa never appeared on Ayatollah Khamenei's website that lists all his fatwas. Furthermore, Islamic scholars believe that a fatwa can be revoked if the circumstances change. Even if the fatwa was not revoked, other ayatollahs could issue their own versions, which might even contradict a previous fatwa.

In December 2001, while addressing the congregation of Friday prayers in Tehran, Rafsanjani was able to square an adherence to the tenets of Islam with the need for the bomb. 'We do not want to fall victim to insecurity, and we do not want a confrontation to turn into World War III. That is the worst that could happen. If a day comes when the world of Islam is duly equipped with the arms Israel has in its possession, the strategy of colonialism would face a stalemate because the exchange of atomic bombs would leave nothing of Israel, while only damaging the Muslim world.'[14] This aggressive declaration must be seen in the context of the preceding months. September had seen the unprecedented terrorist attacks on the US. In October, the US had delivered a decisive response by invading Afghanistan, an Islamic nation and Iran's neighbour. A few weeks later, President George W. Bush's notorious state of the union address would label Iran part of 'the axis of evil'. Meanwhile Israel had threatened that it could attack Iran at will, if pushed. It was an easy moment in history to argue that Iran needed a strategic nuclear deterrent. And soon.

Iran wasted no time. Early in 2002, a CIA report described Iran as the country most actively seeking to acquire weapons of mass destruction.[15] But world leaders had not yet judged Iran's efforts to be a pressing problem. The complacency of the international community was shaken by an announcement on 15 August 2002 from exiled Iranian oppositionists alleging that Iran was building two nuclear facilities. The Mujahedin-e-Khalq Organization (MKO) alleged that a nuclear enrichment plant in Natanz and a heavy-water plant in Arak were already secretly under construction. The MKO had become militant opponents to the point of allying themselves with Saddam Hussein. This alignment with Iraq and their adherence to their cause through violence aroused much hostility among Iranians, and any allegation from the MKO was bound to be met with scepticism. Outside Iran, a number of governments and even the American Congress branded it as a terrorist organization. But subsequent satellite photographs shown on CNN seemed to confirm the existence of the plants identified by the MKO. But even this was not enough to drive the global leaders into action. Because of the unreliability of intelligence from opposition groups, it was not until these rumours were confirmed several months later by President Khatami himself that alarm bells were triggered across the world. In a keynote speech Khatami said that Iran was constructing a large number of nuclear facilities with the intention of mastering the nuclear fuel cycle. He also confirmed the existence of nuclear facilities in Isfahan and Kashan (Natanz) – facilities that were not known to the IAEA. He stated that Iran had plans to produce 6,000MW of electricity and stressed that Iran's programme was aimed at this and other peaceful uses of nuclear technology.[16] Although technically Iran did not need to declare the facility at Natanz to the IAEA until six months before injecting uranium hexafluoride gas into centrifuge machines, the secretive way in which the project had been pursued did not inspire confidence, and suspicion grew that – under the guise of producing electricity – Iran had developed a clandestine nuclear programme. External observers interpreted Khatami's speech as a declaration that Iran intended to master the nuclear cycle – which meant gaining a capacity to produce weapons-grade uranium.

There was also the issue of the speed with which Iran was proceeding with its programme to produce fuel for nuclear power plants that did not even exist. Iran did not posses the capacity to build nuclear power plants, and moreover the Bushehr power plant had been intended to use fuel produced in and imported from Russia. The question of legality would come up time and again in the diplomatic discussions. The Iranians persistently argued that the NPT allowed them to pursue a peaceful nuclear programme. They often went further and put the case that the NPT made it binding on the IAEA and nuclear states to provide member countries with assistance to acquire peaceful nuclear technology – something the Iranians said they had not received even in small measures. And they were correct on that point.

When, a couple of weeks later, the IAEA director, Mohammed ElBaradei, visited the facilities that had been kept secret from his agency, he found what he called 'a sophisticated' and extensive underground facility in Natanz. At the complex, 164 centrifuges had already been installed and there were preparations under way for the installation of another 10,000 centrifuges. Centrifuges can spin hexafluoride gas at high speeds to produce enriched uranium. Uranium with a low grade of enrichment might be used as fuel; highly enriched uranium is more commonly used as the core of nuclear weapons. Everything hinged on the level of enrichment Iran was aiming for. Or, perhaps more straightforwardly, everything now hinged on what the world believed Iran to be aiming for. And many global experts were coming to the same opinion: given the nature of the facility, Iran was working towards nuclear weapons capability.

Leonard Spector, a long-standing expert on proliferation issues, wrote:

Iran had secretly made considerable progress on two different routes to nuclear weapons. First, it had completed a pilot-scale facility to enrich uranium at Natanz using high-speed centrifuges, a demanding technology but one that is now spreading rapidly. If enlarged, the facility would be capable of producing large quantities of uranium enriched to the level needed for nuclear weapons of the type used against Hiroshima. Second, Iran appeared to have completed, or to be near completing, a facility at Arak for the production of heavy water, a product used in reactors designed to produce plutonium. This was the material used in the Nagasaki bomb.[17]

The IAEA report in June 2003 put Iran on notice to cooperate fully with the IAEA or be reported to the UN Security Council for further international action, as the US was already demanding. The report declared that 'Iran failed to meet its obligations under its Safeguards Agreement with respect to reporting of nuclear material, the subsequent processing and use of that material and the declaration of facilities where the material was stored and processed.' The US and Israel adopted a very hard line and threatened military strikes against the nuclear facilities if the diplomatic route failed to halt Iran's progress towards nuclear weapons. Europe was characteristically less robust but was no less clear on the core message: they could not allow a nuclear Iran. The response from Iran was that the only way to encourage the state to review its nuclear ambitions was through diplomacy rather than ultimatums and military posturing.

There followed several anxious months in which the international community increased pressure on Iran to suspend its sensitive nuclear enrichment work and come clean on all its activities, its purchases from abroad and its diverse facilities. By way of a concession, Iran reluctantly agreed to the so-called 'Additional Protocol'. This agreement gave IAEA inspectors the right to visit any facilities they wanted at short notice. Yet Iran also refused to divulge fully all its activities or the details, including locations, of some facilities. Many important questions remained unanswered. Iranian officials treated the UN inspectors with a good deal of suspicion. Occasionally a newspaper article or editorial would describe them as spies for Israel or the US. Inspections were often a tense cat-and-mouse game that created a lot of bad blood between Iran and the IAEA and led to more suspicion abroad.

On 15 November 2004, Britain, France and Germany, on behalf of the European Union, succeeded in convincing Iran to suspend its nuclear enrichment activities while the search for a diplomatic solution continued. At a late-night meeting in the former palace of the Shah in northern Tehran, the suave white-turbaned senior clergyman, Hassan Rohani, a powerful figure heading the important Supreme National Security Council, agreed with the ambassadors of the three European powers to suspend fully all of Iran's nuclear enrichment activities. A spokesman for the Iranian side, Hussein Mussavian, said the agreement could usher in an important change in Iran's relations with Europe and much of the international community. But he also added that Iran's voluntary suspension of its programme would be short-lived and was only intended to build confidence between Tehran and the international community rather than sound the death knell for Iran's legitimate pursuit of nuclear power.[18] Despite the caveat, all agreed that this was an important breakthrough for the Europeans in the long-running dispute between Iran and the West. The US remained highly sceptical but the Europeans intended to continue by putting together a package of incentives that would entice Iran to abandon the more sensitive parts of its nuclear programme. In a Middle East rocked by the war on terror and the invasion of Iraq, the global community preferred the carrot to the stick.

What crisis?

Iran's enrichment programme was still suspended when Mahmoud Ahmadinejad won the presidential run-off in June 2005. It was clear that the suspension would not last much longer.

Ahmadinejad had been forthright in his criticism of Hassan Rohani and his negotiating team all through his election campaign. In the eyes of the future president, these men had been ineffective and cowardly in the face of pressure from Western countries. 'Those who are handling the talks are terrified, and before they even sit down at the negotiating table they retreat 500 kilometres,' he complained bitterly. He vowed to take a far harder line in negotiations with the EU to defend Iran's pride and its nuclear programme. 'A popular and true Islamist government,' he added, 'will quickly change that.'[19] Western eyes are always on Middle East power shifts but the 2005

Iranian presidential election took on even greater significance in light of the nuclear issue. Diplomats close to the EU–Iran nuclear talks watched closely. 'We're holding our breath,' one told AFP in the run-up to the second round. 'If Ahmadinejad is elected, it will be very uncertain what will happen.' Another diplomat seemed to consider the result of limited importance. 'In any case, our position will stay the same. If Iran decides to break its nuclear commitments, we are going to the Security Council.'

Ahmadinejad seemed either oblivious to the trouble Iran was in, or he believed bravado was the way to win the hearts and minds of the electorate. 'I don't agree with those who say the nuclear issue has created a crisis for the country. What crisis? Nuclear technology is our right and no one can deprive us of it. We have come so far, and, God willing, we will need just one more push.'[20] On another occasion he said it was impossible to stop a nation's scientific progress. He described Iran's march towards nuclear capability as 'a flood which cannot be stopped by a matchstick'. Rhetoric such as this has a tendency to frighten diplomats and provoke strong responses from the international community, but Ahmadinejad was careful to always continue to offer the possibility of diplomacy. 'We will hold talks from a rational point of view and if they accept our legitimate right, we'll cooperate,' he said about the negotiations with the EU3.

Ahmadinejad's positioning on the nuclear issue made it very evident that, should he be elected, the chances of military action against Iran by the US and/or Israel would be greatly increased. Even before the votes had been counted there were reports that both nations were preparing for military strikes against Iran's nuclear facilities. Yet Ahmadinejad repeatedly rejected this notion. 'Analysts say no country, no matter how powerful they are, can attack Iran. They are right. It would be suicidal for a country to attack Iran ... so we must not bow to threats,' he said. But the trouble was that Ahmadinejad had not seen much of the world outside Iran and knew little about the dynamics of international relations.

There was no softening of his stance once he was declared president. If anything, Ahmadinejad's view hardened after he took office. He piled criticism on the nuclear negotiating team. His hard-line supporters – and there were many of them now that he had been elected – went even further. They described the agreement to suspend all of Iran's enrichment activities as worse than the infamous Turkmanchai Agreement. It was an emotive comparison. The Turkmanchai Agreement in 1828 led to the Qajar dynasty, defeated in a war with Russia, ceding Iranian territory to its expansionist northern neighbour. These territories were never regained and now form parts of the republics of Azerbaijan, Armenia and Georgia. In the eyes of the re-energized hardliners and conservatives, the agreement to suspend the nuclear enrichment programme was another attempt by internal traitors to sell Iran down the river to its imperialist enemies.

From day one of his presidency, the nuclear problem was a major issue. Ahmadinejad and Islamic hardliners were agitating for a resumption of enrichment activities. As he took office, Iran officially asked the IAEA to remove its seals from the machinery at the Isfahan Uranium Conversion Facility. The enrichment programme was back in business. Iran went even further and threatened to start up work at the more sensitive enrichment plant at Natanz if the Europeans continued to stall.[21] In fact, the EU3 had not even finished formulating what they hoped would be a set of incentives capable of convincing Iran to abandon its enrichment plans. They hurried through the incentive package, and a few days later the British, French and German ambassadors delivered the proposals in a document entitled 'The Framework for a Long-Term Agreement'. The document laid out proposals for long-term energy cooperation with Iran, as well as commitments to promote trade and investment and to help Iran enter the WTO. Promises were heaped upon promises in an attempt to dissuade Iran from carrying on down the road to nuclear capability. It did not take long for Ahmadinejad's government to respond and to respond definitively. In their eyes the proposals were 'a big insult to the government and the people of Iran'.[22] There would be no replay of the Turkmanchai Agreement.

Iran expected a far higher reward for abandoning its nuclear programme. For Ahmadinejad this was the time to play tough. To do that he had to take the driver's seat in nuclear policy. Hitherto, policy had been carefully and painstakingly drawn up based on consensus at the Supreme National Security Council, whose members included the country's top leaders. In addition, any decision would have to be approved by the Supreme Leader, Ayatollah Khamenei. In this decision-making process, there was no room for bickering or factional opportunism. But Ahmadinejad's election had changed the whole political orientation of Iran, tilting everything to the right. He immediately assumed a position that was even more extreme than Khamenei's. Until then, Khamenei had played a balancing act as the hardliner who stood up to some of the demands of the moderates who dominated the government. With Ahmadinejad now leading the government and talking tough, it looked as if he was outflanking Khamenei. And certainly, to advise caution in this atmosphere of bravado would make any leader sound feeble.

Ahmadinejad had made it known that he wanted to change the whole negotiating team. He wanted a new team to take 'a brave and unwavering stance on the nuclear issue'. Very quickly, Hassan Rohani resigned as leader of the negotiating team and was replaced by Ahmadinejad's election rival Ali Larijani. In his previous position as head of IRIB, the state broadcaster, Larijani had criticized Rohani for agreeing to suspend Iran's nuclear enrichment activities. He described the agreement as 'like getting sweets in exchange for a polished pearl'.[23] There could be little doubt what stance Larijani was going to take in the talks with the EU3.

With the IAEA removing its seals from the Isfahan Uranium Conversion Facility, work began on producing more hexafluoride gas as feed for centrifuge machines in Natanz. But the facility in Natanz was still out of commission and sealed by the IAEA as part of the November 2004 agreement. The international community watched with growing concern as Iran made noises about resuming work at Natanz. If reopened and equipped with sufficient centrifuges, Natanz could enrich uranium to the level required to make nuclear weapons.

The nuclear issue now seemed to be turning into a nuclear crisis. The proposals had been rejected. The negotiations were being railroaded by a new hardline Iranian team. Military conflict seemed unavoidable. It was at this point that Ahmadinejad travelled to New York to speak at the UN General Assembly in September 2005. This speech was heralded as an 11th-hour reprieve. In the unnecessarily mysterious and theatrical way that was to become Ahmadinejad's trademark, he announced that he had a new proposal to put before the General Assembly which would serve to defuse the crisis. But when Ahmadinejad arrived and delivered his speech, it was immediately apparent that he had either misjudged the mood of the global community or was being deliberately provocative.

The speech was a curious blend of the disingenuous and the overtly aggressive. Ahmadinejad reiterated that Iran's programme was peaceful. He attacked the attempts by foreign powers to prevent Iran from enriching uranium as the imposition of 'nuclear apartheid'. Significantly, he threatened to consider pursuing nuclear weapons if pressures on Iran continued. 'Those hegemonic powers, who consider the scientific and technological progress of independent and free nations as a challenge to their monopoly on these important instruments of power and who do not want to see such achievements in other countries, have misrepresented Iran's healthy and fully safeguarded technological endeavours in the nuclear field as pursuit of nuclear weapons. This is nothing but a propaganda ploy,' claimed Ahmadinejad. 'However, if some try to impose their will on the Iranian people through resort to a language of force and threat with Iran, we will reconsider our entire approach to the nuclear issue.'[24] However, the Iranian president did, as promised, have a proposal of sorts to make to the UN. He suggested that South Africa and Iran establish a joint venture to enrich uranium on Iranian soil. He believed that this would reassure the international community, as joint production would prevent Iran from diverting uranium into a weapons programme. The scheme was naively ill conceived, not least because Ahmadinejad had not even bothered to run the idea past the South African government. Neither did the idea convincingly calm fears about diverting the uranium. With three months' notice, Iran could pull out of the NPT, eject South African technicians and assume sole control of the facility, easily enriching the uranium as needed.

If this speech was intended to soothe the crisis, then it failed miserably. The president's uncompromising words and his clear threat to acquire nuclear weapons only convinced diplomats that the issue now needed to be referred to the Security Council. What made his visit to New York even more of a failure was that, to the horror of much of the international community, he also offered to share Iran's nuclear expertise with other states. This broke the international consensus on nuclear secrets. With just a few words, Ahmadinejad established a reputation as a loose cannon. His words after meeting with the Turkish prime minister, Tayyip Erdogan, did nothing to reassure the world. 'With respect to the needs of Islamic countries, we are ready to transfer nuclear know-how to these countries,' he told the Turkish leader.[25] Again, the Iranian president was thought to either be a deliberate agitator or incredibly foolish and naive about international affairs.

To many in the UN and in the West this was beyond the pale and smacked of irresponsibility. The way that Ahmadinejad offered nuclear expertise around like drinks at a party pointed to the clear and overwhelming proliferation dangers of Iran possessing such technology. The world had agreed on the nuclear Non-Proliferation Treaty as a means of preventing the spread of nuclear technology which could be used for making weapons. According to the NPT, such transfers of peaceful technology were allowed only between member states of the NPT and under the strict approval and monitoring of the IAEA. Yet here was a member state, a signatory to the NPT, under strong suspicion of striving to make nuclear weapons and – seemingly oblivious of its obligations under the treaty – promising to transfer unilaterally its nuclear knowledge to other states.

But this was Ahmadinejad's way of insisting that he would not subscribe to 'nuclear apartheid' – like the student revolutionary who wanted to be the hero of the underdog. And this was no one-off error of judgement. He repeated the offer many months later when he met a top Kuwaiti envoy.[26] The generosity of bestowing nuclear gifts on others became infectious. The Supreme Leader made the same offer to Sudan's hardline Islamic leader, Umar al-Bashir. 'The Islamic Republic of Iran is prepared to transfer the experience, knowledge and technology of its scientists,' Khamenei told the visiting al-Bashir.[27] Ahmadinejad's bluster now had the blessing of the highest authority in the land.

While in New York, Ahmadinejad also met the foreign ministers of the three European powers that had been negotiating with Iran until he halted the discussions on taking office. Again the Iranian president was not in the mood for reconciliation and discourse. He railed against the three European foreign ministers, accusing them of being lackeys for their 'American masters'. The ministers were shellshocked. 'No one could quite believe what had just happened,' one official said. 'All the rules that we had been playing to – and have been playing to for years – had been overturned. He was just not speaking our language. It was as if he had just walked in from the boondocks covered in dust.'[28]

Ahmadinejad returned to Tehran just as the IAEA board met to discuss Iran's dossier. The US and several European countries were in favour of reporting Iran to the Security Council immediately, but there was resistance to this idea from Russia and China and some members of the Non-Aligned Movement in the IAEA who wanted to give diplomacy a fair chance. With the IAEA board gathered round the table, Larijani warned that if reported to the UN Security Council, Iran would reconsider its membership of the NPT. This would effectively destroy the toe-hold external powers had in Iran. If Iran withdrew from the NPT, UN inspectors would no longer be allowed to visit the state's nuclear sites or suspected facilities. Such a move could have only one implication: Iran had chosen to pursue nuclear weapons.

Ahmadinejad's trip to New York was a failure, diplomatically, politically and in terms of public relations. Or at least, that was how the West viewed it. But in Iran the president was a returning hero, certainly among the hardliners. The official line was that the discussions had been an incredible success. Iranian television showed night-time pictures of thousands of Ahmadinejad supporters welcoming him back on the tarmac. They held posters of Ahmadinejad and flashed placards praising his unwavering stand at the UN General Assembly. Some of his supporters at the airport were particularly impressed by Ahmadinejad's invoking of the Mahdi at the world forum. They saw this as spreading the message of Shia Islam throughout the world, using the high-profile platform of the UN.[29] Ahmadinejad was now the champion of Iran's quest for nuclear technology.

Sanctions

But reality was about to catch up with Iran. The IAEA eventually reported the country to the UN Security Council. After months of deliberations and arm twisting, the Security Council agreed unanimously to impose sanctions on Iran on Christmas Eve 2006. The Security Council planned to increase the pressure on Iran by imposing greater sanctions every two months. They hoped that these incremental turns of the screw would force Iran to comply with the wishes of the international community. The sanctions were imposed under

Chapter VII of the UN Charter, which deals with 'action with respect to threats to the peace, breaches of peace'. Importantly, Article 42 of Chapter VII allows for the use of force to impose peace. Implicitly, war was now an option.

The sanctions in Security Council resolution 1737 were mild in essence. But they had serious psychological repercussions. They included a ban on the sale of any material to Iran that could be used for nuclear or missile programmes. They also imposed a travel ban across international borders for 12 individuals who were named in an annex to the resolution for having been involved in the development of those programmes. This list of 12 included the top commander of the Revolutionary Guard, Major General Yahya Rahim Safavi. The resolution also called for the freezing of the foreign assets of these individuals and also of seven Iranian companies involved in Iran's nuclear and missile production activities.[30] It called on Iran to suspend its enrichment activities and all efforts connected to a heavy-water reactor under construction in Arak. The Security Council threatened to meet again in 60 days and impose more sanctions if Iran failed to comply.

But Iran was not backing down. Ahmadinejad denounced the Security Council as a tool of the world powers, describing the resolution as 'a useless scrap of paper' that would not deter his country from pursuing its legitimate right to peaceful nuclear energy. He threw the threat of sanctions back in the UN's face, noting that Iran had already thrived under the US sanctions imposed in the wake of the hostage crisis in 1980. Iran had survived and advanced under these sanctions for nearly 30 years. More sanctions would simply help Iran learn self-reliance. 'Whether the West likes it or not, Iran is a nuclear country and it is in their interests to live alongside Iran,' asserted the president.[31] At home, the stand-off with the international community and the UN was doing Ahmadinejad many favours. 'The UN resolution lacks validity and is completely political and unlawful,' he told a cheering crowd in the southern city of Ahwaz. 'It is a political resolution adopted under pressure from the United States and Britain, although the content of the resolution is not very significant.' The nuclear issue, rather like the Al-Qaeda attacks on the US in 2001 had done for President Bush, had drawn all attention away from a dodgy election process and unified the nation against a common external foe. The attitude of defiance became endemic among the politicians of Iran. Officials claimed that the state would raise its enrichment activities to an industrial level by installing 3,000 centrifuges. Parliament tabled a motion to reconsider the level of Iran's cooperation with the IAEA. Within Iran, the president's resistance to what he was pleased to describe as arrogant foreign nations was proving very popular.

But Ahmadinejad was careful not to miss the opportunity to gain even more ground on his internal critics. Talking of the UN resolution, he remarked that 'it was adopted with two objectives. Firstly, to create psychological war and propaganda against Iran and also to give some an opportunity to frighten the people in the country with this hollow resolution.' [32] There was no doubt who he meant by 'some' – his election rival, Rafsanjani, who headed the powerful Expediency Council. The Council had been created many years earlier during the Iran–Iraq War to arbitrate on important national issues on which there was no consensus. Ahmadinejad was aware that he needed to pre-emptively outmanoeuvre the Council and Rafsanjani on the nuclear issue to ensure that he continued to enjoy the public's undiluted support. Rafsanjani had already described the UN Security Council resolution 1737 as 'a dangerous resolution', which he said indicated that world powers had designs on Iran.[33] Thus, in direct contrast to Ahmadinejad's glib and careless dismissal of the resolution as meaningless, Rafsanjani was attempting to portray himself as the concerned statesman. In order to not appear to be carrying the nation to the brink of disaster, Ahmadinejad had to assure the people of Iran that there was no real possibility of a military move against the state by either the UN or by individual nations, particularly the US.

It was a gamble on Ahmadinejad's part. But there were sanctions and they had their bite. Although they did not affect ordinary Iranians directly, a feeling of doom and gloom descended on the country. Several foreign banks stopped dealing with Iran, and, under pressure from the US, other banks called on their Iranian customers either to withdraw their funds or convert them to a currency other than the US dollar. The transfer of funds became increasingly difficult. Businesses, which were already reeling under government mismanagement, faced increasingly serious obstacles. Iran's financial relations with the outside world became more and more difficult by the week as greater numbers of foreign banks joined the sanctions against Iran and refused to handle money to and from Iran. Many businesses were on the verge of collapse. Iran felt itself slipping back into the role of pariah nation – a role from which it had begun to extricate itself through the reforms of recent years.

Psychologically the effect was considerable, and fear and uncertainty gathered momentum. Soon rumours circulated that merchants in the big bazaars in Tehran and other provincial cities had begun hoarding. Prices of basic foodstuffs rocketed. Domestic anxiety fed into anxiety about national security. There was considerable alarm about allegedly imminent US strikes on nuclear and military targets. Reports said the US was sending more troops and a second and a third aircraft carrier to the Persian Gulf. Ahmadinejad was happy to respond with displays of Iranian military might. State television repeatedly showed pictures of manoeuvres with rockets and images of missiles being fired. Iran seemed to be on a war footing. Ayatollah Khamenei issued a warning to the Western nations that if Iran came under attack oil shipments through the Persian Gulf would be stopped and US interests across the world would be targeted.

The stalemate between the global community and Iran was mirrored by the practical frustrations to Iran's nuclear dream. Although Iran could cling to its *right* to a nuclear programme, it could not make it happen without some outside support. The Russians were now openly dragging their feet over the construction of the Bushehr nuclear power plant, more than 12 years after they had started work on it. Iran did not divulge how much it had paid the Russians already for the construction of the power plant, but many observers put the cost at over $1 billion. That was costly for a completed nuclear power plant; it was simply ridiculous for a useless building site, which was what Bushehr remained. It was clear that under international pressure, the Russians were not going to complete the work and were only stalling in order to extract a good price from the West for toeing the line. At the same time, to cover themselves, Russia insisted that the power plant would present no risk of diversion to a military programme.

Pausing for thought

By early 2007, Iran was shunned by the international community, subjected to ever increasing UN sanctions and brought to the very brink of conflict with the West. How had it reached this point? Almost single handedly, Ahmadinejad had pushed Iran on a path of confrontation with much of the international community. His statements on Israel and his denial of the Holocaust (see Chapter 5) had stirred huge controversy that helped harden attitudes against Iran. And his undiplomatic language castigating the West for a range of real and imaginary crimes had not helped either. But it was the nuclear issue that mattered the most. World leaders would not become too anxious if a Middle Eastern religious zealot started badmouthing Israel and the Jews or sounded off about international conspiracies against Islam. But as soon as the word 'nuclear' was mentioned the stakes were raised.

For his part, in order to win popular support after an election of dubious legitimacy, Ahmadinejad had elevated the nuclear programme into an issue of national honour. It was simply politically impossible to back down or even engage in serious negotiations. By speaking on the subject at every opportunity, he turned himself into the *de facto* spokesman for Iran on the nuclear issue. Iran's nuclear policy was inextricably entwined in the person and personality of the president. His intimate involvement with the debate had completely undermined the Supreme National Security Council – run by Larijani – which was previously the sole policy-making body on the nuclear issue and whose decisions would normally be approved by the Supreme Leader. Ahmadinejad was a natural populist and had applied his knack for populist tactics to the nuclear issue. His exuberance bordered on fantasy and his eagerness to play the populist at times raised questions about his grip on reality. In one speech delivered at a mosque, he told the story of a 16-year-old schoolgirl who had managed to produce nuclear energy at home by buying a few simple implements from the bazaar. 'That girl is now one of the top scientists of Iran's Atomic Energy Organization, with security guards, a chauffeur, and other trappings of high office. This is belief in one's self,' Ahmadinejad said.[34]

Rhetorically, the president has likened the nuclear issue to Iran's struggle against colonialist Britain in the 1950s to nationalize its oil. He has delivered firebrand speeches on the subject all over Iran. In doing so, he has helped the nuclear question to become not just a national but a nationalist issue. 'The nuclear issue is even more important to us than the nationalization of oil that they opposed,' he said, referring to Western powers.[35] He compared giving up enrichment to giving up Iran's independence and stressed the moral importance of not backing down. 'We are not only defending our rights, we are defending the rights of many other countries,' he claimed. 'By maintaining our position, we are defending our independence.'[36] All this played well with the mass of the public and, as with all populist rhetoric, there was considerable political calculation behind the apparent rants. But with his tactics Ahmadinejad made it politically unacceptable to capitulate on the issue and left the negotiators with no room for discussion with the UN. Whenever there seemed to be a ray of hope for a diplomatic solution, Ahmadinejad would shut it out with tough rhetoric, stating that 'no Iranian official has the right to back down an iota'. And again, 'We know well that a country backing down one iota on its undeniable rights is the same as losing everything. ... We will not bend to a few countries' threats. Their demands for giving up our nation's rights are unfair and cruel.'[37]

When his internal critics said Iran needed to proceed with caution and wisdom, Ahmadinejad accused them of cowardice and weak resolve. Under his instructions, the Supreme National Security Council wrote to newspaper editors warning them against debating the nuclear issue – a warning heeded even by reformist newspapers for fear of being closed down. Newspapers were even banned from discussing the US military movements in the region – movements which Ahmadinejad described as psychological warfare. Internal debate had been stifled under the veneer of national security; only the hardliners had a public voice and that voice seemed to be madly shouting for a stand-off.

Even then, some could not keep silent, particularly in the face of Ahmadinejad's increasingly extravagant claims. The president suggested that nuclear technology would push the country forward by 50 years, even though a punitive response to its development might set them back ten.[38] This prompted a rare rebuke from one reformist journalist who reminded his readers that Pakistan's nuclear achievement had not propelled it 50 years forward, nor had the Indian tests helped eradicate poverty in India. But critical arguments were very few, and they did not matter anyway. Iran under Ahmadinejad had made its choice: nuclear or bust.[39]

Joining the nuclear club?

In April 2006 an elaborate ceremony was held in the holy city of Mashhad, where a beautiful golden dome on a sprawling shrine marks the tomb of Shia Islam's Eighth Imam. The ceremony was a thanksgiving of sorts. The president was thanking God for helping Iran to join the nuclear club – or at least approach it. The government had reported that Iranian scientists had enriched uranium for the first time, albeit to a low degree. Ahmadinejad was claiming the glory and announcing the news to an auditorium packed with officials, Guard commanders and clergymen flown to Mashhad for the occasion.

'At this historic moment, with the blessings of God almighty and the efforts made by our scientists, I declare here that the laboratory-scale nuclear fuel cycle has been completed and young scientists produced uranium enriched to the degree needed for nuclear power plants,' Ahmadinejad said. Behind him, a huge backdrop poster showed white doves in flight to emphasize the peaceful nature of Iran's intentions. (When India tested its first nuclear device in 1974, setting off fears of a nuclear race in the region, they had called the effort 'the Buddha Smiling'. The title was meant to convey that the test had increased the chances of peace rather than conflict.)

'I formally declare that Iran has joined the club of nuclear countries,' he told the audience. The ceremony was broadcast live on state television as the crowd in a large auditorium broke into cheers of 'Allah O Akbar!' or 'God is great!' Some stood and thrust their fists into the air.[40]

The announcement led to many official celebrations up and down the country. At some schools the next day bells were rung to mark Iran's new-found 'power and authority'. At some universities, the Basij militia students, who over the years had been admitted in order to intimidate other students and control student politics, distributed yellow-coloured cakes to mark Iran's progress from producing treated uranium (yellow cake) to producing enriched uranium. *Kayhan* announced in a banner headline that the West was 'checkmated'. It repeated Ahmadinejad's words that Iran's technological feat would 'change all the power equations in the region and beyond, turning Iran into the biggest power in the Middle East'. It claimed that Iran had only to reproduce the success to reach 'industrial scale enrichment'.[41]

While there was certainly considerable PR spin put on the announcement that Iran had joined the nuclear club, there was also sufficient credence in the claim to worry the West. A short time later an IAEA report to the UN Security Council said its inspectors' examinations 'tended to confirm' that Iran had used a cascade of 164 centrifuges to enrich uranium to the level of 3.6 per cent by feeding hexafluoride gas into the centrifuges.[42] The term 'nuclear club' usually describes the group of several nuclear weapon states around the world. By that definition Iran had not joined 'the club' – not yet. But Ahmadinejad was leading Iranians into a make-believe world in which their country had now obtained a seat at the high table of the nuclear powers. His eagerness to reach this status flew in the face of claims that Iran did not intend to become a nuclear weapons power.

In fact, so keen was Ahmadinejad to create the impression that Iran had joined the nuclear club that exactly one year to the day – now known as National Nuclear Day – he made the same announcement. The announcement was almost an exact repeat of the previous occasion. The president invited a large group of diplomats and journalists to hear that Iran now had the capability to enrich uranium on an industrial scale. An emotional Ahmadinejad, who had been caught by cameras shedding a tear moments earlier, told the audience in a big hall in the Natanz nuclear facility that Iran had 'joined the nuclear club' – yet again. 'With great honour, I declare that as of today our dear country has joined the nuclear club of nations and can produce nuclear fuel on an industrial scale.'

Later the IAEA confirmed that Iran's centrifuges were increasing by the thousand. The general consensus was that Iran needed tens of thousands of centrifuges to work around the clock for two years before they could produce enough highly enriched uranium to build one nuclear bomb. By the end of 2007, it was confirmed that Iran had around 3,000 centrifuges in operation. This placed nuclear weaponry several years away from Iran's grasp. But it did make the idea of a nuclear Iran a serious possibility.

By mid-2007, the IAEA chief ElBaradei was concerned that Iran's head-long move towards nuclear capability, ignoring all international calls for it to stop, could end in disaster. He repeatedly called on Iran to halt enrichment, at least temporarily, as a confidence-building measure. ElBaradei also warned the rest of the world against an attack on Iran, describing it as 'an act of madness'.[43] But there could be no denying that Iran was 'building a capacity, a knowledge' of enrichment that was irreversible. Not only that but Iran had also failed to furnish the IAEA with all the information it had asked for.[44]

Throughout his warnings ElBaradei stressed that he did not know for sure that Iran intended to build a bomb. Despite Ahmadinejad's sabre rattling, Iran had not formally declared an intention to acquire nuclear weapons and – it must be remembered – such a decision would not be for the president alone to make. It was a feature of Iran's constitution that decision-making powers were diffused, with the Supreme National Security Council ultimately functioning under the Supreme Leader. It was inconceivable therefore that, for all his bluster, Ahmadinejad would be able to embark on a nuclear arms policy solely on the basis of his decisions. ElBaradei would have been well aware of these constraints when sounding his warnings. 'Even if Iran wants to have a weapon they are three to eight years away,' he said, citing unidentified intelligence sources for his estimate. But 'the longer we delay, the fewer options we have to reach a peaceful solution'.[45]

In an interview on a BBC radio programme, he gave more details of his concerns about a war breaking out. 'I wake every morning and see a hundred Iraqi innocent civilians dying,' he said. 'I have no brief other than to make sure we don't go into another war or that we go crazy in killing each other. You do not want to give additional arguments to "neocrazies" who say "let's go and bomb Iran".' Asked who the 'neocrazies' were he replied, 'Those who have extreme views and say the only solution is to impose your will by force'.[46]

Iran was still some way from a bomb. But in Tehran, some observers were convinced that, with the insistence of Ahmadinejad and the hawks in the Revolutionary Guard, Iran was wasting no time in its goal of testing an atomic device. Those monitoring the statements of the Iranian leaders were convinced that Iran was concentrating all its efforts on testing a first device, ignoring the international community which was piling on sanctions. With such a test, Iran would truly join the nuclear club – something the hardliners believed the country had to do, come what may. Such a test would deter any US military strikes and change the balance of power in the region in Iran's favour.

In Washington it was thought that diplomatic efforts and the imposition of sanctions had done little or nothing to convince Iran to terminate its enrichment programme. Citing unnamed senior administration officials, the *New York Times* said that the debate had pitted Secretary of State Condoleezza Rice and her deputies against the few remaining hawks inside the administration, especially those in the office of Vice President Dick Cheney, who were pressing for greater consideration to be given to the idea of military strikes against nuclear facilities before spring 2008.[47]

CHAPTER 5

AHMADINEJAD VS. THE WORLD

We do not defend the War; we in fact condemn it. Sixty years ago there were people in power and they did what they did. But why should today's generation be burdened – burdened politically culturally and economically? Why must they continue to pay a ransom? Pay a ransom to whom? To a group of Zionists! What for? To suppress the Palestinians! I have no doubt that the great German nation cannot be happy about this.[1]

A world without Zionism

For no more than a few weeks every autumn the winds pick up in Tehran to push away the blanket of toxic carbon monoxide that usually hangs over the city, giving it a real autumn feeling. The quieter streets lined with trees are covered in yellow leaves. The atmosphere is serene, and, briefly, the metropolis rediscovers the magic of its sleepy early twentieth-century past.

Wednesday, 26 October 2005 was one such sunny peaceful day. Against this placid backdrop Mahmoud Ahmadinejad was to mount the podium of an obscure student conference and drop a rhetorical bombshell whose shockwaves would be felt around the world.

So what did Ahmadinejad actually say in this ill-fated address? The words most commonly reported outside Iran were: 'Israel must be wiped off the map'. This suggests taking an active part in the wiping out, which clearly implies violence. Not surprisingly, the world in general, but in particular Israelis and Americans, were shocked.

Was this a sign of genocidal intent? In the context of the Holocaust-denial language emanating from Ahmadinejad and his followers, it was no surprise that the interpretation put on his words was the most horrific. The 'Israel must be wiped off the map' language provoked swift and furious reactions. To the Israelis, this was the final evidence of Iran's malign intent towards the Jewish state. To the Americans and the rest of the world, Ahmadinejad's outburst underlined the importance of putting an end to Iran's nuclear ambitions. Indeed the affair could not have come at a more convenient time for those advocating a strong line against Iran.

Ahmadinejad's words created a climate that seriously threatened peace in the region, although there is considerable debate whether his speech was accurately translated and whether in fact he threatened war on Israel. The Persian words he used, quoting 'our dear Imam [Khomeini]', were: 'Een rejimeh eshghalgareh Quds bayad az safeyeh rouzegar mahv shavad.' Literally this translates as 'this Jerusalem-occupying regime must disappear from the page(s) of time.' The key phrases are 'az safeyeh rouzegar' and 'mahv shavad'. 'Shavad' means 'must become'. 'Mahv' is the crucial word. It can mean 'disappeared', 'obliterated', 'vanished'. It is a word whose nuance is difficult to convey in English, but it does not uniquely imply violence. If moonlight is obliterated by clouds or fog, the moon becomes 'mahv'. A man who disappears into a thick crowd or a smokescreen becomes 'mahv'. In occult terms, something which vanishes into thin air becomes 'mahv'. But it does not imply action on the part of a third party, inducing a state of 'mahv'. For this reason it is wrong to translate 'mahv shavad' as 'must be wiped off', which implies a specific action on the part of a third party.

In short 'mahv shavad' is a descriptive phrase meaning 'to disappear' or 'to vanish', whereas to convey the action of wiping out, Ahmadinejad would have had to use the phrase 'bayad mahv kard', or 'must be made to disappear or vanish'.

As for 'az safeyeh rouzegar', this has been loosely translated as 'off the map'. 'Rouzegar' means 'time' or 'day and age', so 'safeyeh rouzegar' means – to put it more elegantly – 'the pages of time'.

Thus a literal translation of Ahmadinejad's words would be: 'this Jerusalem-occupying regime must vanish from the pages of time'. This is hardly a friendly or reassuring message to the Israelis, but nor is it as aggressive and blood-curdling as 'Israel must be wiped off the map'. Moreover it is not the first time that an Iranian leader has expressed such views.

The Revolution of 1979 had abruptly put an end to the regime of the Shah, which had close economic and military relations with Israel. The new clerical leaders of Iran, committed to fundamentalist Islam, wasted no time in cutting these relations with Israel. The Israeli legation building was closed down and was then given to the representatives of Yasser Arafat's Palestine Liberation Organization (PLO). All trade relations, including oil exports, between Iran and Israel were terminated. Arafat travelled to Tehran to greet Supreme Leader Ayatollah Khomeini in the very early days of post-revolutionary Iran, cementing the Islamic nation's anti-Israel credentials. Very quickly, an anti-Zionist lexicon became common, as did anti-Israeli slogans and demonstrations. At rallies and large Friday prayer gatherings, hardliners shouted 'Death to Israel' alongside the more commonly heard 'Death to America'. Slogans to the same effect were painted on walls and bridges up and down the country, where Israel was referred to as 'the Zionist entity' or the 'Quds-occupying regime' (Quds is the Arabic name for Jerusalem).

However, the Islamic Republic under Khomeini was always careful to differentiate between Zionists and Jews. Although Islamic clerics harboured a deep-rooted religious suspicion of Jews, the Koran is very clear in its teachings. The Jews are People of the Book. They are fellow monotheists and followers of the Abrahamic faith. They are to be tolerated and allowed to practise their religion and adhere to their customs in peace. In contrast, Zionists were labelled as secular nationalists who had usurped Palestinian land illegally. In the official Iranian orthodoxy, the occupation of Palestine had nothing to do with Jews and everything to do with Zionists. It was a distinction that was also made by many Jews in Europe and America as well as by many non-Jews.

To mark the inherent support of the Iranian regime for the Palestinians in their nationless plight, the leader of the Islamic Revolution, Ayatollah Khomeini, named the last Friday of the Muslim fasting month of Ramadhan as Quds, or Jerusalem Day. The day was designated as one of nationwide demonstrations against Israel and support for the Palestinian struggle. Khomeini was unstinting in his criticism of the Israeli state and described it as 'a degenerative tumour' in the region that must be excised. On another occasion, he preempted Ahmadinejad by using the language that Ahmadinejad was later to echo about Israel disappearing from the pages of time.

However, Iran's actions never matched the rhetoric. Throughout the 1980s, Iran was engaged in a devastating war with Iraq. It was careful not to make another enemy of Israel, which would have been tantamount to suicide. During the war, when Iran became desperately short of weapons, the nation swallowed its pride and bought American-made weapons from Israel, albeit clandestinely. Ayatollah Khomeini promptly broke off this short-lived relationship when it all came to light, causing massive political embarrassment to the Iranian leadership. In fact, this Faustian pact was humiliating for all the parties, and the Iran–Contra affair – as it became known in the West – was the biggest political scandal of Ronald Reagan's presidency of the USA. It emerged that his administration had persuaded Israel to sell Iran some US-made weapons in exchange for Iran's good offices in securing the release of six American hostages in Lebanon. Encouraged by the success of the enterprise, the US administration began to sell weapons directly to Iran and diverted the proceeds to anti-Sandinista counter-revolutionaries in Nicaragua. Israel at this time was happy to see this relationship develop, as it was believed that it would draw Iran back into the Western fold.

But it was not to be, and the brief period of uneasy détente remained just a blip. With the end of the Iran–Iraq War, Tehran became deeply involved in the setting up of Hezbollah to increase its influence among the Shiites of southern Lebanon. And when in 1989 Ayatollah Khomeini died, his younger and more energetic successor, Ayatollah Ali Khamenei, personally took charge of Iran's policies in the Arab world. A veteran of the Iran–Iraq War, Khamenei was more militant and hardline than his predecessor. There would be no more deals with the US and certainly no financial arrangements with Israel.

The collapse of the Soviet Union sent a wave of optimism around the world that even succeeded in penetrating the incendiary Middle East. The peace process had swept up the Arab governments, even Iran's closest ally Syria, and threatened to isolate Iran. Globally, the US was basking in its victory and relaxing into its position as the world's sole superpower. In the face of this New World Order, Khamenei did what came naturally and aligned himself and Iran with the most hard-line elements in the Arab world in opposition to the peace process, which he denounced as selling the Palestinians down the river. Total rejection of the peace process and any compromise with Israel became the official policy of Iran and now – with a weakened and unpopular Iraq – Iran felt strong enough to back the rhetoric with action. Iran stepped up its support for radical Palestinians groups such as Hamas and Islamic Jihad, groups that the US and Western countries regarded as terrorist organizations and impediments to peace.

By this time Israel had lost all hope of making an ally out of Tehran and now saw Iran and 'Shiite terror', as the pre-eminent problem on its doorstep. And Iran was only too happy to oblige in the role of Israel's public enemy number one. In December 2001, former president Rafsanjani threatened Israel with nuclear annihilation. The man who three and a half years later was to stand as the moderate alternative to Ahmadinejad remarked at the time that 'one bomb is enough to destroy Israel', and went on to assure the congregation at the Friday prayers in Tehran that 'in due time the Islamic world will have a military nuclear device'.[2]

Meanwhile moderate President Khatami attempted to steer the nation into calmer political waters and declared that Iran would accept the two-state solution, ensuring the creation of a Palestinian state alongside Israel, providing that Palestinians accepted the formula. Yet in theocratic Iran, the executive branch's authority on key foreign policies is far from absolute. Khatami may have extended the olive branch but it was Ayatollah Khamenei that led Iran's policies in the Middle East, and Tehran continued to distance itself from Arafat's PLO and the Al-Fatah organization. Arafat was seen as too ready to compromise with Israel, and the Iranian newspapers occasionally referred to him as a traitor to his cause. Iran's involvement in Palestinian politics grew so deep over the years that Iranian leaders even refused to speak to Arafat, always favouring the more extreme Hamas over Al-Fatah and the PLO. On Friday 12 November 2004, when world leaders gathered in Egypt for Arafat's funeral, and millions of Palestinians thronged the streets in the occupied territories and elsewhere to mourn him, Iranians held their Quds Day demonstrations in support of the Palestinian cause without a mention of its dead leader.

Since the start of the second intifada in September 2000, Iran's verbal attacks on Israel had grown more vitriolic and hardline. Ayatollah Khamenei repeated his predecessor's statement but with added rhetorical garnish. Now the situation seemed to have worsened and Israel was a '*cancerous* tumour' that must be surgically sliced out of the region. If there was any doubt on the subject, Khamenei clarified it further in January 2001 by pronouncing that, 'it is the mission of the Islamic Republic of Iran to erase Israel from the map of the region'.[3]

The next logical step in the anti-Israel process was taken some months later on 24 April 2001 when Khamenei joined an illustrious cast of revisionist historians and neo-Nazis to became the first Iranian leader to express doubts about the Holocaust. This was a topic that his predecessor had prudently avoided. Khamenei declared:

> There is evidence which shows that Zionists had close relations with German Nazis and exaggerated statistics on Jewish killings to solicit the sympathy and lay the ground for the occupation of Palestine. This was to justify the atrocities of the Zionists. There is even evidence that a large number of non-Jewish hooligans and thugs of Eastern Europe were forced to migrate to Palestine as Jews. The purpose was to install in the heart of the Islamic world an anti-Islamic state under the guise of supporting the victims of racism, and to create a rift in the Islamic world.[4]

Thus Khamenei in 2001 had already articulated the same kind of reasoning that Ahmadinejad would express in October 2005. Yet somehow his words failed to cause international uproar. Clearly the autumn of 2005 was a much more brittle world than the spring of 2001 – a world that had not yet seen 9/11 and where Iran's nuclear ambitions had not yet been fully developed. And it was a world which had become accustomed to aggressive Iranian rhetoric being expressed by familiar faces who were known to be in the last resort cautious figures willing to go so far and no further. Ahmadinejad was a different proposition.

In the aftermath of the terrorist attacks against the US on 11 September 2001, the West's 'war on terror' made Iran feel threatened. It rapidly stepped up its missile programme, producing Shahab 3 missiles that could carry nuclear warheads and reach Israel. Hostilities between Iran and Israel grew deeper in late 2002, when Iran's nuclear programme came to light for the first time. Israel now saw Iran as a

major threat and warned Tehran that it might resort to unilateral pre-
emptive strikes to prevent Iran from developing a nuclear-weapons
capability. The Israeli prime minister at the time, Ariel Sharon, had
gone to Washington to impress upon President Bush the urgency of
the threat from Iran. A grim-faced Sharon had taken a top Israeli
general with him to the White House to show Bush aerial pictures,
diagrams and charts to prove that Iran's nuclear programme was far
more advanced than the Americans had thought and that within a
year or two Iran could develop nuclear warheads. The halcyon days of
Israel selling US weapons to Iran seemed very distant.

Relations between Iran and Israel – if you can even call them
that – continued to steadily deteriorate, so it is perhaps unsurpris-
ing that Iran in October 2005 should be hosting a conference with
the provocative title 'A World Without Zionism'. Organized by pro-
government high-school students, it was yet another excuse for a glut
of anti-Israeli speeches and slogans under the very thin guise of a
session of academic lectures and symposia. Few journalists bothered
to cover it, even though the main speaker, Mahmoud Ahmadinejad,
less than three months into his presidency, was still a novelty to many.
There were doubts whether the president would speak at all at the
conference. There were last-minute reports that he would only send a
message.

But he did turn up to speak. And after he had finished, Iran found
itself in a new phase of confrontation with the outside world. With
the election of Ahmadinejad, the gradual radicalization of much of
Iran's politics had taken a leap forward, and his diatribe against Israel
at the conference reflected this. If the majority of Ahmadinejad's
countrymen did not know his views on Israel prior to the conference,
they certainly did now.

Standing at a podium with a huge backdrop of an hourglass herald-
ing that Israel's days were numbered, Ahmadinejad spoke in simple
language readily understandable by the school children who had
packed the auditorium. He said a historical fight had been under way
for the past several hundred years between what he called 'the world-
dominating powers' and Islam. In this fight there had been many ups
and downs for both sides, he said, but, unfortunately, in the past 300
years, Islam had been continuously giving ground. A hundred years
ago, he continued, the world-dominating powers established a bridge-

head by placing Israel in the heart of the Islamic world. This intrusion was intended only to expand their domination over the whole of the Islamic Middle East. Therefore, the president explained, the battle under way today in Palestine was a crucial fight at the front line of the war between Islam and the world powers.

In no uncertain terms, Ahmadinejad stated that the students had to believe in the possibility of a world rid of the twin evils of America and Zionism. He told the auditorium that he was convinced such a world would materialize, and soon. He held up the Shah's regime in Iran, Saddam Hussein's in Iraq and the Soviet Union as examples of how seemingly invincible powers had collapsed.

'As Imam [Khomeini] has said, this Jerusalem-occupying regime [Israel] must vanish from the pages of time. And his is a perceptive statement, as the issue of Palestine is not one that we can compromise on [by trading] a part of its territory,' declaimed Ahmadinejad. He warned other Muslim countries against a compromise over Palestinian territory, saying, 'Anyone who recognizes the existence of this regime will have in effect signed the document of capitulation and the defeat of the Islamic world.' As usual with the new president, geopolitics were simplified into stark black and white. 'I have no doubt that today there is a new insurgency in our beloved Palestine, and with the new wave of awakening in the Islamic world today, and the spirituality that has engulfed the whole Islamic world, this shameful blot will soon be removed from the Islamic world. This is doable.'

Ahmadinejad also explained his formula for resolving the issue: the Palestine question would be resolved only when a Palestinian government was established over the whole of the Palestinian territory, refugees returned to their homes, and there were free elections in which all people from all races and religions could vote and choose a government. 'Of course, those who have come from far-away lands with an eye to plunder have no right to have a say over Palestine,' he added, dispelling any possibility of equal self-determination for Palestinians and Israelis. It was time to take an eraser to the map of the Middle East and strike out the mistakes of the mid-twentieth century. 'I hope the Palestinian nation will continue with its vigilance, as it has done over the past ten years or so of very intensive struggle against the occupation forces. If we can put this latest phase behind us with success, then, God willing, the task of erasing the Quds-occupying regime will

High-school days, early 1970s, caught up in the times of relative
social tolerance. Ahmadinejad is first on the right (top)
and first on the left (bottom).

The football-mad young Ahmadinejad (bottom right)
with his university team, mid-1970s.

An undated photograph from the
early years of the Revolution.

Odd friends – with the ultra-orthodox anti-Zionist Jews of
Neturei Karta during a conference in Tehran that controversially
challenged the accepted history of the Holocaust – December 2006.

President and Mrs
Ahmadinejad during an
official visit to Malaysia,
March 2006. She is even
more religious than her
husband.

Telling his hardline Islamist comrades in a mosque in Tehran that he is 'connected to God' – October 2006.

Ahmadinejad's new allies in a poster produced by Basij students. 'The world's dispossessed must unite whatever their religion or creed.'

be like a walk on a smooth downhill slope.'

By the time of the conference, Israel had already withdrawn from the Gaza Strip in a move considered unthinkable and politically impossible only a few years before. In light of the changing political landscape and the emergence of a potentially more conciliatory Israel there were rumours that Pakistan and Libya were considering establishing diplomatic relations with the Jewish state. This was anathema to Ahmadinejad and, warming to his own rhetoric, he used more vitriolic language to ram his message home, warning other Arab and Muslim countries: 'If anyone takes even one step towards recognizing this regime either under pressure from world powers or under misapprehension or naivety, or, God forbid, out of self-interest or material gain, they should know that they will burn in the fire of the Muslim nation's fury. The Islamic nation cannot allow its historical enemy to live in the heart of the Islamic world and have its security guaranteed.'

The European powers – especially Britain, Germany and France – who had spent the past few years urging a diplomatic resolution to the nuclear dispute between Iran and the UN were listening intently. And after exerting all their energies to keep the hawkish US at bay and prevent them taking Iran to the UN Security Council for its violations of the IAEA resolutions, Ahmadinejad's words came as a slap in the face.

'Those who insist on transferring the Iranian nuclear dossier to the UN Security Council have received an additional argument for doing so,' Russian Foreign Minister Sergei Lavrov observed soon after the comments were reported. Iran had been counting particularly on Russia and China to frustrate attempts by the US to impose sanctions on Tehran. Indeed, Moscow's relationship with Iran had reached the point where Russia was comfortable assisting in the construction of the first Iranian nuclear plant. But Ahmadinejad's speech at the conference had completely undermined Russia's relations with Iran. 'What I saw on television was unacceptable,' added Lavrov.[5] In Washington, the US was for once restrained in its criticism of Iran, perhaps feeling vindicated by other nations' condemnation of the Islamic Republic. State Department spokesperson Sean McCormack said Ahmadinejad's speech 'underscores our concern and the international community's concerns about Iran's pursuit of nuclear weapons'.

Israel, on the other hand, was not interested in mincing words or tempering its reaction and immediately called for the expulsion of Iran from the UN. Shimon Peres said, 'Iran presents a danger to the entire world, not just to us.' He urged China and Russia to join Western efforts to impose sanctions on Iran in light of the comments. Prior to the furore, the two countries had been reluctant to back such proposals in the UN Security Council. 'If all world powers are united against Iran, military action can be avoided,' Peres claimed. 'We can prevent all of this threat, without weapons, if there will be unity.'[6] While most Muslim and Arab capitals remained silent about the president's remarks, a few spoke out – including Palestinian chief negotiator Saeb Erekat. 'Palestinians recognize the right of the state of Israel to exist and I reject his comments,' Erekat told the BBC. 'What we need to be talking about is adding the state of Palestine to the map and not wiping Israel from the map,' he concluded.[7]

Iran appeared genuinely surprised and a little confused by the international outcry caused by the conference in general and the president's keynote address in particular. For those who wanted to hear them, anti-Israeli diatribes were commonplace in Iran. It seemed that political and social isolation had blinded the Iranian leadership to what was and what was not acceptable on the world stage. Ahmadinejad seemed to enjoy the attention without displaying any particular insight into the responses he was provoking. When questioned a few days after the speech, he took the opportunity to reiterate his position and to stress that he had expressed the popular feelings of the nation. 'My word is the same as that of the Iranian nation,' he told the official IRNA news agency. 'They are free to say whatever they want, but they lack credibility,' he said, pointing to expressions of outrage in the West. Iran's Foreign Minister, Manouchehr Mottaki, weighed in to calm the climate by pointing out that Ahmadinejad's speech reflected Iran's 'policy and strategy in the past 27 years'. And it was a point that was very difficult to argue against. That said, there were few in Iran who wanted to argue with Ahmadinejad on this point. Even the reformists who quietly believed Ahmadinejad was unbalanced, kept quiet about the damage he had inflicted. Ahmadinejad was expressing, in albeit harsh words, sentiments about the ambitions of Israel and the plight of the Palestinians which sat well with many Iranians. This was not the issue on which to challenge him.

Naturally the hardline Islamists and conservatives of Iran rallied to Ahmadinejad's support. 'The honourable President has said nothing new about Israel that would justify all this political commotion,' wrote Hassan Shariatmadari, the editor of *Kayhan*, which, thanks to the victory of the hardliners in the presidential elections, was now the single most influential newspaper in Iran. If some Iranians had doubts about what Ahmadinejad had meant, Shariatmadari had no hesitation. 'We declare explicitly that we will not be satisfied with anything less than the complete obliteration of the Zionist regime from the political map of the world,' he said in his bylined editorial.[8]

But there were attempts to contain the impact of the vitriol from Ahmadinejad – from surprising corners. Ayatollah Khamenei – concerned at the impact of Ahmadinejad's speech on the nuclear programme – felt the need to warn Iranian officials, without naming names, against falling into the traps laid for them by the enemies of Iran – in other words, excessive anti-Israeli rhetoric would be playing into Israeli hands. Akbar Alami, the MP for Tabriz and a member of the parliamentary National Security Commission, noted that Iran's top officials were expected to be 'more measured, more farsighted and more insightful when dealing with foreign relations'. Alami continued to water down the president's emphatic words: 'You cannot take these remarks which have been made on the basis of emotions and under the impact of the atmosphere as a threat against another country.'

But no wise words could water down for Iranians the impact of their new president's views on Israel. Ahmadinejad had stood up on the world stage and caught the eye and ear of every nation, simply by stating his beliefs. Better still, he had managed to boost his popularity at home and had received nothing more than the gentlest of rebukes.

New calculations

Although he continued to protest that he simply could not understand what all the fuss was about, Ahmadinejad was politically astute enough to see how he could turn the Western media's susceptibility to his controversial statements to his advantage. His understanding was that the media outside Iran loved a maverick making wild suggestions. It made good copy. He brushed aside suggestions that his remarks had damaged Iran's interests and image abroad. It was time to turn the tables on the West, using its own media to counter what the Iranian leadership believed to be a long-running psychological war against Iran through newspaper columns and international broadcasts. A robust-sounding Iran was surely more likely to protect its interests than an Iran anxious – yet again – to please the foreigners The president was also very aware that he could enhance his popularity at home, where the issue of Israeli excesses in the occupied territories had become an emotive one.

Ahmadinejad was a fervent admirer of Ayatollah Khomeini and was particularly impressed by the way in which the Ayatollah used anti-Americanism as a galvanizing and unifying force in the early days of the Islamic Republic, exploiting it to consolidate his own power base. Ahmadinejad must have been thinking of the Ayatollah's support for the student capture of the US embassy in 1979. With Khomeini's support, the students took 52 diplomats and staff hostage and held them for 444 days, setting Iran off into uncharted territory. Ahmadinejad, now 50, would have remembered well witnessing how the occupation of the embassy changed the course of the Iranian Revolution.

The embassy crisis dominated global headlines and characterized the upheavals in Iran as an anti-American revolution. The hostage taking also generated considerable publicity for the Islamic hardliners who were hugely outnumbered in the internal power struggle against leftist and liberal forces. The Islamic hardliners – not the leftists – were seen as the leading anti-American faction; they stole the popular ground occupied previously by the left-wing socialist revolutionaries. Before long the left-wing factions were on the defensive in the post-revolutionary upheavals in Iran. Liberal forces were also marginalized, with the government of moderate prime minister Mehdi Bazargan collapsing as a result of hardline action. Bazargan had been trying to stop the Revolution from spinning out of control but ultimately had to resign over the embassy affair.

Ahmadinejad had styled himself as a Khomeini-type revolutionary in this election campaign and had promised to rekindle the early days of the Revolution under the Ayatollah. Now the reaction to his comments about Israel showed the president a potential way to construct for himself an image of a revolutionary in the mould of the Ayatollah. As well as being a matter of personal ambition,

Ahmadinejad also reckoned it would raise his popularity at home with his constituency of hardliners as well as with the poor. By positioning himself as the revolutionary successor to Khomeini and the salvation of Iran's poor, the president could shake off and marginalize his reformist opponents and hardline detractors in parliament and elsewhere in the government. Somehow, through an unstable blend of cunning and naivety, Ahmadinejad had convinced himself that taking an unshakeably hard line on Israel, and trumpeting his views publicly, would enable him to silence his critics, strengthen his own position and drive his personal popularity.

But Ahmadinejad's brainchild was based on a fundamental misassessment of the long-term impact of Khomeini's 'Second Revolution', as the hostage-taking period became known. Many years later, most observers inside and outside Iran agreed that his support for the hostage takers represented the Ayatollah's biggest strategic mistake. Although he had certainly cemented his position within Iran, he had also managed to alienate almost the entire world and had transformed the nation into a pariah state. The hostage taking so polarized the world against Iran that Iraq was able to generate sufficient global support to feel comfortable about launching an invasion of Iran. In many ways, the eight years of destruction and death rained down upon the region during the war with Saddam's Iraq was the ultimate outcome of the hostage crisis in 1979/80. Relations with the US were made impossible and the suspension of diplomatic ties remains in place to this day. The resulting imposition of a series of US sanctions and other pressures have also dogged Iran ever since, leaving it in a desperate economic situation and in political isolation. More importantly, the hostage taking exposed the morally and politically unsound foundations on which the Islamic Republic of Iran was erected – a construction whose fault-lines and weaknesses are all too evident today. Internally the event radicalized the politics of the country. The measure of this radicalization is best illustrated by the fact that most of the hostage takers are today considered moderate in their political outlook compared to those in power. Ultimately the seizing of the US embassy injected violence and lawlessness into Iranian society. The country continues to suffer decades later.

Now Ahmadinejad, undeterred by the lessons of history, wanted to unleash the 'Third Revolution'. In his mind, Iran had to go on the offensive, in the same way that Khomeini went on the offensive with the seizure of the American embassy. Ahmadinejad, who in his first press conference two days after his victory in the presidential elections presented a relatively moderate image of himself, had very quickly stepped up his vitriolic language against 'the enemies of the people of Iran'. The same Ahmadinejad who had not uttered a word about Israel or Zionism during his campaign now focused all his energy on them. One of his first rhetorical assaults was to throw Israel's violent suppression of the Palestinians back in the face of all Western powers critical of the Iranian human rights record. 'All of you stand accused. All of you must be put on trial as war criminals,' he would say in rallies in provincial towns while wagging his finger at world leaders, accusing them of all manner of crimes against humanity.

The Third Revolution was under way and it immediately began to achieve the desired effect. Headlines around the world were screaming about the radical new president of Iran. Many Iranians seemed to register a brutal pride in their leader's face-off with the West. Yet every speech was another dagger in the heart of the efforts to find a diplomatic solution at the IAEA. But so far, Ahmadinejad had just been singing from the same hymn sheet as every previous Iranian leader and key political figure. He had not said anything that was genuinely new – yet.

Move Jews to Europe!

A few weeks after his controversial and inflammatory speech about Israel, and hours ahead of a visit to Saudi Arabia, Ahmadinejad went to see Iran's Supreme Leader, Ayatollah Ali Khamenei. It was customary for the president to see the Supreme Leader at his heavily guarded residence in central Tehran before important foreign trips. In public, Khamenei had made no comment about Ahmadinejad's controversial statements. But now Ahmadinejad wanted Khamenei's approval for his new political offensive. And, judging by the uncompromising verve with which he threw himself into it, Ahmadinejad had received the green light from the Ayatollah. It was time for the next stage in the Third Revolution.

On 8 December 2005, Ahmadinejad decided to add a little more detail to the standard Iranian line that Israel ought to be wiped off the map of the Middle East. Not only was he undeterred by the bad publicity Iran was getting abroad, he was positively encouraged by it and revelled in this next volley at Israel and much of the international community. This time he chose a two-day summit of the Organization of the Islamic Conference in the holy city of Mecca in Saudi Arabia. In an interview with the Arabic channel of Iranian state television – Al-Alam – he explained that Israel should be re-located to Europe. His logic – such as it was – was simple. If Germany and Austria felt so terribly responsible for massacring Jews during World War II, then the state of Israel should be established on their soil.

'Now that you believe Jews were oppressed, why should the Palestinian Muslims have to pay the price; why did you come to give them a part of Islamic land and the territory of the Palestinian people?' he asked of Germany and Austria and Europe in general. 'You oppressed them, so give a part of Europe to the Zionist regime so that they can establish any government they want. We would support it,' he said. 'So, Germany and Austria, give one, two or any number of your provinces to the Zionist regime so that they can create a country there which all of Europe will support, and the root problem will be solved. Why do they insist on imposing themselves on other powers and creating a tumour so that there is always tension and conflict?' [9]

The president was still being reasonably cautious in his rhetoric. The description of Israel as a tumour was a standard phrase in radical Iranian discourse on the subject. Similarly, the question as to why the Palestinian people had paid for the crimes of Nazi Germany with their own blood and land was one that had been hanging in the air for many decades in the Middle East. It was a particular favourite of hardline clerics casting around for a reasonable argument against the existence of Israel. While this was familiar ground for private discussions or public debates between like-minded individuals, this was the first time that such opinions were being officially aired and endorsed by a head of state, and especially in such undiplomatic and – to some – patently offensive language.

The fantastical suggestion that Israel be moved across the Mediterranean was new and shocking in its audacity, but Ahmadinejad was to take another bold step in the same interview. 'Is it not true that European countries insist they committed a Jewish genocide? They say Hitler burned millions of Jews in furnaces,' Ahmadinejad told

Al-Alam. 'Then because the Jews have been oppressed during World War II, therefore they [Europeans] feel they have to support the occupying regime of Quds. We do not accept this.'

The president then went on to leap to the defence of the academic integrity and freedom of speech of Holocaust deniers, stating that European countries 'believe in this [the Holocaust] so much, and are so determined, that any researcher who denies it with historical evidence is dealt with in a most harsh way and sent to prison'. He was referring to the claims of those who had been jailed in the West for inciting hatred and denying the Holocaust – something illegal in a number of Western countries.

Again Ahmadinejad was not being as radical as the global media portrayed him – at least not by Iranian standards. State television had for several years held interviews with mainly European Holocaust deniers or revisionist historians. Challenges to the accepted view that Nazi Germany slaughtered an estimated 6 million Jews between 1933 and 1945 were not unheard of in the mainstream media. This contrasted heavily with Europe and other parts of the world where such statements could indeed land a person in jail. But even in an Iran high on anti-Zionist rage, there was still some sense of the distinction between the comments made by near-anonymous quasi-historians and the head of state himself. In an unprecedented move, the president of a UN member state and a leading Middle East country was publicly and very deliberately expressing doubts about the extent – if not the existence – of the Jewish Holocaust. Ahmadinejad was walking a dangerous moral tightrope on the international stage and seemed to be enjoying the thrill of it greatly.

But Ahmadinejad was not yet satisfied. He was determined to make his mark on the two-day conference. In Mecca the next day he took his defining step. He chose to challenge the accepted figure of 6 million Jewish deaths in the Holocaust. 'Some European countries insist on saying that during World War II, Hitler burned millions of Jews. And they insist so strongly on this issue that anyone who denies it is condemned and sent to prison,' he said, repeating his contention of the previous day. 'Although we don't believe this claim,' the Iranian president continued, 'let's suppose what the Europeans say is true ... let's give some land to the Zionists in Europe or in Germany or Austria. We will also support it.' He added, 'They faced injustice in

Europe, so why do the Palestinians have to face the consequences?'

Most of this passage was a repetition of what he had already said – provocative, rhetorical but inoffensive. But it was here that for the first time he uttered the fateful words: '... *we don't believe this claim*'.

The remarks drew an angry response from the summit host, Saudi Arabia. This was an embarrassment for them. They wanted the conference to project a moderate, tolerant and modern image of Islam to the world. Holocaust denial and fairytale suggestions of moving whole countries were simply not supposed to feature on the agenda. The Associated Press captured the Saudi attitude to Ahmadinejad's comments: 'Privately, Saudi officials were furious. Three senior Saudi officials who spoke to the Associated Press complained that the comments completely contradicted and diverted attention from the message of tolerance the summit was trying to project. They spoke on condition of anonymity because of the sensitivity of the kingdom's cool but correct ties with Tehran. Saudi newspapers ran excerpts of Ahmadinejad's news conference where he praised the summit, but they dropped the references to Israel. One Saudi official, visibly angry, compared Ahmadinejad to Saddam Hussein and the Libyan leader, Moammar Qadhafi, whose renegade statements frequently infuriated other Arab leaders.'[10]

And it wasn't only the Saudis who were genuinely aggrieved by the Iranian president's comments. The political class of Tehran had never embraced Ahmadinejad and had – at best – held back in their criticism because of the enormous support he enjoyed among the poor and the religious establishment. Yet even members of parliament who might normally support Ahmadinejad began to distance themselves. A firm message had already been handed to Ahmadinejad when parliament rejected three of his candidates for the key post of oil minister. Now many members were beginning to question the wisdom of Ahmadinejad's inflammatory pronouncements.

Even fellow hardliners thought that the president should mind his language in public. The leader of the hard-right Islamic Coalition Society and one of Ahmadinejad's close political associates, Hamid Reza Taraqi, commented that, 'The president has to choose his words carefully. He can convey his message to the world in better language.' Prominent political analyst Davoud Bavand also weighed in: 'The ruling establishment should do something about this man.

Ahmadinejad speaks as if he is a spokesman of a hardline vigilante group. His words don't fit with those of a responsible president.' Masud Behnud, a veteran Iranian journalist, believed Ahmadinejad's remarks were calculated: 'I think this shows that Ahmadinejad wanted to hit the headlines. He wanted to cause uproar and become a personality in the radical world. And I believe that he has achieved his goal.'

There were distinct rumblings in the media, the parliament and the general public about the image of Iran being presented to the world by a president who seemed to be increasingly preoccupied by his own international status. Yet, as is often the case in Iran, only one opinion truly mattered: the Supreme Leader's. And the silence coming from Khamenei on the subject of the Holocaust was deafening. He gave not even the mildest hint of a rebuke. So, without any censure at all, the president would simply go further and further.

The myth

Like a Chinese whisper or an ugly rumour, Ahmadinejad's public baiting of Israel and the Jewish world grew slowly with each retelling. On 14 December 2005, he delivered a speech in the southwestern Iranian town of Zahedan, one of the most underdeveloped areas of Iran and with a Sunni majority. This speech was relayed live by Iranian television. Despite the irrelevance of the subject to either the place or the occasion, the president took the opportunity to move his provocative language up another notch. For the first time, he referred to the Holocaust 'myth'. His exact words were: 'Today, they [Europeans] have created a myth in the name of the Holocaust and consider it to be above God, religion and the prophets.' Again, he stopped short of out-and-out Holocaust denial. Returning to his favourite idea of the wholesale removal of Israel to another continent, the president widened the geographical net, bringing North American nations into the plan. 'This is our proposal: give them a part of your own land in Europe, the United States, Canada or Alaska so that Jews can establish their country.' He explained to his listeners, who had never heard of David Irving or David Dukes, that the West dealt severely with anyone who denied the Holocaust, but those who deny God, religion and the Prophet go unpunished by the law.[11]

The president was now travelling beyond the bounds set by previous leaders about Israel. He was now re-writing the Iranian stance not only on Zionism and the Holocaust but on the right of Jews to a natural presence in the Middle East. He was also leaping into bed with a range of individuals and groups not commonly thought of as fundamentalist Islam's friends: European neo-Nazis, anti-Semitic Holocaust deniers, white supremacists and outright racists. There were expressions of deep indignation from around the world. In Iran, there was little in the way of open and public debate, yet many privately felt that their president's outbursts were only harming the state and damaging its reputation and status internationally. Most baffling of all to many Iranians was the sheer pointlessness of Ahmadinejad's crusade.

What most critics – especially those outside Iran – failed to recognize as they leapt on Ahmadinejad's apparent anti-Semitism was the most interesting aspect of the issue, namely that while Ahmadinejad was revelling in his Israel-baiting and becoming ever more charged as the Western outrage became stronger, he was completely failing to grasp that this was more than an angry response to a political insult. Ahmadinejad's lack of knowledge of the world outside Iran blinded him to the significance his remarks would be accorded and the extent to which he was exposing himself and his country to the traps which his adversaries around the world hoped he would fall into. He simply did not understand that by laying himself open to the charge of anti-Semitism – a term laden in the West with terrible memories – he was weakening his own position internationally and undermining his country's interests. What he could not see was that by playing the Holocaust card he was making the American and Israeli hostility to Iran appear reasonable and justifiable.

But Ahmadinejad did achieve one thing. He managed to insult the Jews of Iran. There had been a Jewish community in Iran for the better part of 2,500 years, making it one of the oldest such communities in the world. Whereas other nations had expelled, oppressed, converted or simply slaughtered their Jewish minority populations, Iran had accommodated its Jewish community for millennia, along with the plethora of different communities that make up Iran, with very little discord. As a result, Jewish Iranians were proud of their heritage, resisted emigration to either the US or Israel and considered themselves as much Iranians as Jews. And most certainly, they were not Zionists.

Under the Shah the Jewish community totalled 85,000 in Iran, making it one of the largest outside Israel, Europe and the US. During the revolutionary years and the post-revolutionary period under Khomeini, although many Jews did leave, those who stayed felt reasonably secure in the distinction that the new regime drew between the Jews – as fellow People of the Book – and the Israelis – as occupiers. In this tacit compact between the Jews and the Muslims of Iran, there were some things that were off limits – and Holocaust denial was clearly one of them. Now Iranian Jews felt offended and more insecure as a result of Ahmadinejad's ill-informed comments. Despite the oppressive political atmosphere of Iran that certainly discourages, if not directly forbids, public dissent, the Jewish community decided to tackle the issue head on. Haroun Yashayaie, the leader of the Iranian Jewish community, penned a daring letter to the president in which he openly attacked him for challenging 'one of the most obvious and depressing human episodes in the twentieth century'. Yashayaie explained that the president's words had 'struck panic and fear in the small Jewish community in Iran'. The letter went on to ask the Iranian leader 'how it is possible to ignore all the undeniable evidence that exists of the killing and exile of the Jews in Europe during World War II'. Yashayaie said that the fashion for hosting Holocaust-denial seminars (see below) did no favours for Iran, Palestine or the international Muslim community. 'It just soothes the complexes of racists,' he said.

This was the first time since the 1979 Islamic Revolution that the Jewish community in Iran had spoken out against the government. It reflected the depth of hurt and fear the community felt. While they were used to being sidelined, they were not used to rhetoric which might spell the beginning of real persecution. Jews who remained after the removal of the Shah found Iran an imperfect but permanent home. Jews in Iran were largely free to hold religious ceremonies and to own cemeteries, kosher food shops, schools and synagogues. The country's constitution even guaranteed a member of parliament, as it did for all religious minorities. The current holder of that seat was Moris Motamed and he called a press conference to denounce Ahmadinejad's denial of the Holocaust.

'Denial of such a great historical tragedy that is connected to the Jewish community can only be considered an insult to all the world's Jewish communities,' he said. Even so, Motamed was eager to draw on his proud heritage and on the strong friendship between Iran and its Jews. He argued that Holocaust denials by a few extremists would not have a negative impact on Iran's Jewish community. 'Iranian Jews have been present in this country for a long time, for some 2,700 years [sic]. During these 2,700 years they have always been in full understanding with the society, they've lived in friendship and brotherhood, so therefore I don't think that bringing up such an issue could damage the Jewish community in Iran.'[12] Several months earlier, Motamed had criticized state television for broadcasts whose anti-Israeli and anti-Zionist tone could easily spill over into creating anti-Jewish sentiments in Iran. Again, there was no direct action or aggression towards Iran's own Jews but the broadcasts had caused emotional upset and, most significantly, had led to increased emigration.

Ignoring the offence the president had caused in Iran and much of the world, the Foreign Ministry in Tehran rushed to support Ahmadinejad. 'What the president said is an academically correct issue. The West's reaction shows their continued support for Zionists,' the Ministry spokesman, Hamid Reza Asefi, declared. 'Westerners are used to conducting a monologue but they should learn to listen to different views.' Asefi was not alone. Others in the Ministry expressed the same opinion. Foreign Minister Manouchehr Mottaki said the remarks were a reflection of the official Iranian government's position on the issue. 'The words of Mahmoud Ahmadinejad on the Holocaust and on Israel are not personal opinions, nor isolated statements, but they express the view of the government,' he said. This was in fact incorrect. Denying the Holocaust had never been part of Iran's policy towards Israel. Until the moment Ahmadinejad made his speech, there had always been an unspoken but inviolable distinction drawn between the secular state of Israel and the world religion of Judaism. This important distinction was now being called into question.

'The Europeans have to understand that the current Iranian government doesn't have any intention of playing the role of someone who listens without having the right to reply,' Mottaki said, adding that if Europe wanted to have relations with Iran 'it has to learn to listen to our opinions and take them into account.' Although a seasoned diplomat, Mottaki was not known for his perceptive statements. Describing Holocaust denial as part of Iran's foreign policy, and then saying 'if Europe wants to talk to us, it should listen to our offensive words' was clearly missing the point: that in Europe (as well as the USA) the Holocaust had acquired such an iconic, emotive status that to deny it, however irrationally and however marginal the deniers, was guaranteed to arouse the same emotional intensity as denying God to a devout Muslim.

This move towards Holocaust denial also discarded 26 years of Iranian foreign diplomacy. Until this row erupted, Iran had always adopted a friendly, pro-European stance in an attempt to distance Europe from the US. This was particularly true in the years of nego-tiations relating to the nuclear crisis. Iran had counted on Europe to gain some leverage against the hawkish US, which appeared hell-bent on taking Iran to the Security Council.

Despite support from within Ahmadinejad's government, his comments aroused considerable criticism inside Iran. Former Iranian president Khatami – though a cleric, a much more travelled and world-aware figure – clashed with Ahmadinejad and described the Holocaust as 'a historical reality'. He conceded that the Holocaust might have been exploited by opportunistic Zionists to pile enormous pressure on the Palestinian people but he refused to countenance that the genocide had been concocted by European Jews in collusion with the Nazi party. It seemed nothing short of childish gibberish. Khatami was adamant: 'We should speak out if even a single Jew is killed. Don't forget that one of the crimes of Hitler, Nazism and German National Socialism was the massacre of innocent people, among them many Jews.'

The biggest reformist political party, the Mosharekat Front, said the president's remarks were 'costing Iran dearly on the economic, political and security' fronts. The party urged 'leaders and officials who care about Iran' not to allow 'adventurism and incompetence' to replace Iran's policy of détente with the outside world, as pursued by President Khatami for the previous eight years. The Mosharekat Front attempted to inject some pragmatism and common sense into Iran's position: 'The unjustifiable provocation of the sensibilities in the West, and the bringing up of issues that at present will neither benefit Iran and Iranians, nor improve the lot of the oppressed Palestinians, will only incite the Palestine-occupying regime and rally its supporters to form a united front against Iran.'[13] The message was daring in the Iranian context. Even though it was in code, no one could mistake its message. By referring to 'the leaders and officials who care about Iran', the statement was desperately urging Ayatollah Khamenei to break his silence on the matter.

But with every speech and every step on the road to Holocaust denial, Ahmadinejad understood the Supreme Leader's enduring silence as a sign of approval. This was not an unreasonable supposition on the president's part. Most of what he had said coincided with Khamenei's own personal beliefs. The Ayatollah had publicly expressed his own doubts about the reported figure of 6 million Jewish deaths in the Holocaust as early as 2001. He had alleged that there was a Jewish conspiracy to solicit the sympathy of the world in order to lay the ground for the occupation of Palestine and to justify the atrocities of the Zionists. But it was a measure of the desperation of the moderates and reformists that they could imagine that the Ayatollah would speak out for international Jewry in order to undermine his president – a president whose views he at least shared and perhaps had directly inspired.

Ahmadinejad had opened the floodgates. Now Iran's political and religious hardliners rushed to echo his radical sentiments. Parliament's speaker, Gholam-Ali Haddad-Adel, a close relation of the Supreme Leader, asked: 'If, hypothetically, it is true that the Jews were oppressed in Germany, why should Islamic nations pay the price of the oppression which was committed in another continent by another country?' The remarks were an almost word-for-word echo of Ahmadinejad's. Holocaust denial had spread like wildfire in Iran, with politicians and all those in the government toeing the line and expressing their doubts.

While Ahmadinejad was riding high with the Supreme Leader and the masses, his reformist and moderate antagonists were in despair. They feared the damage his bigotry and aggressive posturing before the global community were doing to Iran. 'His comments have seriously tarnished the image of a great nation in the world,' said the outspoken reformist writer Ahmad Zeidabadi. Others were quick to discern the link between Ahmadinejad and the Ayatollah. 'There is no doubt that the president is acting in close coordination with the leader,' said parliamentary representative Emad Afrouq, attempting to calm things, adding that 'Ahmadinejad is the closest president to Khamenei in the last 16 years'. Afrouq claimed the president's comments were 'part of a strategy' to influence international public opinion about Israel's occupation of the Palestinian territories. He argued that the battle was to be entirely rhetorical rather than factual. Even Ahmadinejad did not want to actually go to war with the well-armed and well-connected little Jewish state. 'The bottom line is he wants to keep anti-Israeli sentiments alive,' Afrouq said. 'He doesn't think of military action.'

Some critics believed that Ahmadinejad's rhetoric was simply part of an effort to boost his weak standing in Iran's complicated power structure and to deflect attention from his handling of basic domestic issues such as unemployment and the economy. It was, in this view, nothing more than the standard populist warmongering – one of the easiest methods of consolidating political support. 'He wants to reinforce his position,' said analyst Saeed Leilaz. 'Rhetoric against Israel is the only thing he can say without strong challenge.'

Criticism of the president and his new-found interest in the Holocaust was by no means limited to his political opposition. University professor Mahmoud Kashani, an Islamic conservative like Ahmadinejad, said the president's stance on Israel and the nuclear programme were creating enemies, not friends, for Iran. 'People in the capital, Tehran, can't breathe because of high air pollution, and the economy is in tatters,' said Kashani, a one-time presidential candidate. 'Ahmadinejad's job is to solve these problems, not to create tension in foreign relations.'

Strange bedfellows

Ahmadinejad had certainly placed himself in the illustrious company of Nazi sympathizers – the Holocaust deniers, or historical revisionists as they prefer to call themselves.

The Holocaust deniers insist that the Nazis did not have a deliberate policy of exterminating Jews. They claim that no one was killed in the infamous gas chambers – these, they believe, were there only to delouse prisoners. They deny that 6 million people perished at the hands of the Nazis. Although crimes were committed, the Nazi regime bore no central blame, and the wealth of documentary evidence to the contrary was fabricated in order to advance the interests of the Jews who, together with the Americans and the British, had conspired to create the whole 'myth'.

The darlings of the Holocaust-denying community were soon to become the academic heroes of Ahmadinejad's fiercely anti-intellectual government. Pre-eminent among the pseudo-historians is the German Ernst Zundel, who immigrated to Canada in 1958 and there established a small publishing house printing pro-Nazi material. His publishing catalogue includes pamphlets such as 'The Hitler We Loved and Why', and 'Did Six Million Really Die?' Zundel was jailed on a number of occasions in Canada before ultimately being deported to Germany in 2005. He was charged and imprisoned in Germany for his links to illegal neo-Nazi groups including 'the Aryan Nations'. After discovering Holocaust denial, Iran took to defending Zundel and even accused Canada of violating his human rights by extraditing him to Germany.

While Zundel has not yet reciprocated Iran's support with kind words for its president, self-proclaimed Nazi-sympathizer Norman Lowell has publicly congratulated Ahmadinejad on his remarks about the Holocaust. He has also repeatedly gone on record to describe Hitler as 'a hero'. He has found himself continually in trouble with the police and judiciary of his home country of Malta, mainly for his incitement of racial hatred and his writing of extreme anti-Semitic articles. Lowell subscribes to the view that the US is now entirely run by Jews, who control the nation's government, media and financial institutions. Renegade US university professor Arthur Butz is another 'revisionist' who has commended Ahmadinejad. 'I congratulate him on becoming the first head of state to speak out clearly on these issues and regret only that it was not a Western head of state,' wrote Butz, author of a 1976 'history' text that described the Holocaust as nothing more than a hoax.

Arch conspiracy theorist Michael A. Hoffman II also came out in support of Ahmadinejad. With a penchant for identifying cross-cultural occult plots against the liberty of the 'white European' and a taste for neologisms, Hoffman wrote: 'Now on the world stage returns the President of Iran, Mahmoud Ahmadinejad, so recently in the news for upsetting the sacred cows of Holocaustianity. Yet, instead of backing off, he has again stuck his thumb into the eye of the Cyclops, even deeper than before, and in so doing has given us all an opportunity to smile at the expense of the mandarins of Judeomania.' Hoffman was also happy to offer the Iranian president some advice: 'Follow through on your laudable defiance in a substantive manner: open your nation to revisionists, bring us to your nation (all of us who are not yet in jail in 'freedom-loving, democratic' Europe and Canada), and have us conduct a news conference for broadcast around the world, and then have us conduct teach-ins, seminars, symposia, TV shows and documentaries and beam these, also by satellite. Establish the Revisionist University of Iran. Translate the books of Arthur Butz, Germar Rudolf and Robert Faurisson into Persian and Arabic.' [14]

Within weeks of Hoffman issuing this call to arms, the Iranian government announced that it was to hold an international conference on the Holocaust, to be organized by Iran's Foreign Ministry. Spokesman Hamid Reza Asefi said the time had come for Western leaders to hear comments not to their liking. 'For over half a century, those who seek to prove the Holocaust have used every podium to defend their position. Now they should listen to others.' The Islamic Republic of Iran was about to host a jamboree of racism and Nazism. The circus was coming to town.

As the Holocaust-denial controversy gathered momentum it became increasingly clear that Ahmadinejad, his closest advisors and those hardline clerics who were backing him had not the slightest grasp of how damaging all this was to Iran. This fazed Ahmadinejad not a bit, as he positively relished tweaking the beard of Uncle Sam and his acolytes. More importantly his failure to understand the low-grade level of his Western, Holocaust-denying friends was a clear indication of Ahmadinejad's disconnection with the world outside his own very limited provincial experience. If a man could – as others would see it – seriously consider his new bedfellows as desirable witnesses to his cause, could he seriously be viewed as a negotiating partner? With such poor judgement in choosing his friends, could he be counted on to behave sensibly and rationally in furthering his country's interests?

The circus

It was 11 December 2006. Snow was falling on the white stucco building of the conference centre on a hilltop in north Tehran. Below, delegates from a host of countries were arriving for a two-day programme of discussions, lectures and debates. Nowhere else in the world could you find such a mixed bag: American white suprema-cists, European Nazis, fundamentalist Muslims and ultra-orthodox anti-Zionist Jews milled around, exchanging handshakes and smiles. It was Iran's International Conference to Review the Global Vision of the Holocaust. This was the day on which Ahmadinejad finally alienated the international community and drove his country into the backwaters.

In the centrally heated entrance hall covered with red carpets and lit by brass chandeliers mingled the suits of Americans and Europeans, the tall black hats and long coats of the ultra-orthodox Jews and the turbans and flowing robes of the Iranian clergy. Bearded Iranian offi-cials with their dark suits and collarless white shirts bustled about playing host. None of them had anything in common with any other except a deep-seated hatred for the state of Israel and suspect academic credentials.

Journalists, enjoying full access for a change, were already inter-viewing some of the guests who were picking up their name badges from the organizers' desk. Many of the delegates were only too happy to give interviews. Others shunned the cameras, fearful that the publicity might land them in trouble with their own authorities when they returned to their own countries. The conference delegates had been shrouded in a necessary anonymity. No names had been released in advance for fear of the delegates' governments attempting to prevent them travelling to Tehran. Not even the journalists, let alone the average Iranian, had a clear idea of who these 67 invited guests actually were. Iranian television had set up transmission facili-ties in the entrance hall to broadcast the opening of the conference live. The national 24-hour news channel and its Arabic-language twin Al-Alam ('The World') were preparing to interview the visiting 'histo-rians'. Upstairs on the first floor, an exhibition had been set up of photographs, books, CDs and posters contrasting the alleged lies and the truths of the Holocaust, while a big screen played out a presenta-tion of a 'revised' account of the Holocaust. Also on display was a model of Auschwitz, 'demonstrating' that it was physically impossible to kill the large numbers of people reported to have been killed in its gas chambers.

A few days ahead of the conference, the deputy Foreign Minister in charge of the education and research department, Dr Manouchehr Mohammadi, had told the media that the conference would try to answer the question of whether or not the Holocaust ever happened. Mohammadi claimed the conference was a scientific exercise to get to the truth of 'this phenomenon' and that historians and scientists on 'both sides of the divide' had been invited. He continued by stating that if it were proved that the Holocaust had indeed happened, the conference would try to investigate why the Palestinians had been forced to pay for the crimes of the Europeans. On the eve of the conference, Moris Motamed, the only Iranian Jewish MP, made an angry public statement, unable to conceal his anger. He declared that he simply was unable to understand why Iran was doing this. He feared for his people and denounced the conference as a 'a big insult to all Jews'. He warned that 'holding conferences of this kind and questioning the historical issues of the Jewish people ... will inevitably dismay them and might trigger another wave of migration from this country'.

On the streets of Tehran, few people were aware that such a conference was about to begin its work in the capital. Iran was in the last days of campaigning for the local council elections. Posters of the candidates had been put up prominently everywhere, and newspapers were preoccupied with endless speculation about how the reformists or conservatives would fare in the elections. The supposed Holocaust question was not the foremost political issue in the minds of the average Iranian. Apathy or ignorance were more common responses than denial or active anti-Israelism. The younger generation of Iranians simply did not know enough about the Holocaust to take a position one way or the other. European history is no more on the Iranian curriculum than is the history of the Persian empire in European and American secondary schools. And national newspapers are hardly vehicles for raising the awareness of readers on international issues.

When asked, most young people said they did not know much about it. But those who had been around during the war or in the decades immediately afterwards were more aware of the historical significance of the Holocaust. 'It's a historical fact. It's not something for you and me to deny,' said a retired Oil Ministry official, pointing to William Shirer's book, *The Rise and Fall of the Third Reich*, which has been translated into Persian. A woman out shopping with her young daughter was surprised to learn that such a conference was being organized in Tehran and remarked, 'We must not get involved. We have many problems of our own that need to be addressed. We do not need to make any more enemies than we already have.' Her young daughter, an unemployed university graduate, agreed. 'Since President Ahmadinejad has come to power, our problems have multiplied. There is no need to make any more enemies for ourselves. In this way, nothing will get better here.'

Meanwhile over at the Institute for Political and International Studies – an affiliate of the Foreign Ministry – Iranian Foreign Minister Mottaki was opening the conference. He affirmed the Iranian government's central role in organizing a conference that would be illegal in many countries. He took the opportunity to castigate the West for allegedly 'stifling open debate and research about the Holocaust'. It was the perfect moment to crow over the freedom of speech Iran enjoyed in comparison to Western nations. Mottaki then detailed the political agenda of the conference. 'If the official version of the Holocaust were to be thrown into doubt, then the nature and the identity of Israel would be thrown into doubt.'

But the veneer of historical impartiality had to be maintained and Mottaki made it clear that the conference was not designed to prove or disprove the Holocaust. 'The main aim of this conference is to provide an opportunity to thinkers who in Europe, which claims to be free, have no chance to express their opinions on a historical phenomenon.' But in reality Iran was giving a soapbox to a ragtag collection of bigots and racists for seemingly no reason except to provoke its Western critics and yet again to proclaim its dislike of Israel. And it certainly was not lost on the president that by taking an international high-profile position on Israel he was reaching beyond Iran and the West. In the Arab world, among the masses and the dispossessed, Ahmadinejad's rhetoric was striking home.

The rostrum of radicals

Only now as they sat listening to their foreign minister and receiving the programme of events did the Iranian media grasp the full extent of the two-day conference. Presiding over one of the panels was the former Iranian interior minister and founder of Lebanon's Hezbollah,

Ali Akbar Mohtashamipour. A senior Shiite cleric in black robe and turban, he had no time to debate the 'facts'. He baldly announced to the conference that 'all the studies and research carried out so far prove that there is no reason to believe that the Holocaust ever happened, and that it is only a fable'.

For Western observers, the most immediately recognizable individual in the rogue's gallery of outside participants was the former leader of the American white supremacist group the Ku Klux Klan (KKK), David Duke. He told journalists he was in Tehran to defend freedom of expression. To him, it was abhorrent that some of his fellow 'revisionists' were in jail because they wanted to exercise their right to free speech. In reference to his past life as Grand Wizard of the KKK, Duke explained that he had changed and matured. It seemed unlikely that the organization's past history of burning down the homes of non-whites or planting burning crosses on their properties would endear Duke to Muslim Iran. The question for many observers was, 'Why on earth was Iran associating itself with the likes of Duke?' But no one would accept official responsibility for choosing the speakers. When Foreign Ministry officials at the conference were asked why Duke had been invited, they pleaded ignorance. Ultimately, some time after the conference, the Foreign Ministry said it would investigate Duke's attendance and discover how a committed racist could have been given such a prominent platform by the Iranian government. But Duke was not the only guest whose presence at the conference could give Iran a bad name. A number of right-wing extremist politicians from Germany's neo-Nazi NPD party had also been invited, but Berlin had barred them from attending. And quite a few of the delegates had either criminal records or were awaiting the outcome of court cases.

An associate of Duke's, George Kadar, was also present at the conference. An American of Hungarian origin, Kadar was a member of the white supremacist, anti-immigrant group 'American Springs' in the late 1990s. At the time of the conference, he was writing for the anti-Semitic newspaper *American Free Press* as well as being an active participant in the white supremacist Stormfront electronic forum. Kadar has been a leading figure in anti-immigration circles, organizing rallies on the US–Mexican border. These agitators maintain that Hispanics have 'flooded' the state of California, which they dub

'Mexifornia', and that they bring with them lawlessness, drugs, disease and every other shade of immorality.

Another guest speaker was Lady Michelle Renouf, a friend of David Irving, the Holocaust-denying historian who at the time of the conference was languishing in a jail in Austria for his statements on the Holocaust. Married for a short spell to the New Zealand financier Sir Frank Renouf, Lady Renouf had been the glamour queen of the far right. A model, dancer and beauty queen in her prime, she was now speaking at the conference in Tehran about her objection to Jews, and distributing DVDs of Irving's court case. She told journalists that she was delighted to be at the conference in Iran, which allowed free speech, while many were in jail in the West for their opinions.

Herbert Schaller, a lawyer for pro-Nazi Holocaust deniers including David Irving and Ernst Zundel, participated in the conference in place of, and at the request of, another Holocaust denier, the Austrian Gerd Hosnik. Hosnik was a fugitive from an Austrian jail who was recently arrested in Spain, to which he had fled in 1992. He has numerous convictions in Germany and Austria for his efforts to reactivate the National Socialist Party, his perpetual Holocaust denying and his book *Exonerating Hitler?*. In the book, he recounts the statements of 36 'witnesses' who have rejected the existence of gas chambers, and he argues that Hitler, therefore, should be acquitted of all charges. He claims in another book to have proven that there exists a huge conspiracy to dilute the white race with blacks and Asians in order to facilitate the Jewish subjugation of the master race. However, it was not this overt racism that kept Hosnik from coming to Iran and mixing with his racial inferiors. He apparently had no valid passport.

The roster of less than illustrious names continued with Veronica Clark, the organizer of the Adolph Hitler Research Society. Clark presented a paper which the conference programme summarized as follows: 'In this article, Clark sets out to paint a different picture of the Holocaust and to show that in actuality Hitler was very lenient with Jewry and took serious measures not to condemn decent Jews to internment or deportation.' On her website, replete with pictures of Hitler and Iron Crosses, she declares: 'We believe National Socialism to have been a movement that was rich in love and Christian brotherliness.'

Perhaps the most active of the guests at the conference was the

German-born Australian Holocaust denier Fredrick Toben. He is responsible for a Holocaust-denying website that acts as a contact point for all fellow deniers around the world. Toben was jailed in Germany in 1999 under laws that forbid Holocaust denial. Among other crimes, he was charged with declaring the Nazi extermination of Jews to be an 'invented legend' and sentenced to nine months in prison. In 2002 an Australian judge found that Toben's website 'vilified Jewish people' and ordered him to remove the offending articles. One sympathetic website describes Toben as being interested 'in exonerating the German people from the anti-German racism of the Holocaust legend'. A regular visitor to Iran, Toben had been on lecture tours of universities there and had met many Iranian officials before. He also acted as the linchpin of Holocaust deniers around the world, following their court cases on his website and maintaining contact. He was certainly in a position to help the organizers of the conference to bring together the Holocaust deniers that were now in Tehran.

A mentor of other Holocaust deniers, the veteran Robert Faurisson was the special guest of the conference. Faurisson has the honour of five convictions in France for denying crimes against humanity. He has claimed that no gas chambers were used in Nazi concentration camps. When at the conference a lone affirmer of the Holocaust, an Iranian professor by the name of Gholamreza Vatandoust, said there was ample evidence to show that the Holocaust did happen, Faurisson got up on his feet, shouting and demanding to see 'one piece of evidence'. Presenting his paper Faurisson, a former literature professor, told the conference that 'the myth of the Holocaust may be dying', burning itself out as more and more people in the West were becoming aware 'of the hazards imposed on the international community by such prolonged submission to the false religion of "the Holocaust"'.

Dr Christian Lindtner, a former professor of religious history at Copenhagen University, and an advocate of the superiority of the white race, was another invited guest. Lindtner wrote in an article entitled 'The Aryan Humanism' that Islam, Christianity and Judaism posed 'an enormous threat to the progress of Aryan, or European, civilization'. His quest to prove the Holocaust never happened stems from his desire to exonerate the white race. 'Now, this accusation, that "the

Aryans" are somehow responsible for the so-called Holocaust of the Jews, is a very serious one indeed. If "the Aryans", or at least those in Germany, were responsible for the abominable murder of six million Jews, who, then, must not detest the Aryan ideal of virtue? But what if the allegation is not true? In that case, we must be dealing with what is surely one of the most obnoxious cases of calumny in history. ... In order to defend themselves, or rather in order to defend their ideals of truth and decency, it is, therefore, the obvious duty of all Aryans to study the alleged Holocaust in a scientific manner,' he wrote.

The Swiss Holocaust denier Jürgen Graf had also been invited to the conference, but failed to show up. In July 1998, a Swiss court had convicted Graf and his publisher of breaking anti-racist laws. Graf was sentenced to 15 months in prison and fined $5,500. He and his publisher were ordered to hand over the proceeds from the books, which totalled $38,000. In November 2000 Graf fled to Tehran and later to Moscow after his appeals against the 1998 conviction for inciting racial hatred were rejected. However, Graf's friend, Wolfgang Fröhlich, a former member of Austria's far-right Freedom Party, did attend the Tehran conference but, on the advice of his lawyer, chose not to speak. In 2000 he had also fled to Tehran, claiming that he was about to be arrested by the Austrian police. The Holocaust-denying fraternity said he had gone to Tehran 'as the guest of Iranian scholars'. More than a year earlier, Fröhlich, an engineer, had testified as 'an expert' in Graf's trial in Switzerland. He had also distributed a CD-ROM entitled 'The Gas Chamber Swindle', denying the Nazis had used gas chambers to exterminate Jews. On 21 June 2003, he was arrested in Vienna after three years as a fugitive. A few months later, he was put on trial and was eventually sentenced under the Nazi prohibition law to three years' imprisonment. The German neo-Nazi groups and websites reacted angrily to his arrest and trial, describing him as 'a dissident scientist' and branding the trial 'an inquisition'.

The Frenchman Georges Thiel, an apologist for Hitler, took part in the conference while still awaiting the result of his appeal in the Supreme Court in France against a conviction on Holocaust-denial charges. He said at the conference that the Holocaust was 'an enormous lie, a complete fabrication'. Theil wrote in a 2002 pamphlet that the Nazis never had a genocidal agenda against the Jews, and that any repression of Jews under Nazi rule was merely a reaction to 'the

Jewish takeover of the German economy after the First World War', which was a Jewish 'declaration of war' against Germany. He said at the conference that he was hoping the government of Iran would buy the rights to his book to rescue him from total financial ruin, as the French court had also fined him more than $100,000. His optimism was rooted in a number of similar cases where the government of Iran had bailed out convicted Holocaust deniers in Europe by paying their fines.

Also at the conference, the American writer Don Heddesheimer expounded on his book *The First Holocaust*. He argued that the 6 million figure dated back to a Jewish fundraising campaign that started during World War I and reached its peak in the mid-1920s. During those years, Jewish groups in the US spread the rumour that millions of Jews had died already and many more would face a lingering death.

Henri Roques argued that the accusations of Kurt Gerstein – the enigmatic Third Reich functionary who claimed to have witnessed mass gassings of Jews in 1942 – were groundless, and that post-war academics have deliberately falsified key parts of Gerstein's testimony. 'I am not a neo-Nazi, I am not an anti-Semite,' declared the 65-year-old retired Roques. 'But I do doubt that six million Jews were killed in Nazi gas chambers. I live in a free country, I have a right to doubt.' He has the distinction of being the first man in the nearly eight-century history of French universities to have his doctorate revoked by government order.

Patrick McNally from Tokyo, whose colourful language makes his Holocaust denial particularly pungent, presented a paper to the conference that described the Holocaust as 'a vicious lie'. 'During World War II JudeBolsheviks in Poland and the Soviet Union made up the Holocaust story to stir up anti-German hatred,' he said in the summary of his paper. McNally believes it was the Jews who declared war on Nazi Germany. 'Nazi Germany did what it could to help Zionists by permitting them to set up separate camps to train Jews to do useful work in Palestine, to publish Zionist newspapers in Germany, and to publicly display the Zionist flag. Germany wanted to help settle Jews in Palestine and Jews declared war on it,' he said.

If nothing else, the conference enlightened the world on the depth and variety of anti-Semitism, but what continued to puzzle observers was why the Iranians had given a platform to so many misfits and fantasists. Was it really genuine ignorance and naivety? Or had calculated Israel-bashing got out of hand? For example, in what way could V.T. Rajshekar have possibly furthered Iran's interests? A former journalist and the leader of the Dalit Voice movement that seeks to end the caste system in India, Rajshekar believes that the upper-caste Brahmins who form much of the ruling class in India are of the same racial stock as Jews. He presented a paper to the conference arguing the 'Jews of India,' – or the Brahmins – have perpetrated a 3,000-year Holocaust and 'kept it secret, buried under mountains of lies called Gandhian non-violence'.

Or take the case of the British writer Alexander Baron, with links to the far right, Islamists and anti-Zionist Jews, who also attended the conference. A former member of the ultra-nationalist British Movement, Baron is bizarrely also a current associate member of the Islamic Party of Britain. He is known to have attended and addressed the meetings of the far-right British National Party. In December 1997 Baron was charged with violation of the Malicious Communications Act. He was fined by a magistrates court in London in January 1998 for sending anti-Semitic leaflets to members of the Jewish community and to police stations and for publishing thousands of pages of racial hatred on the Internet, including anti-Semitic booklets.

Another guest of the government of President Ahmadinejad was Bernhard Schaub, who describes himself as a 'right-wing extremist'. A regular speaker in far-right and neo-Nazi circles in Switzerland and Germany, Schaub was indicted in 2005 for his anti-Semitic speech during a march of the far-right groups in the town of Aarau in the German-speaking sector of northern Switzerland. Schaub is a leading member of the far-right National Party of Switzerland, PNOS. Another white supremacist, he has declared, 'Europe is the homeland of the white race.' He has warned of a conspiracy that was under way under the banner of the 'New World Order', which, he says, is a vision of 'one world, with one government, one [mixed] race. ... This campaign is by no means finished. Its goal will be reached only when little Switzerland and all of Europe are finally forced into submission, ruled by one "chosen" people, one god (Yahweh), and one cult – the Holocaust.' He told the conference in Tehran: 'We European strugglers for right and truth here want to call out to the Islamic realm:

We have the same enemy! It is the corrupter of humanity who with the help from his American battle-elephant desires to subject the entire world to Jewish capital, and who desires to destroy all sovereign nations, cultures and religions until nothing is left but a faceless mass of spiritually and mentally inferior slave workers, there to toil for Zion. That must never be! We will fight the enemy and his lies and liberate ourselves – so help us God!'

The German self-styled 'national-Anarchist,' Peter Topfer, looked more respectable at the conference than in the pictures he has posted of himself sporting a Mohican-style haircut – the shaved skull and spiky strip favoured by young anarchists and skinheads. He was convicted in 1995 in Germany for publishing hate material in an anarchist magazine *Sleipnir* that has since ceased publication. A police raid on the magazine offices and the home of the editor of the magazine, Andreas Roehler, in 1995 found Hitler memorabilia and Nazi literature.

But perhaps the most bizarre delegates at the conference were the seven ultra-orthodox anti-Zionist Jews from New York and Vienna, members of the notorious Neturei Karta, a Jewish faction of some several thousand adherents first established in 1935. Dressed in the traditional Hassidic Eastern European dress of long black coats and black hats, the Neturei Karta stood out. They are not Holocaust deniers. They believe in the full horror of the Holocaust but object to the establishment of Israel on religious grounds. In their interpretation, the Torah specifically forbids the establishment of an exclusively Jewish state before the return of the Messiah. Rather than a man-made secular Israel, they are holding out for a Messianic holy homeland. While many Hassidic and other extreme-orthodox Jewish factions eventually became reconciled to Israel, the Neturei Karta kept the flame of enmity burning for 60 years. They steadfastly maintain that Jews have no right to set up a Jewish state whose creation is the sole job of the Jewish Messiah when he returns. But unlike other ultra-orthodox Jews, members of Neturei Karta have resorted to some extreme actions to publicize their views and oppose the state of Israel. They publicly mourn the anniversary of Israeli independence. They defended their participation in the conference by insisting that Iran was not denying the Holocaust but merely questioning why the Palestinians had to pay for the crimes committed in Europe.

Reaping the whirlwind

If Ahmadinejad wanted to provoke the ire and indignation of the global community with this conference, he was immensely and unsurprisingly successful. What was more surprising, and certainly more reassuring to a horrified world, was the extent of domestic criticism. Two weeks after the conference, parliament took up the issue at a closed-door session with Foreign Minister Mottaki.

The session had been originally organized to discuss Iran's next steps in the wake of the UN Security Council resolution that had slapped sanctions on the country for continuing its nuclear enrichment activities. But parliamentarians, and among them hardline supporters of Ahmadinejad, piled in to criticize the minister for having made the passing of the unanimous resolution against Iran politically easier by holding such a conference on the run-up to the vote. Even previously neutral countries felt bound to vote against Iran.

Leaks from the closed session detailed that most parliamentarians held that if the aim of the conference was honestly to hold a scientific study of the Holocaust, then a non-government organization or even an academic forum should have been chosen for the discussion. They said the minister's speech at the conference, as well as his Ministry's involvement in holding the conference, had given the event a political status. Parliament was unambiguous in its verdict: the conference had severely undermined Iran's position at a critical time, just as the UN Security Council was considering imposing sanctions.

The Baztab website, associated with the Revolutionary Guard, went even further. It broke an important taboo by explicitly and strongly upbraiding the president for involving himself with the issue of the Holocaust, describing it as 'adventurism at the cost of national interests'. It even suggested that foreign intelligence services had infiltrated Ahmadinejad's circle of advisors to spur the president on in this course of action that was proving so harmful to the republic. Whatever the motivation and whatever the objective, Baztab rejected out of hand the value of government involvement in the question of the Holocaust, even if the president's advisors had identified it as the Achilles heel of the West. Baztab reminded its readers that the founder of the Islamic Revolution, Ayatollah Khomeini, had never doubted the Holocaust.

Although Baztab's conspiracy theory regarding the president's advisors was far-fetched, they did finger the primary exponent of the Holocaust conference: Mohammad-Ali Ramin, one of Ahmadinejad's closest advisors. Of the need for the conference Ramin said: 'The aim of the conference was to question the [political] system that the West has imposed on us using the Holocaust. We are talking about the forming of a strategy, not a tactic or a physical act.' In an interview with Baztab, Ramin explained the need for a new strategy and its importance at that particular moment: 'The US has reached the end of the line as a sole superpower, and the Zionist domination throughout the world is facing revolt in global public opinion. New powers are taking shape that are shaking the status quo. Meanwhile the Islamic Republic has attained a completely new status in the Middle East. If we cannot use our status, we may lose the opportunity for ever, and they will force us back into our former passive position, and even worse.'

Ramin's words about the new strategy of putting Iran on a new level vis-à-vis the rest of the world were familiar. It was the sort of thing the hardliners around Ahmadinejad said whenever they confronted criticism of their actions on the international scene. And Ahmadinejad – who kept repeating that Iran would soon sit at the high table of nuclear powers – had spoken of Iran's new status in the Middle East region. Outside Iran, some independent analysts were also pointing to Iran's growing influence in the region in the aftermath of the American debacle in Iraq and the strong position of pro-Iranian Iraqi Shiites, as well as Israel's failure to unseat Hezbollah from southern Lebanon, especially during the failed conflict of August 2006.

Ahmadinejad's remarks had appealed to millions of ordinary Arabs throughout the region. They saw him as a hero, in the mould of Nasser of Egypt, who had revived Arab nationalism and Arab self-respect. This confluence of circumstances – America's seeming impotence in the Middle East and Ahmadinejad's growing regional stature – gave the hardliners momentum and pushed Ahmadinejad further to the right. Evidently Iran had decided that the conference in Tehran was only the beginning of its involvement with the Holocaust deniers, despite the international outcry.

Ramin was a name that anyone who followed Iranian politics was beginning to hear bandied about with increasing frequency. But who was he? With receding red hair, trimmed red beard and green eyes,

Ramin does not look like a typical Iranian. His complexion is significantly fairer than that of most Iranians, almost as if his years spent in
Europe had physically altered him. He is of medium height and build
and is always dressed immaculately in a dark suit and the collarless
shirt favoured by Iranian diplomats. He exudes a calm that is at odds
with his abrasive politics. He has been banned from public speaking
in Germany because his virulent attacks on Israel and Zionism fell
foul of the country's anti-Semitism and Holocaust-denial laws.

In Iran, Ramin has evolved as the authority not just on revisionist
Holocaust theories but on the entirety of Jewish culture and history.
All this makes his swipes at Israel all the more worrying, such as his
assertion that 'throughout history, the Jewish Tribe inflicted the
biggest damage to humanity, and continues to do so'. That his output
is labelled 'history' and 'knowledge' is a reflection on the cultural and
intellectual climate among Iran's current political leadership. A typical
'historical' assessment of Jews is Ramin's response to a question and
answer session at Gilan University: 'Throughout history Jews were the
targets of many accusations. It has been said they were responsible for
the spread of plague and Typhus, as Jews are a very dirty people.'[15]

Ramin has coopted into his vehement anti-Zionism all the traditional strands of Western anti-Semitism and its language. Conspiracy
theories abound in his worldview: Hitler and the Nazis were the product of Jewish capitalists; World War II was a masquerade engineered
by the West and Stalin to justify the creation of Israel; the British
and the Americans, envious of the rise of Germany, concocted the
Holocaust to discredit the Germans; the British and the Americans
created Israel to anger and provoke the Muslim world into wiping
out Jews – a task they could obviously not handle themselves; even
the 2006 avian flu scare that gripped the world was dreamt up by the
British and the Americans to divert attention away from the Middle
East, and thus it was that 'tens of millions of poor chickens paid for
this with their own holocaust'.

The fantastical imagination of Ramin makes him gloriously and
uniquely impervious to the charge that his brand of anti-Zionism is
leaving his country open to accusations of ancient Western-style anti-
Semitism. His rhetoric and reasoning is much closer to the sort of
language that used to be common currency in Europe and is now
confined to sociopaths in Europe and America. Iran has always had

its own brand of passionate bigotry – its Bahai community can testify to the many prejudices it has had to endure in the last 150 years – but the sort of rhetoric being spouted by Ramin about Jews has never been heard before from any part of Iran's political elite in any era – even in the highly charged post-revolutionary years when Israel became a demon state in the eyes of Iran's new leaders.

Ramin certainly had the ear of the president, and his key position within the close circle of advisors and friends of Ahmadinejad was evident when he was chosen to direct the campaign of Ahmadinejad's supporters in the local elections in December 2006. In the event, the campaign of the pro-Ahmadinejad candidates, who included Ahmadinejad's sister Parvin, was a general failure, with many of the candidates losing to opponents of the president, but this did not affect Ramin's continuing closeness to Ahmadinejad.

Ahmadinejad and Germany

The setting in April 2006 for Ahmadinejad's third press conference since taking office was the auditorium at the presidential office in central Tehran. It had been decorated with a backdrop picture of a boy holding a ball of light in the air, signifying Iran's mastering of nuclear technology. The diminutive president sat behind a table covered with dozens of colourful microphones sporting the logos of Iranian and international TV stations. Smiling broadly, and seemingly in a good mood, Ahmadinejad expounded a theory that 'greedy Zionists' had exploited Germany for more than 60 years since World War II.

> Sixty years ago a war took place. Some 60 million people were killed from both sides ... but the people of Palestine are still paying for the war in which they had no role; the German people are still paying for the war in which they had no role. The question is this: let us assume that 60 years ago, some people started a war in Germany and that some crimes were committed. But three generations later, what has the present generation of Germans done to deserve to be humiliated in this way and be prevented from playing an independent part in international relations? This generation is constantly given to believe that their fathers were criminals. In all countries, there is a symbol of [national] pride, and they proudly show them off to tourists. But in Germany, they have set up symbols that imply to every German that passes through a park that his or her father was a criminal, and that this is why they have to be humili-

ated. Why? Why should this be imposed on a nation? The same is true for Austrians. We do not defend the war; we in fact condemn it. Sixty years ago there were people in power who did what they did. But why should today's generation be burdened politically, culturally and economically? Why must they continue to pay a ransom? Pay a ransom to whom? To a group of Zionists! What for? To suppress the Palestinians! I have no doubt that the great German nation cannot be happy about this. The war ended some 60 years ago, and yet they are still demanding a ransom from a nation. Why should there be such relationships? We say these relations are unjust ... the people of Germany are dear to us. Why should an intelligent nation be humiliated in this way because of its history? Germany should enjoy the highest positions in scientific, cultural and political relations in the world. After 60 years they are still hostage to the very same people who plotted all the events of those days.[16]

Ahmadinejad's words echoed the sentiments of neo-Nazis in Germany. What made this speech even more ill judged was that at the exact same moment Berlin was working with the five permanent members of the UN Security Council to try to find a way out of the nuclear impasse with Iran.

But ever unmoved by the demands of diplomacy and emboldened by the attention he was getting both inside and outside Iran, Ahmadinejad now felt he could ram home his offensive against Israel, Zionists and the Holocaust. He had set his sights on Germany, the country he believed had paid dearly for a sin it did not commit. As inconceivable and as comically crude as it might appear to European observers, Ahmadinejad was using this press conference in Tehran in April 2006 to initiate an anti-Israel alliance with Germany and Austria. This time it was no audacious attempt to shock the world: it was a genuine diplomatic initiative by a national leader whose grasp of international relations and world history was, to put it mildly, unformed. He waxed lyrical about the unfortunate people of Germany and Austria who had been held back from realizing their potential. He explained that he had taken pity on 'an intelligent people' who could have created wonders, and instead had been held hostage to their past and regularly shamed for something that had been invented by Zionists for their own designs.

Most feebly of all, the president appeared to be gently resurrecting one of the most spurious racial conceits ever: that Iranians and Germans were both part of a common Aryan race. German diplomats found it amusing that every time they met Iranian officials, the question of the 'shared' Aryan race would be brought up by the Iranian side in a casual attempt to break the ice.

The root cause of this purported connection can be found in an inscription over two and a half thousand years old. Darius I – one of the early founders of the Persian empire – had declared himself of the Aryan race in 500BC. His words, carved in stone on a rock high above the plains of today's southern Iran, declared:

> I am Darius, the great king, and the king of kings
> The king of many countries and many people
> The king of this expansive land,
> The son of Wishtaspa of Achaemenid,
> Persian, the son of a Persian,
> Aryan, from the Aryan race.

This carving was made at a time when ancient Persia was at one of its peaks of glory and the Persians were known to many in the region and beyond as Aryans, that is, descendants of one of the great migrations south and west by peoples from inner Asia. In modern times the term 'Aryan race' is more commonly associated with the German National Socialist movement. For the Nazis, on the basis of highly dubious historical analysis, the Aryan race represented Nordic Europeans, in contrast to the Slavic and Latin Europeans and the Semitic Jews. The vision of Aryan perfection – as rather imperfectly expressed in the person of Hitler – was a blond-haired, blue-eyed Adonis. In the minds of the Nazis, the race spread to northern Europe, Iran and India. Obsessed with racial purity and its classifications, the Nazis were comfortable with the idea of the Iranian and Indian Aryans as Indo-Europeans. While the suggestion of a shared heritage – genetic, cultural or historical – between Iran and Germany on the basis of words uttered by an ancient king 2,500 years ago and the ideologues of a twentieth-century fascist movement stretches the imagination, for Ahmadinejad shared blood with the Germanic peoples of northern Europe seemed to be a reality and a potential route into an intercontinental anti-Israel alliance.

This was no provocative act for the cameras of the international media. This was a reflection of the president's real beliefs. Only this can possibly begin to explain what he did next: he wrote a personal letter to the German chancellor Angela Merkel, putting forward a proposal.

Letter to Chancellor Merkel

With his controversial remarks about Israel and the Holocaust echoing around the world, in May 2006 Ahmadinejad wrote a personal letter to Chancellor Merkel proposing, in all seriousness, an alliance of the two countries against 'the victors of the Second World War'.

Foreign Minister Mottaki handed over the ten-page letter in a sealed envelope to a top German diplomat in Tehran. Its contents were not made public immediately. By this time, Germany had joined the five permanent members of the UN Security Council to offer Iran a package of incentives in return for Tehran suspending its nuclear enrichment activities. It had also been made clear to Iran that if it did not take the offer, the UN Security Council would consider imposing sanctions.

The letter was part of Ahmadinejad's plan to communicate directly with world leaders to suggest 'ways to resolve world problems'. It followed hot on the heels of a letter penned a few weeks earlier to US president George W. Bush, which had been virtually ignored in Washington – at least publicly (see Chapter 6). But if this dismissive reception had wounded the Iranian president, he certainly did not allow it to deter him from writing to Chancellor Merkel.

When, a few weeks after being delivered, the contents of the letter to Merkel were released to the media, it went largely unnoticed. Few people bothered to read it, and it had already been dismissed by Merkel and was no longer a newsworthy item for either the Iranian or the international media. But for those who took the trouble to read it, the letter yet again betrayed a serious lack of understanding of international relations, as well as a serious delusion of grandeur on the part of Ahmadinejad.

Ahmadinejad told Merkel that the wicked victors of World War II had terrorized, degraded and humiliated Germany. They had then invented the Holocaust to hold Germany to ransom. His proposal was simple: since Iran too had been wronged by the same powers and given the gathering storm over Iran's nuclear programme, the time was ripe for Iran and Germany – two powerful God-fearing nations – to get together to put these powers in their place, restore world order and resolve many of the world's problems.

'I believe we and you have both been the subject of tyranny. They do not respect your rights and want us also to forgo our rights,'

Ahmadinejad said, referring to the victors of World War II. 'Together we must end the present abnormalities in international relations ... the type of order and relations that are based on what the victors of World War II imposed on the defeated nations. ... With the coop-eration of our two governments and the support of these two great nations we can make great strides in alleviating the problems and abnormalities of our world today.'

In his letter, Ahmadinejad again dismissed the Holocaust. 'I do not intend to argue about the Holocaust. But, does it not stand to reason that some of the victorious countries of World War II intended to create an excuse on the basis of which they could continue keeping the defeated nations of World War II indebted to them?'

Ahmadinejad was seeking an alliance with a chancellor who only a few months earlier had compared him to Hitler. She had said that the world had to act immediately to stop Ahmadinejad before his coun-try developed a nuclear bomb, and had disregarded as 'disgusting' and 'totally unacceptable' the president's remarks about Israel and the Holocaust. She had been emphatic and unambiguous: 'I say it as German chancellor: a president that questions Israel's right to exist, a president that denies the Holocaust, cannot expect to receive any toler-ance from Germany.'[17] It affords us some insight into Ahmadinejad's single-mindedness and tenuous grasp of international affairs – not to mention the quality of advice he was receiving – that he could seri-ously believe Merkel would be receptive to his proposal.

Completely ignored was the half-century of German NATO membership and that, as a founding member of the G8 group of industrialized nations, Germany was now essentially and intrinsically part of the world order that the Iranian president wished to under-mine. It is not impossible to suppose that he had only a very limited awareness of the G8, only a cursory understanding of Germany's post-war history and the close and mutually beneficial Cold War rela-tions between a contrite West Germany and a Soviet-obsessed US and Britain. But what seemed even more strange was that the Iranian pres-ident did not seem to even be conscious of recent political events. Had Ahmadinejad asked for the advice of his Foreign Ministry officials, or anyone familiar with international affairs, they could have told him that in the few months since she had become chancellor, Merkel had established very strong relations with President Bush, had met him three times and had declared that she was in complete agreement with him on a range of issues, including Iran. They could have told him that Merkel had gone on the record stressing that Iran's actions had made the cooperation of the European negotiating partners – France, Great Britain and Germany – with the United States all the more necessary.

In her first comment after seeing the letter, Chancellor Merkel said it did not deserve an answer. 'He's repeating the old thinking, which is totally unacceptable to us,' she declared. 'Israel's right to exist is a key part of our state policy and he calls this into question time and again; and at the same time our offer – an offer which really gives the Iranian people hope for the future – is not mentioned once,' she added, referring to the package of incentives designed to encourage Iran to abandon uranium enrichment.[18]

Tehran of course had its ready answer to the rebuff from Merkel. A senior aide to Ahmadinejad, the ultra-conservative Hamid Reza Taraqi, told an Iranian news agency that it was only to be expected. 'Their response is understandable in view of the indebtedness they feel towards the Zionists.'

CHAPTER 6

A WOLF AND A SHEEP: US—IRAN RELATIONS

Recently they have asked us for direct talks over the issue of Iraq. We agreed, because Iran, today, is not speaking from a position of weakness. And apparently they have understood that they cannot speak to the people of Iran from a position of strength. This is Iran.[1]

The wall of mistrust

The noise was deafening. Fifteen thousand people had packed the indoor sports hall at the Azadi ('Freedom') stadium on the outskirts of western Tehran. All of them were on their feet, cheering at the top of their voices. In the central wrestling ring stood the 31-year-old diminutive American wrestler Zeke Jones from Arizona. He was wearing a red and black tracksuit and waving a small Iranian flag in a dramatic display of camaraderie at the end of the tournament. The crowd went wild. They began shouting and howling Jones's name. The Iranian audience were thanking the American team for coming. The wrestler himself just wanted to thank the home crowd for being so generous in their welcome. 'I came here for sport and friendship. But you know what, it will probably go further than that, and why not?' Jones said.

It was the evening of Friday 20 February 1998 on the final night of the International Takhti Cup Freestyle Wrestling Tournament – a night when the 19 years of simmering hostility between the US and Iran looked as if it might be drawing to a close. Culturally, emotionally and psychologically for participants on both the US and Iranian sides, the games had been an extraordinary breakthrough. The Iranian crowds had cheered the visiting Americans as much as the home team, and now at the end of the games the five Americans were paying that support back. They each ran a lap around the sports hall, as many in the cheering crowd leaned over the barriers to touch their outstretched hands. They were like homecoming heroes. Kevin Jackson, originally from Lansing, Michigan, gave high fives to hundreds of Iranians fans. At the medal ceremony, another of the American wrestlers, Melvin Douglas of Topeka, Kansas, held up a portrait of Supreme Leader Ayatollah Ali Khamenei. It was another extraordinary display of emotion for the home crowd. 'Iranians wanted me to carry it, so I did. It was a great honour,' 33-year-old Douglas said. Earlier, after his match with his Iranian rival, Abbas Jadidi, he had crossed the ring to embrace his opponent in front of the adoring crowd. 'If people back home could see what happened at the arena – that was pretty incredible – a lot of mistrust between the countries would be gone,' said Larry Sciacchetano, the manager of the US team.[2]

That such a thing should be taking place at all was amazing. And the event was even more strange considering the demographics of the audience. These were Iran's ordinary urban working classes. They were not middle-class moderates or wealthy West-leaning elites. These were the ordinary men of Iran. They loved their national sport of wrestling and they loved the US athletes for visiting, for competing and even for winning. The bitter rhetoric and geopolitical wranglings of their leaders seemed stale and lifeless compared to the energy and warmth of this emotionally charged competition. In this sporting arena, the gap between the two nations was closed in the space of only a few hours; both sides were reconciled through their common humanity and a love of wrestling.

It was the first time in more than 20 years that American sportsmen had been in Iran. The hostage crisis had ended formal diplomatic relations between the two countries. During the 444 days when 52 US diplomats and embassy staff were held, Ayatollah Khomeini had described the US as 'the Great Satan', saying that Iran had no need for relations with the US. President Jimmy Carter similarly imposed sanctions on Iran that continue to this day. It was the beginning of decades of animosity. Now it seemed, just as table tennis had paved the way for US president Richard Nixon's historic visit to Communist China, that wrestling might open up the possibility of a new Iran–US relationship.

Many had tried to stop the wrestling tournament from taking place. An editorial in *Jomhuri Islami* (Islamic Republic) outlined the objections of the few hardliners who had come to disproportionately represent the Iranian people. 'People are asking why have American wrestlers been invited to the tournament. ... Is this not making a fool of a nation whose blood is on the criminal hands of America?' The paper was appalled by the presence of US competitors. The gravest concern related to the symbolism: 'If the American wrestlers win their matches, would it not be humiliating to hear the American national anthem being played out or see the American flag raised?' it thundered.[3] But when a US wrestler did indeed win the gold medal and the US flag was raised and the national anthem played, rather than erupting in violent indignation at this 'humiliation', the Iranian spectators were overwhelmed with a spirit of sportsmanship and camaraderie – a spirit that was entirely alien to the religious and political hardliners.[4]

But that is not to say that the event was wholly apolitical and spontaneous. The inclusion of the US had come about through the intervention of Iran's newly elected moderate president, Mohammad Khatami. He had invited them as part of a broad push to normalize relations with the US. Weeks earlier he had given CNN's Christiane Amanpour an interview in which he had spoken of his wish to bring down 'the wall of mistrust' between the two countries. 'There must first be a crack in this wall of mistrust to prepare for a change and create an opportunity to study a new situation.'[5] It was a speech that cautiously extended the hand of friendship and reconciliation.

So in 1998 there appeared to be a confluence of outlook and attitude between the administrations of Iran and the US. In the person of Khatami, Iran had the first president since the Revolution who was likely to offer the olive branch to the US, and, in President Clinton, the US had the man most likely to accept it. Clinton met with the five American wrestlers after their return, to draw more attention to the huge welcome Iranians had given the American wrestlers. 'What we want is a genuine reconciliation with Iran,' Clinton said. 'We believe Iran is changing in a positive way, and we want to support that.'[6]

In September that same year, another US wrestling team arrived in Iran to play in the World Wrestling Championship. Again, Iranians were ready to cheer the American team as their own. The US national anthem was played and the stars and stripes raised in the sports hall to the delight of the 12,000 spectators who repeatedly shouted 'Amrika, Amrika!' To the hardliners this was beyond the tolerable limit. But there was more. Abbas Jadidi, Iran's top wrestler in the 213-pound class, took to the mat to the roar of the crowd, then approached and embraced American Melvin Douglas, further exciting the fans. Both wrestlers showed grace rarely seen in wrestling matches. When the match ended with Jadidi winning 3–0, the Iranian refused to have the referee raise his arm in victory and walked over to Douglas, rais-ing the American's arm along with his own. It was one of those rare moments in history where all elements had come together to augur a historic shift. A moderate president had come to power with a huge mandate for reform and a promise to improve Iran's relations with the outside world. In the US a Democratic president was in office who genuinely wanted to make a fresh start with Iran.

But it was not to be. Islamic hardliners, who had been dealt a humiliating defeat in the presidential elections in 1997, did everything in their power to stop the reformist government of President Khatami in its tracks. Just as American tourists and academics found it easier to get visas to visit Iran, Islamic vigilante groups attacked a bus full of US academics with sticks and stones in the middle of Tehran, putting an end to the cultural and academic exchanges that were supposed to make cracks in 'the wall of mistrust'. Hardline newspapers attacked every little sign of rapprochement between Iran and the US. The judiciary, dominated by the hardliners, closed down reformist news-papers, which had called for better relations with the outside world. Even some of President Khatami's ministers were not spared. His one-time interior minister and key ally, clergyman Abdullah Nouri, was jailed for allegedly insulting Islam. Astonishingly, he was also charged with and jailed for advocating links with the US. Yet this was not a crime, at least not according to the law books. The prosecutor had quoted Ayatollah Khomeini, rejecting any notion of relations with the US and describing the relationship between the US and Iran as one between a wolf and a sheep.[7] A leading reformer, Abbas Abdi, was jailed after a court found him guilty of spying when all he had done was to conduct a public opinion poll for a US polling company. Abdi had found that that 74 per cent of the people in Iran wanted their government to talk to the US. (Ironically, 20 years earlier, Abdi was a leading member of the hardline students who had seized the US embassy in Tehran and took its diplomats and staff hostage.)

Even though the reformers had control of the executive branch of government, they were resisted and their efforts frustrated by the conservatives, who still enjoyed considerable power through their presence in the clergy and the judiciary. The pressure on President Khatami increased to levels that largely paralysed his government. By the time he was in the middle of his second term of office, Iranians could only look back on the early stages of his first term – a period of hope and vitality fraught with missed opportunities – with nostalgia. In Iran, Khatami and his administration were driven into a position where they had to cool their approach to the US if they were to save their political careers. When Khatami went to New York to speak at the UN General Assembly, he was careful to avoid bumping into President Clinton in the corridors of the UN building.[8] And when the US Secretary of State Madeleine Albright officially apologized on behalf of the US for its role in the 1952 coup, her Iranian counterpart, Kamal Kharrazi, said Iran would sue now that the US had admitted to the crime.[9]

The Islamists saw Iranian anti-Americanism as the key to their political survival. Across the Arab and Muslim world, Iran's robust stance against the US had won much admiration. Many saw Iran as the plucky David standing up to the US imperial Goliath. Fundamental to the Iranian Islamists' hopes for the future was Khomeini's belief that the Islamic Revolution had to be extended throughout the region and beyond. Being the international symbol of resistance to US global hegemony appeared to be an effective means of propagating the Revolution. The Islamists were supported in their opinions by Ayatollah Khamenei, who frequently undermined Khatami's reform agenda and moves towards détente with the US. A week after Khatami had spoken of his wish to see cracks developing in the wall of mistrust with the US, Khamenei rejected any ties or talks with the United States, saying that this would be harmful to Iran's independence and to Islamic movements around the world. 'The American regime is the enemy of [Iran's] Islamic government and our revolution.

It is the enemy of your revolution, your Islam and your resistance to American bullying,' Khamenei told worshippers at the Friday prayers in Tehran.[10] Much of his worldview had been affected by what he had seen during the Iran–Iraq War in the 1980s. He had witnessed many young Iranians go to their deaths, hit by weapons that the US and other Western countries had sold to Saddam Hussein. He remembered how a US cruiser, USS *Vincennes*, had shot down an Iranian passenger plane over the Persian Gulf in 1988 in the last months of the Iran–Iraq War, killing all its 290 passengers, including 66 children. There could be no argument compelling enough to sway the Supreme Leader. Even the argument of self-interest and the potential lifting of sanctions, which would allow Iran to engage in lucrative exports of gas and oil to neighbouring countries, failed to sway him.

In the US, the election of George W. Bush did not help matters either. Nor did the Al-Qaeda attacks of 11 September 2001. Designed to place the Western and Muslim nations in irreconcilable opposition, despite Iran's tacit support for Operation *Enduring Freedom* in Afghanistan, the attacks drove President Bush not only to weed out the budding saplings of diplomatic relations with Iran but to push back on any progress made since the days of the embassy hostage crisis. His inclusion of Iran among the three countries he infamously described as the 'axis of evil' removed any chance of a rapprochement with Iran. To the observer, it seemed as though diplomacy between Iran and America was as unpalatable to the emergent neo-conservatives in Washington as it was to the conservatives and hardliners in Tehran and Qom.

The good work of the previous administrations was slowly unravelling. The gradual discovery of Iran's clandestine nuclear programme in 2003 only added to the terrible downward spiral of relations between the two countries. The US demanded Iran stop its nuclear programme and come clean on all its related covert activities. Regime change became the aim of the US administration. A huge build up of US forces in the Persian Gulf, as well as overt and covert operations to undermine the clerical leaders' grip on power, were supposed to speed up the downfall of the mullahs.

US policymakers were certainly about to see a regime change. But it was not in the direction that they had hoped. A relatively young zealot called Mahmoud Ahmadinejad had returned to the capital, having just lost his job as the governor of the northwestern province of Ardabil. He had his eye on political advancement, but who could know where this would lead? The firebrand was convinced of one thing: one day Iran and the US would have to face each other in a war.[11]

Ahmadinejad's journey

When the plane came to a stop on the tarmac at John F. Kennedy airport in New York, Mahmoud Ahmadinejad, now President of the Islamic Republic of Iran, glanced out of the window to find dozens of 'strange cars', many of them with flashing red and blue lights waiting for him. 'I thought they are here to take us to the CIA, and it's all over!' he later joked. But he was soon told that the waiting black utility cars and limousines surrounded by police outriders with flashing lights were part of the protocol and security laid on for heads of state attending the UN General Assembly.[12]

It was his first visit abroad as president of Iran, and the first time ever that he found himself on American soil. Such was the animosity between the two countries that Ahmadinejad's security officials had advised him not to make the trip to New York, where he was to address the 60th General Assembly. They said they could not guarantee his safety. He had only been elected president a few weeks earlier and there had been considerable debate among the top Iranian leaders as to whether or not he should attend the assembly. Some among the president's aides felt that the devious United States and Western governments would use the occasion to put further pressure on Iran. They argued that the Western media would gang up against the pariah nation and would misrepresent anything said or done to fuel their anti-Iranian propaganda machine. Some even suggested that the president might come to harm. The advisors thought it possible that the US authorities would arrest Ahmadinejad as soon as he set foot on US soil for what was still being discussed as his alleged involvement in the hostage-taking saga in 1980. This fear was not as far-fetched as it might sound. The CIA had certainly investigated the issue but, after examining the evidence and its own records, had rejected the allegations of Ahmadinejad's involvement. That said, many hostages continued to insist that Ahmadinejad had interrogated them. The less extreme of the president's advisors suggested against using the presidential plane, as they were worried that the US authorities might impound it.

But Ahmadinejad was undaunted. Characteristically, he was ready for a fight – both with hardliners and reformists at home and with the international heads of states at the UN. He argued that this was a good opportunity to put Iran's case on the nuclear issue forward forcefully, as the speech at the UN would probably be broadcast live around the world. Furthermore, he argued that Iran had to be on the political and diplomatic offensive, rather than keep a timid low profile. He wanted to show the big world powers that Iran would not back down on its nuclear programme, and he wanted to use the opportunity to attack the US and Western countries for their misdeeds. 'It was not an easy decision. After all when one wants to travel to enemy territory, it's not easy,' Ahmadinejad recalled. In fact, the tensions and disagreements over Ahmadinejad's potential attendance at the Assembly had ultimately to be resolved by referral to the Supreme Leader, who finally agreed to the president's visit. Fears were only finally overcome when Iran's experienced representative at the UN, Mohammad Javad Zarif, assured the president that he would be safe.[13]

Ahmadinejad had ambivalent feelings towards the US. He was convinced that sooner or later, Iran and the US would come to blows, and that Iran had to prepare itself for that eventuality. In discussions with Iranian leaders he would argue that the US empire was on the wane and that Iran had to do what it could to speed up its downfall.[14] But some observers noted that he was also keen to be, if possible, the key that unlocked relations with the US.[15] Of course, the first important step was to win some measure of trust in the US and the international community. What Ahmadinejad actually did was the exact opposite: he appeared to be coming to frighten the leaders of the world, increasing the itchiness of the Bush administration's trigger finger.

Ahmadinejad and Bush

It was a graduation ceremony with a difference. In the middle of Tehran's biggest cemetery on the southern outskirts of the capital, a company of volunteer suicide bombers had just finished months of training, and the organizers were giving them their American-style dog tags. There were about 150 of them – men and women – who had covered their faces with Palestinian-style scarves known as kuffiyas, and wore bandanas on their foreheads that bore the legend in Arabic, 'There is no God but Allah'. They were sitting separately on rows of foldable chairs – women on the left, men on the right – facing the stage that had been set up on a patch of grass. The stage had been decorated with a huge colour photograph of rows of coffins draped in the stars and stripes, sitting in the belly of a cargo aircraft – American soldiers killed in Iraq. A smaller banner showed six British soldiers carrying a coffin draped in the union flag.

This was towards the end of May 2006 when reports about an impending US attack on Iran's nuclear sites had reached dizzying heights. A US aircraft carrier and thousands of fresh US troops had been brought into the Persian Gulf. More were on their way. The American officials in Iraq regularly accused Iran of supplying the weapons that killed their soldiers. There were even reports that the US was toying with the idea of using tactical nuclear bombs against some of Iran's nuclear facilities, which had been built deep underground. In the face of this increased US military presence, the Iranian leaders had remained defiant. Ayatollah Khamenei had said that Iran would hit back at the US twice as hard as any attack it suffered. And the reprisals would not be limited to Iran and the Middle East. American interests everywhere in the world would come under attack. All the while, Iran's Revolutionary Guard were holding regular military manoeuvres, test-firing new missiles and weapons and warning that the nation was ready to respond to any attack. There were hints also that Iran might close the Straits of Hormuz, through which a large proportion of the world's oil passes every day. Naturally, this was a major ace up Iran's sleeve and something that unnerved the US considerably more than Iran's military might. But the general feeling was that Iran's biggest weapon against the US would be individuals who were prepared to carry out terrorist attacks against US nationals and interests around the world. And the graduate suicide bombers being given their dog tags in front of the media conveyed that message. The Supreme Leader's threat was reproduced in English on the stage at the graduation ceremony: if attacked, Iran would hit back twice as hard against US interests anywhere in the world.

A shadowy organization with the title of the Headquarters for Commemorating the World Martyrs of Islam had been recruiting suicide bombers for months. The organization claimed it was an NGO, independent of the government or the Revolutionary Guard. But it was clear that its activities would not have been possible without the backing of some state mechanism. Most likely, the organization was a Revolutionary Guard or Basij militia initiative. It certainly had the support of some of the top leaders of the country who openly attended their functions to speak. A couple of months earlier, the organization had invited journalists to the auditorium of a university in Tehran to witness Islamic students registering and volunteering to become suicide bombers. Now it seemed that some of those who had registered had completed their training courses and were ready to leap into action.

At the ceremony, a woman graduate said that the most difficult part of the whole training was the acceptance of death. 'Once you manage to come to terms with death, then you will be able to carry out your mission with the coolness that is required,' she said, only her dark brown eyes showing from behind the kuffiya that masked her face. A male volunteer said that the US threatened Islam and Iran regularly and that this was a necessary and appropriate defence. 'We have to be ready,' he said, adding that he masked his face to avoid identification by foreign intelligence agencies. As the graduation celebrations continued, a group of male singers, members of the Hezbollah militia in Lebanon, sang revolutionary songs in Arabic, regularly invoking the name of the Hezbollah leader, Sheikh Nassrallah.

The army of suicide bombers was not an exceptional event in Ahmadinejad's Iran. These were extraordinary times in which the authorities were resorting to extraordinary means to defend their country and their revolution. There was a feeling that the US fist was hovering overhead; the government was already responding and trying to gain some control over the situation. Newspapers had been ordered by the government not to speculate about the possibility of a war breaking out, and to play down reports of US military preparations and operations. Ordinary Iranians, those who listened to foreign radio broadcasts such as the BBC and the VOA, were deeply concerned. There were reports of hoarding. Some parents – those who could afford it – were thinking of sending their children abroad.

Business activities had reached their lowest point for many years. The economy was drying up as, psychologically, the country began to feel as though it was already at war.

Ahmadinejad had said privately that he and President Bush were locked in a game of chicken – on a collision course and driving at great speed towards each other. The question was: who would chicken out first. Ahmadinejad was resolved that it would not be him and that Iran would remain defiant, even if that meant death and destruction.[16] What made a confrontation likely and all the more dangerous were the similarities of the two opponents at the helm in Tehran and Washington – two fundamentalist presidents who believed they were on a divine mission to advance peace on earth; two presidents who were buoyed by neo-conservatives in their administrations who relished the idea of a war. In this atmosphere of fatalistic aggression, someone had to blink first. Someone had to give a little to allow a release of pressure and to bring the world back from the brink. And then something unforeseen happened.

Letter to the president of the United States

On 8 May 2006 Iran's Foreign Minister Manouchehr Mottaki handed a letter together with its English translation to the Swiss ambassador in Tehran, Philippe Welti. It was addressed to the president of the United States. The government spokesman, Gholam Hussein Elham, said the letter suggested 'new ways to solve current international tensions'.[17] It was the first of a series Ahmadinejad planned to write to world leaders in the year that the Iranian leader, Ayatollah Khamenei, had named 'The Year of the Prophet Mohammad'.

The text of the letter was not initially available. But that did not stop the letter from having the most remarkable effect in Iran, where a gesture like writing a personal letter to a US president was unprecedented and even seen as taboo. There had been no overt or covert high-level contact between the two countries for 27 years, and the hardliners would view any such gesture from an Iranian leader with a good deal of suspicion. Under any other administration, the conservatives' first reaction would be that their president was selling out to the Americans. But Ahmadinejad's conservative credentials were impeccable. That he might be kowtowing to the US was unthinkable.

The timing of the letter was critical. Iran's nuclear programme had become the number one concern in Western capitals, including Washington, which was trying to force Iran, one way or another, to abandon its nuclear enrichment activities. Tension between Iran and the US had reached an unprecedented height. For many, this personal letter from Ahmadinejad offered hope. Without knowing the details of its contents, many both inside and outside Iran hoped that it contained ideas for defusing the tension. Many even wondered if this could be the end to 27 years of hostilities.

But initial reactions from Washington were not encouraging. Upon seeing the letter, US officials described it as 'rambling'. Secretary of State Condoleezza Rice said that it changed nothing. 'This letter is not the place that one would find an opening to engage on the nuclear issue or anything of the sort,' she said. 'It isn't addressing the issues that we're dealing with in a concrete way.'[18] As for the US president, the only official response he gave to the letter was that he believed Ahmadinejad was 'a very strange man'. There did not seem to be any real spite on Bush's part when he made that comment: he appeared genuinely confused. State Department officials said that the letter offered a window into the mentality and thinking of Iran.[19]

There can be no doubt that Ahmadinejad had expected a very different reaction. In his mind, the nuclear crisis had made Iran America's number one priority. Perhaps in his mind, he imagined that he now had the status of the USSR at the height of the Cold War and that this letter was his equivalent of the old red telephone hotline between the Soviet and US leaders. Yet the US cold shoulder bordered on the rude, and Ahmadinejad was quietly dismayed. How could they not respond to his gesture of friendship?

The reasons became clearer when the text of the letter was published a few days later. Those in Tehran who read the letter were struck first with disbelief and then - once the shock had worn off - concern. The letter suggested that either Ahmadinejad was deliberately trying to provoke the US or - and this alternative seemed far more likely - the Iranian president genuinely held a deeply odd and worryingly simplistic worldview, peppered with severe delusions of grandeur. It was clear that Ahmadinejad was not merely addressing the issues of diplomatic relations, defusing of tension or stopping a war. As well as laying out Iran's grievances with America, along with some of the standard conspiracy theories, Ahmadinejad seemed to be trying to convert the US president to Islam. The 'very strange man' described by Bush was there on the page for all to see.

Page after page of Ahmadinejad's letter was devoted to blunt evangelizing. 'Mr President, according to divine verses, we have all been called upon to worship one God and follow the teachings of the divine prophets.' Yet again Ahmadinejad was demonstrating his weak grasp of world affairs and his own terribly inflated sense of importance. Evidently, Ahmadinejad hoped to follow in the footsteps of many great men in history who had urged world leaders and opponents to submit to the will of Allah and convert to Islam. These attempts had begun 1,400 years earlier when the Prophet Mohammad sent emissaries to kings and emperors far and wide to invite them to embrace Islam. More recently, Ayatollah Khomeini had written to President Mikhail Gorbachev in 1989 to suggest, 'Islam could fill the intellectual gap that the demise of Communism has created for the Soviet Union.'

Although the letter was ignorant, opinionated and naive, it was also hopeful and honest. The writing of a letter to President Bush was not much less momentous than Ahmadinejad picking up the phone and calling the White House. It showed that the previously impenetrable and isolated conservatives of Iran were now trying to open lines of communication. History may well judge rather harshly the blanket rejection that came from Washington.

The letter enjoyed remarkable support from Iranian hardliners. One such supporter was Ahmadinejad's powerful backer, Ayatollah Ahmad Jannati, head of the constitutional Guardian Council and one of the rotating Friday prayer leaders of Tehran. A long-time admirer of Ahmadinejad, Jannati told the congregation at the Friday prayer in Tehran that the letter was the result of a 'divine inspiration' to Ahmadinejad and that he had bravely told the president of the United States that America's power was on the wane. 'God is kind to Iran and every time God wants to make Iran powerful, he makes this sort of divine revelation,' he said. 'This man [Ahmadinejad] is truly a brave, God-fearing and powerful figure. Who could have written such a letter that would astonish everyone?' Jannati even suggested that the letter be made part of the syllabus at schools and universities.[20]

The letter, however, achieved nothing. President Bush did go on to describe it as 'interesting' and certainly refrained from passing overtly negative comments. He also failed to convert to Islam. And he never replied. The non-response injured Ahmadinejad's pride but did not deter him from his course. Months later he challenged Bush to a live television debate, similar to those in US presidential elections. 'I suggest holding a live TV debate with Mr George Bush to talk about world affairs and the ways to solve issues,' he said. 'The debate should go uncensored in order for the American people to be able to listen to what we say, and they should not prevent the American people from hearing the truth.' White House spokeswoman Dana Perino dismissed Ahmadinejad's proposal, saying 'Iran may want to look first to allowing free expression and open debate within its borders, as opposed to the current practice of crushing dissent.' [21]

Escalating tension

The operation began just before dawn on Thursday 11 January 2007. Using darkness as cover, five US helicopters converged over a building in the town of Arbil in northern Iraq. While three of the helicopters hovered low to provide cover, dozens of Marines in the other two lowered themselves on to the roof using ropes. On the ground, a dozen Humvees and armoured personnel carriers blocked the roads in the area and laid siege to the building – an Iranian liaison office. Once in place, the Marines used loudspeakers to call, in Arabic, English and Persian, on the occupants to come out. When no one came, the Marines broke windows and threw in stun grenades. Smoke billowed out of the shattered windows. This was the cue for the Marines to break down the doors. [22]

As the Marines entered the building, President Bush in Washington was delivering a keynote address to the nation. 'Good evening. Tonight in Iraq, the armed forces of the United States are engaged in a struggle that will determine the direction of the global war on terror and our safety here at home. The new strategy I outline tonight will change America's course in Iraq, and help us succeed in the fight against terror.'

Bush announced that an additional 20,000 troops were to be deployed in Iraq in a new attempt to bring the situation under control.

He left little doubt as to who the main targets of the new push were going to be. 'This begins with addressing Iran and Syria. These two regimes are allowing terrorists and insurgents to use their territory to move in and out of Iraq. Iran is providing material support for attacks on American troops. We will disrupt the attacks on our forces. We'll interrupt the flow of support from Iran and Syria. And we will seek out and destroy the networks providing advanced weaponry and training to our enemies in Iraq.' There could be no doubt: US toler-ance of Iranian involvement in Iraq was at an end. Radical Shiites helped by Iran had formed death squads in Iraq, Bush claimed. 'The consequences of failure are clear,' he warned gravely. 'Iran would be emboldened in its pursuit of nuclear weapons. We will prevent Iran from gaining nuclear weapons and dominating the region.'[23]

As the domestic and international pressure piled up on Bush, and his administration was being pressured to sort out Iraq and provide a solution to the nuclear problem, the US president and his people had responded the only way they knew how: with a bravado show of force. They wanted to tell the world that the gloves were off with Iran. And the raid on the building in Arbil, just as the president unveiled his new plan, was a new and dangerous escalation in the hostilities between the two nations.

The US Marines in Arbil netted six men. A few hours later, they released one of the men, who was an Iraqi guard. The US raiders also took documents and computers. They were trying to arrest top commanders of the Revolutionary Guard's Quds Brigade who were operating in Iraq. The next day, Marine General Peter Pace, the joint chiefs of staff chairman, accused Iran of providing Iraqi insur-gents with weapons designed to kill American troops. 'We will do all we need to do to defend our troops in Iraq by going after the entire network regardless of where those people come from,' he said at a news conference with Secretary of State Condoleezza Rice.[24] Rice played the good cop, offering to meet with her Iranian counterpart 'anytime, anywhere' to discuss 'every facet' of US–Iranian relations. There was only one condition. Iran had to stop enriching uranium as part of its nuclear programme. Until then, Rice explained, 'the United States will use all our power to limit and counter the activities of Iranian agents who are attacking our people and innocent civilians in Iraq'.[25]

The Iranian liaison office in Arbil was in the process of being given consulate status. An Iranian flag had been hoisted on top of the building and it was already issuing up to 250 visas a day to Kurds who wanted to travel to Iran – mostly for medical treatment. The Kurdish authorities in northern Iraq were furious at the raid. It had taken place without their knowledge, in their territory and against the representatives of a country that had helped them during many difficult years under Saddam Hussein and Ba'ath rule. There were a few hours of tense stand-off between the US and Kurdish forces at Arbil airport where the US Marines were transferring the five Iranians on to a plane destined for Baghdad. The two sides nearly opened fire on each other. 'A massacre was avoided at the last minute,' said Iraqi Foreign Minister Hoshyar Zibari.[26]

But there was worse news to come. It later emerged that the raiders had in fact missed their targets. They had wanted to grab two high-ranking Iranian security officials, who were not in the building at the time of the raid. Instead, they had arrested five Iranians who many months later were identified as relatively junior officials. According to Kurdish and American sources, the targets were Mohammad Jafary Sahrarudi and Manouchehr Foruzandeh.[27] Sahrarudi was the deputy secretary of the Supreme National Security Council in Tehran. He had previously been the commander of the ground forces of the Revolutionary Guard. Many years earlier Austrian authorities had indicted Sahrarudi in his absence for involvement in the murder of the Iranian Kurdish opposition leader, Abdurrahman Ghassemlu. Foruzandeh was the top intelligence commander of the Revolutionary Guard. The two were on an official visit to Iraq to discuss security issues. They had met with both Iraqi president Jalal Talabani in Baghdad and, on the night of the raid, with the president of the Kurdish regional government, Massoud Barzani.

The botched raid nevertheless marked the beginning of a new chapter in relations between Iran and the US. Iraq was fast turning into an unofficial battlefield between the two. US soldiers on the ground had already worked out that they were not just fighting Iraqi rebels. There was Iranian military might involved as well. Although the US presence was restricted to Iraq, Iran was aware that they were in the firing line. The nuclear issue had enabled the US to push a range of sanctions against Iran through the UN Security Council. And these were set to increase incrementally as long as the stand-off continued. Iranian leaders were divided as to how to respond to the new escalation in the tension. Foreign Minister Mottaki told parliament that American threats were serious and not just part of a psychological war. 'Both limited and unlimited attacks on Iran are possible,' he said days after the arrest of the five in Arbil and the announcement of the US's new policies in Iraq.[28] Former commander of the Revolutionary Guard Mohsen Rezaie, one-time rival of Ahmadinejad in the 2005 elections, told state television that a war with the US was inevitable: 'The US has entered a new phase of serious confrontation with Iran and we will probably see the first signs in a couple of months.' He believed that while Iran should not underestimate the enemy and be taken aback by the psychological war the US had waged, it should prepare for confronting this threat.[29] The deputy speaker of parliament, Mohammad Reza Bahonar, said: 'There could be an attack at any moment; we must be prepared.'[30]

The whole country and its government were on red alert. War was perhaps only moments away. But at least one man in Iran remained unfazed. 'No, I am not worried at all,' Ahmadinejad said coolly in a lengthy interview on national television. 'Americans are not in a position to attack Iran. They would love to cause trouble for us but they cannot. Furthermore, in America there are some wise counsellors [who would advise against it].' Challenging Ahmadinejad, the television presenter reminded him that Bush had not paid any attention to the recently issued Baker–Hamilton report which had called for US dialogue with Iran. Implicitly, the presenter seemed to be saying that the US president was displaying the same type of arrogant calm as Ahmadinejad. 'They [American leaders] do listen to [the advice of the counsellors] to some extent. I do not think the Americans are capable of attacking Iran. They are waging a psychological war,' the president insisted. He also let it be known that Iranian political and military analysts were watching American moves in the region around the clock. His self-assuredness was designed to calm ordinary Iranians across the country.[31] But many were not reassured.

Yet war did not come in the early days of 2007. The escalation in tension actually turned into a release of tension. The US perhaps felt consoled by the fact that it had acted at all, even if that action had not been a success militarily. The Iranian people, once war failed to materialize, also felt calmer. Perhaps their president was right. Perhaps the US could not afford to go to war with Iran. But it was the Iraqi government that had helped to ease tension, struggling to avoid a fully fledged civil war in Iraq. Baghdad was desperate to stop its territory becoming the battleground for Iran and the US. It began a series of diplomatic efforts to bring Iran and the US together to talk about security in Iraq. Iraqi Foreign Minister Hoshyar Zibari travelled to Iran and the US to convince the two sides to meet. It seemed like a fool's errand. The two nations had had no diplomatic relations for decades and now their relationship was possibly at its lowest point ever. Yet, remarkably, the Iraqi efforts bore fruit. The two sides seemed eager to step back from the brink. On Monday 28 May 2007, top Iranian and US diplomats sat across the table for the first official face-to-face talks between the two countries in almost three decades.

Direct talks

In the late afternoon of 23 May 2007, without prior notice being given to the Iranians, a flotilla of nine US warships, including two nuclear-powered aircraft carriers carrying hundreds of aircraft and 17,000 soldiers, moved in tight formation though the Straits of Hormuz and into the Persian Gulf. This was a big show of force to Iran, which was, according to American officials, helping to kill US soldiers in Iraq while racing to make atomic weapons. The ships, flying large American flags and moving against the backdrop of the setting sun in the narrow waterway not far from the Iranian coast, was a dramatic display of American naval power.[32] Evidently, direct talks with Iran – the first since the 1979 Islamic Revolution – would not happen without a show of force from the US and some bravado from Ahmadinejad. The US felt that its tough stance on Iraq over the nuclear issue, as well as UN sanctions and threats of military strikes, had brought Iran to the negotiating table. In some ways, the talks were being interpreted as a vindication of US policies rather than as an attempt to change them.

The movement of the US ships through the Straits of Hormuz unsettled the markets. Two-fifths of the world oil supplies pass through the straits. Its global importance cannot be overestimated. The US military presence pushed the price of oil towards $70 a barrel, which was close to an all-time high. At the same time the IAEA reported to the UN Security Council that Iran had not only ignored the demands of the Security Council to stop its uranium enrichment activities but had actually stepped them up. Iranians played down the theatrics in the Persian Gulf, with Defence Minister Mostafa Mohammad Najjar saying that Iran would respond to any threats with a 'powerful answer'.[33]

But all eyes were on the direct talks. The historic meeting took place in the offices of the Iraqi Prime Minister Nouri al-Maleki in the Green Zone compound in Baghdad. US ambassador to Baghdad Ryan Crocker and a few aides met with the Iranian ambassador, Hassan Kazemi Qomi, whose delegation had been strengthened by senior officials from the Foreign Ministry in Tehran. Prime Minister Maleki shook hands with representatives of the two sides, who then shook hands with each other. Then they all sat down around the same table. It was a simple event, yet one which could define the future of the region and the world. Maleki, a Shiite with close relations with Iran, made a short speech before leaving the session to allow the Iranians and Americans to talk to each other. He told both sides that the US forces were in Iraq at the invitation of the government to help build up the army and the police. This was to forestall the Iranians from accusing the US of occupying Iraq. To reassure the Iranians, Maleki also made it clear that Iraqi soil would not be used for an attack on any of its neighbours. He explained that Iraq wanted a stable country free from foreign forces and regional interference.

When the two sides finally got down to their bilateral talks, there were no fireworks. Both ambassadors read out polite and restrained statements about the need to bring stability to Iraq. The Iranians suggested meeting again for a second time and the establishment of a tripartite commission to look at Iraq's security issues. But both diplomatic teams also said they would have to refer back to their capitals. It was tentative. It was cautious. But diplomatic contact had been resumed. In Iran, the surprise was immense. Despite all preconceptions, the hardliners had achieved something Iranian reformists had hoped for and yet had never dared attempt. Ironically, the reformists had been held back by a fear of the internal hardliners' possible reactions to any diplomatic links with the US. The meeting in Baghdad had confirmed to many in Iran that if anyone could re-establish relations with the US it would be the hardliners.

In less than two years, Ahmadinejad had made several important overtures to the US and to President Bush. He had travelled to the US twice, had spoken to the US Council of Foreign Affairs, had written a personal letter to President Bush, and now had given his government's blessing to direct talks with the US. His actions seemed to speak more loudly than his violent words. 'It's among the ironies of life that the very people who had made a taboo of any talks with the US are today breaking them,' said Mohsen Armin, an ideologue of the reform movement. Ahmadinejad had done all this with the backing of Iran's Supreme Leader Ayatollah Khamenei as well as by a certain amount of verbal gymnastics and trademark bravado. His argument for agreeing to the talks with the US was that Iran was now strong enough to sit across the table as an equal partner of the US. 'Recently they have asked us for direct talks over the issue of Iraq. We agreed, because Iran, today, is not speaking from a position of weakness. And apparently they have understood that they cannot speak to the people of Iran from a position of strength. This is Iran,' he said.[34]

Sensing a backlash from his hardline supporters, Ahmadinejad began a damage-control exercise. He told Basij commanders that 'the sons of Khomeini will never compromise. So long as there is oppression in the world, there is struggle and so long as there is struggle, we are at the forefront of the struggle.'[35] The government spokesman, Gholam Hussein Elham, had argued that people were safe in the belief that Iran under President Ahmadinejad would not sell out to the Americans in any direct talks. 'The people are satisfied that the government of President Ahmadinejad will not sidestep the values of Islam and the Revolution,' he said when asked why the hardliners were not making their usual hue and cry about the planned talks with the US. But the decision to hold direct talks had indeed upset a few of the staunchest supporters of Ahmadinejad.

'Foreign Ministry, Shame on You' read one placard, as dozens of Basij students from a host of universities demonstrated in front of the president's palace, demanding Ahmadinejad reverse his government's decision to hold direct talks with the US. Police quickly moved these agitators on but not before they had made their point. In their slogans and in their placards they said they felt betrayed by the government. It was to them a betrayal of the leader of the Revolution, Ayatollah

Khomeini, who had said there would never be any compromise with America. It was a betrayal of the suffering people and children of Lebanon and Iraq who had pinned their hopes on Iran's unwavering struggle against the US. Although there were only a few dozen demonstrators, they had a significance beyond their numbers. They represented the idealist Islamic revolutionary youth who had been brought up on a diet of Islamic internationalism, anti-Americanism and martyrdom. Their demonstration was a clear warning to Ahmadinejad that he could go only so far.

The disappointment of the students was serious enough for Iran's Supreme Leader to make a speech to allay their fears. He made a bellicose statement saying that Iranian officials were going to the talks only to read out to the Americans their charge sheet. It was necessary to release tension among these young idealists to whom hardliners in power had fed an endless diet of hatred and anti-Americanism. 'Those who imagine that the Islamic Republic of Iran would change its firm, logical and totally defendable policy of abstinence from negotiations and relations with the United States are deeply mistaken,' Khamenei said.[36] This was not just Khamenei calming the students. It was a warning. On America at least, it seemed Khamenei and Ahmadinejad did not see eye to eye. It was the first noticeable divergence in the rhetoric of the two most important individuals in the country.

Ahmadinejad had believed that Iran and the US would eventually come to blows, but he also had a burning ambition to be the man who ended the long-running hostilities with the US.[37] The Iranian president might have been a simple man, with a shaky grasp of world politics, but for all his rhetoric about the unavoidable military clash between Iran and the US, he would not want to throw away the first chance of a bloodless end to the problems between the two countries. Iran and the US had turned an important corner in their relationship and, despite some domestic criticism, the conservative majority were not up in arms against Ahmadinejad. The Great Satan and the Islamic Republic had broken bread and the sky had not fallen in – not yet.

The second meeting between the two countries a couple of months later went relatively well, and the two sides agreed to a tripartite commission to look into security issues. But in the US there was a growing realization that Iran was buying time by engaging in talks with the US over Iraq. Certainly, if the US military in Iraq were to be believed, Iran was stepping up its support for the insurgents. With the US congressional elections getting closer and with both Republican and Democrat candidates talking tough on Iran, the Bush administration once again cranked up the rhetoric against its old enemy. There was once again talk of military strikes, and Ahmadinejad did not help with his statement that Iran was going to fill the void in Iraq left by the Americans and British. At a press conference in Tehran on 28 August 2007, Ahmadinejad said that US political influence in Iraq was 'collapsing rapidly' and that Tehran was ready to help 'fill any power vacuum'. The statement rang alarm bells in the region and beyond, confirming the worst fears of the West and the Arab world.

Iran and the USA were on a collision course once again. Many in Iran were deeply concerned. But Ahmadinejad continued to dismiss the possibility of US military strikes against his country, saying that Washington was not in a position to take such action. Iranians could only pray that he was right.

CHAPTER 7

IRAN IN TURMOIL

Today we have managers in the country who do not believe in the ability of Islam to administer society, managers who approve of liberal ideas, managers who believe in progress only in the framework of individualistic, material and secular initiatives, managers who lack confidence in their own Islamic culture when confronting the cultural onslaught of the West. These managers are weak in front of the enemies and look down on their own people.[1]

A star is born

Within a year of his presidency, Ahmadinejad had dragged Iran up the international agenda and raised his personal profile to within a hair's breadth of that of Ayatollah Khomeini. His U-turn on reform, his strident anti-Israel rhetoric and his aggressive resistance to US and UN pressure to halt Iran's nuclear programme had all won Ahmadinejad a place on the world stage. Somehow he had strengthened his domestic standing with people all across the political spectrum. He had isolated his critics and won the respect of the Muslim world.

Yet here was also a man who wrote incoherent letters to heads of state, who invited neo-Nazis to speak at high-profile events, who was lampooned and ridiculed the world over for believing that he was an agent of the divine, preparing Iran for the arrival of the messianic Missing Imam. Here was a leader whose grasp of geopolitics was rudimentary, a man who seemed not to understand economics, a man who would drag Iran to the brink of an unwinnable war with the West.

Intentionally or not, Ahmadinejad's erratic and sensationalist behaviour had won him considerable global media attention. With his controversial views on the Holocaust and his determination to press forward with the nuclear programme, every newspaper and news channel hung on his every pronouncement, no matter how unusual. CNN International and BBC World, as well as the Arabic channel Al Jazeera, took to broadcasting live portions of Ahmadinejad's frequent speeches on his visits to provincial towns in Iran. Even the most innocuous speech could yield the most amazing insights into this enigmatic world leader. On one occasion, BBC World even opted for the live transmission of Ahmadinejad's press conference in Tehran in preference to British prime minister Tony Blair's, which had been scheduled to take place more or less at the same time in London.

Ahmadinejad's poster appeared on the streets of several European capitals on billboards, advertising the news programmes of major television channels. He was the pin-up of political unrest. *Time* magazine was considering him for Person of the Year and sent a top photographer to do a session with the president in case he was chosen from the list of 26 candidates. Only two other Iranians had been *Time*'s person of the year: Ayatollah Khomeini in 1979 and Iran's fiercely nationalist prime minister Mohammad Mosaddeq in 1952. Ahmadinejad was increasingly viewing himself as the third great revolutionary leader of Iran, after the father of the modern nation, Mosaddeq, and the founder of the Islamic Republic, Khomeini. Somehow he simply was not bothered that this renown was earned for the wrong reasons. Ahmadinejad believed he had begun a new move in the world towards spiritualism. In his way of thinking, attacks on him in the Western media were just a sign that he was on the right track. If you didn't provoke the ire of your enemy, then surely you were doing something wrong.

In the Arab world he was seen as an unambiguous hero, enjoying a standing comparable to that of some of the most popular Arab leaders in history, such as the Egyptian nationalist leader Gamal Abdel Nasser. Many in the Muslim world took great pride in the Iranian president and loved him as a no-nonsense leader standing up to the bullying Western powers. Even taxi drivers in Beijing liked him for his ordinary appearance and his perceived resistance to US imperialism. Because of this, Ahmadinejad was riding high at home. He continued to enjoy the support of the Supreme Leader, Ayatollah Khamenei, and, through the Ayatollah, he had the backing of the clergy, the judiciary and the whole religious conservative establishment. Pro-government newspapers and state-run television loved the exposure Ahmadinejad and Iran were getting, portraying it as a reflection of the power of Iran in the world under its down-to-earth president. The hardliners seized on the international attention Iran was getting to argue that Ahmadinejad had 'checkmated' Iran's enemies – the US, Britain and all of the West – with his unwavering stances on the Holocaust and the nuclear issue. As Ahmadinejad had expected, some doubters in the hardline camp joined him as he consolidated his power base.

Ahmadinejad was also careful not to forget his election goldmine: the rural poor. His provincial tours had became popular with locals, while a series of policies to help the poor won him a good deal of support across sections of the country generally ignored by Tehran. The provincial tours were also the ideal arena in which to try out his even more radical opinions and policies. High on his own success and popularity, and driven by a heartfelt zeal, Ahmadinejad wanted to rekindle the flames of the Revolution and return to the values of the early years. He began to speak openly on his tours of his ambition to unleash the Third Revolution. He travelled to small provincial towns and tried to engage with rural Iran, to understand and attend to their problems. All the while, he adopted a revolutionary persona in the mould of Ayatollah Khomeini in the early days of the Revolution. His language also changed to appeal better to the poor masses in provincial towns. He often used Khomeini-type language, simple but ferocious rhetoric, to denounce the US and Iran's other enemies, criticizing their opposition to Iran's nuclear activities. He championed the cause of Iran's right to nuclear technology. The crowds loved it when he prompted them to shout 'Nuclear energy is our legitimate right'. Deep down, the president was a rabble rouser. In the current climate, it seemed to be politically expedient but, more than that, he positively enjoyed it.

Ahmadinejad was high on adrenaline. He was also very lucky. The unprecedented rise in oil prices following America's Iraq adventure continued to inflate Iran's income from oil exports, allowing him to spend money like there was no tomorrow – a possibility that his policies made all the more likely. As he travelled the country, he followed up his inflammatory remarks about Israel, the Holocaust, the US and the West with promises of increased development budgets for provinces. He pledged sports facilities, roads and bridges for remote towns. He announced plans to create jobs for the unemployed. He also raised the salaries of nurses and workers, increased pensions for retired civil servants and set up a fund to provide wedding loans to the young. His largesse was conspicuous; his generosity with state funds seemingly knew no bounds.

When he was elected, his critics and opponents had given him only a few months in office because of his hardline ideas and his incompetence. Now his reformist opponents were in a state of stunned resignation. Ahmadinejad was loved across the country. He had brought hope to the poor and had won the respect of many in the Muslim world by his repeated pokes in the eye of the West. Although Iran's interests and image abroad had taken a huge battering, his reformist opponents remained largely silent.

Although he been strangely devoid of policy or inspiration during the first round of the presidential campaign, in office Ahmadinejad had a clear objective: he wanted to unleash a revolution.

The Third Revolution

Six months into his term of office Ahmadinejad had created enough uncertainties to plunge the country into chaos and turmoil. But, he believed, that was the price to be paid for a genuine and far-reaching revolution – the Third Revolution. In Ahmadinejad's words, the new revolution aimed to change the country's power structure in favour of social justice at home. He also aspired to bring peace and equality to the entire world – and he really meant it. As he repeatedly made clear, the president believed that he was divinely appointed to prepare both Iran and the whole world for the imminent return of the Mahdi. The Mahdi was to bring about a new global regime of peace and justice, and Ahmadinejad was driven by the belief that his policies and actions would make the Mahdi's task easy once he arrived. 'The Third Revolution has begun. It will revolutionize relations among the people, between the management of the country and the people, and among the managers,' he said after his election as president.[2] In the Iranian revolutionary vocabulary, the first revolution was the Islamic Revolution of 1979 that overthrew the monarchy. The Second Revolution, so designated by Ayatollah Khomeini, referred to the occupation of the US embassy in Tehran, the event which led Iran to turn away from the West.

Now it was time for the Third Revolution. But what exactly did that mean? Ahmadinejad had used the phrase throughout his election campaign and with greater frequency since coming to power. During the campaign, he had explained that the Third Revolution would aim to rid the country of liberal and secular influences and establish a truly Islamic government. 'Today we have managers in the country who do not believe in the ability of Islam to administer society, managers who approve of liberal ideas, managers who believe in progress only in the framework of individualistic, material and secular initiatives, managers who lack confidence in their own Islamic culture when confronting the cultural onslaught of the West. These managers are weak in front of the enemies and look down on their own people.' He said the Islamic Revolution had failed to eradicate poverty, corruption and discrimination. 'Unfortunately we are still facing moral as well as political and administrative corruption.' [3]

Ahmadinejad was certainly right in observing that Iran was dogged by poverty and corruption. He believed the solution was a return to the values of the 1979 Revolution. Ahmadinejad repeatedly criticized the management of the country under presidents Rafsanjani and Khatami, during which social justice had been sacrificed to economic development. This had led to a corrupt bureaucracy, the plundering of the nation's wealth by a few, and the spread of poverty. To make matters worse, the people of Iran had become more and more distanced from their Islamic spirituality. Under the aegis of the Third Revolution against corruption, Ahmadinejad was able to strike out at the political classes who had rejected and ridiculed him in the run-up to the elections. He had received no support from any political party or group during the campaign and this enabled him to talk openly and critically about corruption and the failings within Iran's limited democracy. He presented himself as the voice of the people and argued that Iran was fed up with the bickering of political parties who thought only of their position in the power structure. 'Today our people have shown they are not constrained by the usual political divisions. These divisions belong to those who sit behind closed doors and haggle over their share of power,' he said. [4]

There can be no doubt that from the very day he took power,

Ahmadinejad was committed to inspiring the Iranian people to rise up against the status quo, both nationally and internationally. 'A huge energy has been released in our country and we must put this to good use,' he said. But who were the president's targets, and why?

Internationally, the issue was simple. Ahmadinejad wanted a fundamental change in international relations, particularly at the UN where the five powers with the right of veto had disproportionate control and authority over other countries. But if Ahmadinejad was shouting about 'one member one vote' at the UN, he sang a very different tune domestically. Within Iran, the key target of the Third Revolution was the ruling elite and their ideology of democratic Islam. Ahmadinejad's election had handed the government to the Islamic neo-conservatives. Together with their allies in the Revolutionary Guard and the Basij, this faction wanted – as a first step – to purge the government and the bureaucracy of the reformists who spoke of democracy, the rule of law and the establishment of civil society. These were seen as un-Islamic and therefore unacceptable.

Professor Fred Halliday of the London School of Economics has described what had been happening in Iran with the election of Ahmadinejad as 'a revolutionary spasm', not dissimilar to the symptoms suffered by many other revolutions. 'In a crucial respect, this revolution, like many other upheavals, is moving after twenty years, not into a "reform" phase, but into a "twenty-year spasm" – a second reassertion of militancy and egalitarianism that rejects domestic elites and external pressure alike (as in Russia in the purge era of the late 1930s, China under the "cultural revolution" of the late 1960s, and Cuba in the "rectification" campaign of the 1980s).' [5] In Ahmadinejad's revolution, the wrath of the people should not be directed against the Supreme Leader, and he was very firm in his distinction between the glorious, inspired, revolutionary Islamic leaders and the corrupt, ineffective, bureaucratic, un-Islamic managers of government. 'We have to make the people understand ... that the problems, the weaknesses and the deviations have nothing to do with the leader of the Revolution and the regime. They are the making of managers who have deviated from the Revolution.' [6] One target of his 'revolution' was none other than his old rival in the presidential elections – Rafsanjani and his allies. That Rafsanjani had strong revolutionary credentials did not stop Ahmadinejad smearing his political record and his private character. 'In an Islamic government we cannot have someone who is involved in gigantic economic deals taking the reins of the government or being present in the management of the country,' he said in an obvious dig at Rafsanjani, who had reputedly amassed considerable wealth for himself and whose sons were commercially highly active.[7]

Over the first two years of Ahmadinejad's presidency, the expression 'Third Revolution' gradually gave way to references to 'a second wave of the revolution'. Perhaps this was to emphasize that what was taking place was a direct continuance of the events of 1979 and 1980. Also, while a Third Revolution might be expected to have some clear, achievable goals and to occur within a delineated time-frame, a 'second wave' was a more nebulous concept and more open to interpretation and extension. Central to the Ahmadinejad revolution was a dogged and violent pursuit of his own ideals and morality, without bowing to anyone else.

Throughout this time the Supreme Leader remained silent on the return of the Revolution. Many believed that he had privately given Ahmadinejad the go-ahead for his revolution and that it might even have been Khamenei's idea. Certainly it appeared that the Ayatollah was supportive of a huge purge and a fresh start in Iran. But to do this, Ahmadinejad needed more than cheering and waving from the populace. He needed an Iranian people energized and committed to his vision of the new Iran.

A people's president

On an autumn day in 2006 the afternoon sun cast a warm light over a football field on the edge of the capital. About 4,000 people had turned up to see and hear their president more than a year into his presidency.

As well as borrowing his moral code from the Middle Ages, Ahmadinejad seemed to have adopted the governing style of a peripatetic medieval monarch. He constantly toured the provinces. He said that it was helpful for him to see the daily problems of Iran at first hand. And when he went on tour, it was not simply a PR exercise with rallies and crowds and very little substance. The president would hold his cabinet meetings in the places he visited and attempt – with mixed success – to deliver policy decisions, budget commitments and incentives to immediately deal with the problems seen on those visits. It was a roadshow government offering seemingly endless hits of instant gratification.

At the age of 51 Ahmadinejad still had the stamina for a taxing schedule of travel by road or by helicopter. He was able to move from town to town, making speeches and listening to the people's problems in the remote and less developed parts of the country. These were the parts of Iran that had seen no significant political presence since the first revolution. This was the forgotten Iran, and Ahmadinejad was showing his face and telling the people emphatically that they were forgotten no longer. All this was made even more successful by the decision of state television to follow him on his travels and broadcast his rally speeches live to the rest of the nation. Dominated by Islamic hardliners, the state Islamic Republic of Iran Broadcasting (IRIB) saturated its airtime with footage of the energetic president with his touring circus. Not surprisingly the IRIB had not been so generous with its resources and airtime when President Khatami was in office.

A makeshift fence of scaffolding partitioned the men and women in the crowd in the middle of a playing field. Some of the schoolboys who made up part of the crowd were misbehaving, trying to chat up or tease the girls in black all-enveloping *chadors* on the other side of the fence. It seemed that even the much feared Revolutionary Guard manning the partition were no match for such basic hormonal imperatives. A large group of young women in back *chadors* had turned up with yellow bandanas, inscribed with 'Allah O Akbar' (God is Great). These women were members of the neighbourhood Basij. In the men's section of the audience, the crowd was made up in equal measure of the very poor, plain-clothed young members of the Basij militia, loyalists of the regime and school children. The poor in the crowd were some of the poorest in Iran. Many had come to hand Ahmadinejad letters appealing for help. There was a commotion close to the stage where the president was speaking, as the desperately impoverished thronged in an attempt to hand their pleading notes and letters over to Ahmadinejad's security team. In a typically expansive gesture, Ahmadinejad had said he would attend to every request for help he received. And as a result, every rally was inundated with thousands of the poor and needy, clutching letters detailing their modest demands.

In most of his speeches during his provincial tours, Ahmadinejad would work the crowd by calling out questions and receiving answers back from the audience in unison. This call-and-response catechism followed simple political lines. Ahmadinejad would holler out the question: did the Iranian people want to back down and forgo their legitimate right to nuclear energy in the face of bullying Western powers? 'No' would be the resounding cry of the audience. But the rallies were far from being negative affairs. Ahmadinejad's promises and pledges saw to that. The construction of a new dam, a separate sports hall for girls and boys, a university, or an increase in the local development budget – the promises fell like manna in the desert. Like any performer, the president would remember to praise whichever town or province he was visiting in the most glowing terms. A particular favourite was to laud the crowd for their sacrifices during the Iran–Iraq War. But poverty was the big issue in these rallies, not war or religion or the enrichment of uranium. Always the president would raise the big question: why shouldn't young men and women in the poorer rural areas enjoy the same opportunities as those in Tehran? No act of flamboyant populism was too ridiculous. On one occasion in the middle of his speech, carried live on Iranian television, he asked the local governor what his development budget was. The president then turned to the crowd while addressing the governor and, with perfect theatrical timing, announced, 'Consider your budget doubled as of today!' Understandably the audience erupted in cheers. During another speech in the small town of Gavbandan, some in the crowd held up placards demanding that the town's name be changed. Gavbandan translates as either 'the match-fixing place,' or 'cow-rearing place', neither of which chimed with 'second wave' revolution, twenty-first-century nuclear Iran. The residents wanted the town to be called Parsian, which means 'the Persians'. Ever the showman, Ahmadinejad asked the crowd if they all wanted the change, and when they replied 'yes' in unison, he said, 'I declare that from now on Gavbandan will be named Parsian.' Such erratic and unpredictable events were commonplace with the pantomime president during his tours, which would result in misery and untold complications for Iran's huge bureaucracy.[8]

Sometimes this childish miracle-maker act would do more than simply overburden civil servants and government ministers. On a visit to the southern province of Fars, the president was egged on by chanting locals to apportion the town in which he was speaking to a neighbouring district. Three days of rioting ensued in the district's capital; the inhabitants objected to the sudden ceding of part of their district.[9] But the biggest problem was balancing the books. One report said that during a provincial tour, Ahmadinejad's government had pledged development funds to the tune of $300 million over and above the budget that had been allocated to the province in the annual government development budget. Oil prices were rocketing and it seemed that Ahmadinejad did not see himself as bound by the government's own budget allocations. A *Financial Times* journalist travelling with Ahmadinejad on his tour of the southern Fars province was taken aback by the sheer generosity of Ahmadinejad. 'In this tour alone, the promises amount to $3 billion, including $2 billion in soft loans and $1 billion in spending from the country's oil stabilization fund,' reported Najmeh Bozorgmehr, referring to the fund that had been set up to save some of the oil income for a rainy day.[10]

By that autumn afternoon in 2006, in the football field on the edge of Tehran, the Ahmadinejad roadshow was at its height. The loudspeakers had been turned up to a deafening level to make sure not only that those in the playing field but the whole neighbourhood could hear what the president was saying. A small platform had been built for cameramen and local journalists next to the main stage. As with every Ahmadinejad rally, the crowd had to politely listen to the president riding his particular hobbyhorses first. The crowd did not seem that attentive as Ahmadinejad expounded on his favourite theme: Iran's right to pursue peaceful nuclear technology. Many in the crowd continued their chit chat as he went on about his opposition to a parliamentary bill that would make it compulsory for the airport authorities to fingerprint American tourists when they arrived in Iran. He explained that this was a reciprocal measure against the unnecessary security checks for Iranians visiting the US. But according to the president, Iran had no quarrel with the American people. Few in the crowd seemed to care. But when he turned his attention to local issues, such as building roads and bridges to ease the traffic in this corner of Tehran or to help create jobs, they listened attentively before cheering him enthusiastically. At rallies during his provincial tours, Ahmadinejad had learned to speak about his pet subjects such as the nuclear issue and the Holocaust 'myth' for the benefit of the cameras, before moving to local issues for the benefit of those present. At the close of this particular rally, he announced that his government had set aside the equivalent of $40 million for this Tehran suburb. The show ended in huge cheers from the crowd.

During his first two years in office, Ahmadinejad travelled to all 30 provinces, speaking in more than 2,000 towns. In his visit to the southwestern province of Khuzestan, he spoke in 20 towns and received close to 1 million letters of request for help from a provincial population of some 4.5 million people. A few days after the visit, his officials said they had opened some 300,000 of the received letters, which mostly dealt with requests for jobs. Ahmadinejad's officials had let it be known that the government would provide cash relief to the poor. Of course, the promise of handouts had helped attendance at the president's rallies, with many hoping to be recipients of cash aid. The handout was the equivalent of $40 in grant aid to the most needy and an additional $250 in no-interest loans. Serious illness, having no source of income or being a university student qualified Iranians for cash relief. Ahmadinejad's critics would say he was buying the loyalty of the young students. But the public itself was certainly not complaining. Allegedly, before the presidential circus would hit town, scores of Iranians would rush to their doctors to ask for a letter certifying them as seriously ill so that they could qualify for government aid. Many also discovered that their letters were not treated as confidential, as they were opened by officials and referred to the relevant authorities for follow-up. Some who had complained about a certain official, for example, now found that the official in question knew what they had written to the president about him, opening the way for possible retribution.

Ahmadinejad seemed to be perpetually on an election campaign. On average he spent four days every three weeks touring the provinces. Some of the towns he visited were so remote that journalists had to look them up on the map to see where the president was speaking. His speeches became the president's principal way of putting his messages out to the domestic and international media. They were broadcast live on television and were a popular and useful platform for airing the key beliefs of his Third Revolution. His more remarkable statements attacking the West, defending Iran's right to nuclear energy, vowing not to suspend Iran's nuclear enrichment activities 'even for a day', declaring the Holocaust 'a myth', and attacking his internal critics as weak and faint-hearted or traitors, were all made during speeches at provincial rallies. In rally after rally he told the crowd it was only natural that big powers were angry with Iran. 'We tell these big powers: be angry with us and die of your anger!' he would say.

Ahmadinejad's provincial tours cemented his relations with the poor across the country. Many leaders and politicians before him had largely neglected the provinces in preference for a high profile in the capital. Few made regular trips to remote towns and villages, and when they did, it was mostly for the photo opportunities they provided at the official opening ceremony of a factory or a development project. The provincial tours provided Ahmadinejad with the chance to claim that he was the president of the people – interested not in politicking in the capital but in working to improve the lot of poor people in remote areas. Here was a president in touch with his people, promising a better tomorrow and challenging the world to a fight.

Unfortunately these promises, distributed so liberally, were taking their toll on the nation. Already there were murmurs in parliament and elsewhere that Ahmadinejad's promises were raising unrealistic expectations in the provinces. It was one thing to promise and quite another thing to deliver. Standing and chanting and cheering about increased budgets and new roads, schools and hospitals was all very well, but these things could not happen on their own. Nor could they happen at anything like the rate Ahmadinejad was promising. If he were the Mahdi and his words turned into deeds, then all would be fine. But the president was – despite his beliefs – a mortal being, not a divine one. It had reached the point where parliament speaker Gholam-Ali Haddad-Adel complained that every time he visited a provincial centre he was inundated with requests for more cash. During one provincial visit, he declared upon arrival that his pockets were empty.

Critics of Ahmadinejad said that the provincial visits had not been as successful as they seemed. Many decisions taken during the cabinet meetings in provincial centres were not implemented. Promises of roads and bridges, sports centres for girls and boys, or establishing factories to create jobs in the provinces never came to fruition. Some of the advisors of the president expressed concern that if the situation persisted it would lead to disappointment and that this disappointment would swiftly sour public opinion. One governor of a southern province explained that lack of money was the main reason for the non-implementation of the decisions of the cabinet or the promises of the president. Ahmadinejad was not deaf to these comments and responded to all criticisms by sending some of his closest aides to the provinces he had already visited to follow up on the promises he had made and the cabinet decisions that had been taken.

As with anything else Ahmadinejad instigated, there was a certain slapdash audacity and sheer luck involved, but certainly the intention behind the policy pronouncements and largesse was sincere. His popularity in the provinces continued to skyrocket, and so did his confidence. There was simply no stopping him.

The Islamic populist

As he went up and down the country, Ahmadinejad projected an Islamic populist persona, which was not only new to Iran but also to the Islamic world. He put on the khaki-coloured baggy trousers and the tight vest Kurdish men wear when he went to the province of Kurdistan. He wore the white dish-dash robe and headgear of the Arabs in the mostly Arab-populated province of Khuzestan. At rallies of the Basij militia, he sported the Palestinian-style scarf, the kuffiya, favoured by Basij members. For all his deeply held convictions and his reputation for being radical and uncompromising, Ahmadinejad was also a political chameleon, attempting to be all things to all men.

If he had a trademark item of clothing, it was surely his cheap beige jacket. Immediately following his election victory, the jacket became a must-have fashion item for many of his younger supporters. In the men's clothing shops in downtown Tehran, jackets like his sold briskly. The garment became so much a part of his persona that even he took to describing it as 'an Ahmadinejad jacket'. In one press conference, he joked that journalists wearing 'an Ahmadinejad jacket' could ask two questions instead of one! Such a quip was typical of the president. Iranian journalists seemed to love his sense of humour and his informal style. 'You should know that American culture is trying to impose itself everywhere,' Ahmadinejad told a French television channel in an interview when asked about his trademark jacket. 'If we accept this, we would lose a lot more. We must be ourselves.'[11]

Ahmadinejad worked by instinct, but often, while the sentiment was right, the approach was wrong. As part of his attempt to cultivate the image of a president close to his people, the president gave out both his office telephone number – Tehran 6133 – and his email address – Dr.Ahmadinejad@President.Ir – so that ordinary people could get in touch. It appears never to have occurred to Ahmadinejad that this simplistic approach was doomed to failure for obvious reasons. After he had given out the number, the telephone line was jammed for several months. Despite his obvious glee in courting media attention, the president was – at least from a religious and intellectual perspective – a humble person and, soon after taking office, issued a directive to all government offices to refrain from hanging his photo on the walls, as was customary for the president. He said only the pictures of Ayatollah Khomeini and Ayatollah Khamenei should be hung there.[12] He is a textbook definition of the populist leader.

Even before he was elected president, Ahmadinejad showed his flare for populism when he was mayor of Tehran. He wore the luminous orange uniform of the rubbish collectors – and encouraged his senior officials to do the same – for a photo opportunity to display his high regard for these public servants, the lowest paid in the whole municipality. He described them rather confusingly as 'ambassadors of health', and promised at a meeting with them to improve their pay. But he went even further and told them that he regarded himself as a rubbish collector. 'We will never trade our job as rubbish collectors and servants of the people for anything else,' he told their gathering. This was the beginning of a recurring motif in Ahmadinejad's descriptions of his role in public life. He would always align himself with the everyday public-sector employees, the rubbish collectors, the street sweepers, the anonymous servants who kept Iranian society ticking over.

The most memorable sign of his emerging populism was one of his election campaign videos shown on national television in the run-up to the presidential elections. Ahmadinejad invited the camera into his small and simply furnished house. Inexpensive carpets covered the sitting room. Apart from some wall cushions to sit against on the floor, there was hardly any other furniture. These images were juxtaposed with footage that purported to show the residence of the one-time mayor of Tehran and a stalwart of the reform movement, Mohammad Hussein Karbaschi. Here was a lush and well-furnished home with many creature comforts, with intricate Persian mirror-work covering the walls of an opulent interior. Time and again Ahmadinejad alleged that Karbaschi had spend the equivalent of hundreds of thousands of dollars to redecorate his office. The exact figures fluctuated in accordance with Ahmadinejad's imagination and mood swings. Sometimes the cost was $200,000; at other times $1 million.

As a presidential candidate, Ahmadinejad would criticize government departments for buying or renting opulent buildings in north Tehran, home of the richer residents of the capital. Simple was the lifestyle of the Prophet Mohammad and the Supreme Leader Ayatollah Khamenei, went Ahmadinejad's reasoning, and therefore his must also be simple. This frugal and uncluttered way of life combined with his national tours to create the image of a simple, dedicated Muslim who understood and cared about the plight of the poor. During the election campaign, Ahmadinejad travelled to every corner of Iran, a country five times the size of France. This was in contrast to his main rival, Rafsanjani, who did not set foot outside Tehran during his campaign, claiming that he neither had the time nor the financial resources. This from a wealthy man with wealthy supporters.

Time and again Ahmadinejad would criticize the development and the direction Iran had taken over the previous 16 years. This was a thinly veiled attack on the administrations of Rafsanjani and Khatami. The allegations were always the same. The nation had lost its way. Corruption had spread greatly under them, and they had deliberately encouraged cronyism, which compromised the management of the country. The ordinary and poor people suffered under them, he contested – and he may well have been right on that point. Ahmadinejad would allege that the decadent and indulgent lifestyle of the top managers of the country would not allow them to find out about those who went to bed every night hungry. He said economic justice did not have a place in their Western model of development. He argued that Western political development, which entailed the development of a multi-party political system based on democracy and representation, was alien to ordinary people whose problems were of a different kind.

To the immense irritation of many Iranians who sacrificed a good deal in the 1979 Revolution for a democratic system, he repeatedly said that the architects and foot soldiers of the Revolution had not wanted democracy; they wanted an Islamic state in which Islamic values were the order of the day. And for all his many failings, no one could justly accuse Ahmadinejad of being a hypocrite. On coming to power, he remained true to his ideas and commitments, and frequently repeated them. To those who criticized him for being an extremist, he would say if defending the rights of ordinary people was extremism, then he would own up to it. He went to great efforts to underline his humble background and his simple lifestyle. Soon after his election, he refused to live in the presidential palace and said he would stay in his own small house. Ultimately, security considerations persuaded him to make the move. Perhaps the whole affair had been a stage-managed piece of theatre, but it certainly fitted with his general mode of conduct. He particularly wanted to show that, unlike many Iranian officials, he had not begun amassing personal wealth.

When, according to the law, he publicly and noisily declared his assets on assuming presidency, it turned out that his two bank accounts were empty, that he drove a 30-year-old Peugeot 504 and lived in his own small two-storey house that measured 175 square metres (1,500 square feet) in a lower-middle-class area of east Tehran. Of his two cheque accounts, one was for receiving his salary as a university lecturer; the other had no deposits.[13] Not only did the new president wear his heart on his sleeve, he wore his wallet there too. His government made a huge fuss about a luxury airliner that had been purchased from the Sultan of Brunei when President Khatami was in office and which was delivered under Ahmadinejad. The plane was supposed to be a safe and respectable alternative to the aging fleet of Iran's passenger jets that had suffered from US sanctions and mismanagement over many years. The planes were now falling from the sky with increasing frequency, killing large numbers of people every year. Yet to Ahmadinejad the new plane was a symbol of decadence and luxury. The plane had already been paid for, but to use it would have been an affront, if not to Islam exactly, then certainly to the president's core values, he thought. As a result, the plane gathered dust in a corner of Mehrabad airport for many months until it was quietly brought into service. But Ahmadinejad never travelled in it.

Never before had Iran seen a leader like him. In the early 1950s, Prime Minister Mohammad Mosaddeq had fired up his country against British imperialism. But the high-born aristocratic and European-educated Mosaddeq was not a product of the people. He championed Western-style democracy against an abrasive monarchy. Ayatollah Khomeini led a huge revolution not by appealing only to the poor but to all Iranians who were tired of tyranny and ready to embrace freedom. Ahmadinejad was also an Islamic phenomenon. For many in the Arab and Muslim streets he fast became the leader they wished they had. His posters were sold at street corners and even sweets were named after him.

At his insistence, the national carrier, Iran Air, established a direct flight between Tehran and Caracas although this did not make economic sense as there were very few people who wanted to travel between the two destinations. On the first flight only 19 seats were occupied. One Iranian report estimated that the weekly flight would incur losses of a half a million dollars each flight.[14] The cost was not important to Ahmadinejad. Although he had rejected the Sultan of Brunei's plane, he was keen to ensure that this flight to Venezuela was preserved. He was concerned about the message these decisions would send out to the public.

The axis between Iran and Venezuela, the link between Ahmadinejad's anti-American stance and that of President Hugo Chavez, had to be seen to exist and made to flourish. What better way to broaden this message than an airlink – regardless of its cost?

Aligning Iran with the wave of left-wing and populist leaders that had come to power in Latin America became a cornerstone of Iran's foreign policy. In January 2007 Ahmadinejad paid a visit to South America, especially the three Latin American countries of Venezuela, Nicaragua and Ecuador. The president returned filled with energy for a new anti-imperialist front between all the leaders and their nations. 'Anti-domineering sentiment in Latin America is very strong and the domineering powers are frightened,' he said.[15]

At universities the Basij students published posters that bore the heads of Ahmadinejad and four Latin American leaders: Hugo Chavez of Venezuela, Fidel Castro of Cuba, Daniel Ortega of Nicaragua and Juan Evo Morales of Bolivia. Below the five heads there was a slogan which read in English in bold letters: 'Alliance for Justice'. The Basij held meetings at universities to promote the idea of 'a world resistance front'. They dug up a quote from many of Khomeini's speeches in which he had apparently said that 'the world's dispossessed must unite, whatever their religion or creed'. When Ortega and his wife and children visited Tehran in June 2007, posters went up which showed the two presidents holding each other with one arm and raising clenched fists with the other. Iranian socialists and leftists who had survived years of executions and persecutions in Islamic Iran were outraged. 'Mr Ortega and the other so-called socialists should know that by coming to Iran they step into a land that has had a horrific legacy of killing socialists,' claimed Fariborz Rais-Dana, one of the few political activists in Iran who describes himself as a socialist. It was difficult to see what truly connected Iran to these South American social democracies, except their shared ambitions to be flies in the US ointment. Anti-Americanism was bridging a massive ideological gap.[16]

Champion of the poor

But there was an undeniable – if perhaps accidental – socialist tint to Ahmadinejad's crusade to help the lower classes and battle Iranian poverty. Without much consideration for the broader implications, Ahmadinejad raised the salaries of nurses in government hospitals, increased the pensions of retired civil servants, set a higher minimum wage for workers and established what he called 'the Imam Reza Love Fund', named after Shia Islam's Eighth Imam, to help young people get married, find jobs and set up a home.

There were 150,000 or so nurses working in Iran, a third of them in government hospitals and other health centres. They were among the lowest-paid and hardest-working people in the nation – as is the case in many countries – with an average monthly salary of about $180. The poverty line in the capital was $500 a month at the time. After a series of protests by nurses, Ahmadinejad's government agreed to raise the minimum salary as well as other benefits by an average of 30 per cent, or another $60. Government pensioners and retired civil servants numbered about 750,000. Their average pension of $180 was also raised by 14 per cent with a promise to raise the minimum pension to $220. Although a step in the right direction, these increases hardly lifted the pensioners and nurses out of poverty. In fact, the pension increases were little more than the rate of inflation, which was at 15.5 per cent. They made very little difference to people's lives and the increases were not paid until several months after they were announced. Yet the media had grabbed the ball and run with it. Whatever the truth on the ground, the president had managed to paint himself as the champion of the low-income groups of Iran.

His plan to raise the minimum wage of workers by a significant 50 per cent, however, was not as successful as he had hoped, and smacked of an ill-advised populist impulse. Without much warning, the government announced that with the new Iranian year beginning 21 March 2005, the minimum wage of contract workers would rise by 46 per cent and the wage for pensionable workers by 23 per cent. This would raise their minimum monthly income to Rls1,800,000 (about $200) and Rls1,500,000 (nearly $164) respectively. This sudden, dramatic change threw the whole industrial sector into turmoil as business responded in the only way it knew how. Hundreds of thousands of workers lost their jobs, as employers found that they could only remain afloat by drastically cutting back on their contract workers. Instead of helping, Ahmadinejad had thrown many workers out of work as swiftly and decisively as if he had fired them himself. The issue became a source of embarrassment for the government and in particular for Ahmadinejad. There was no other possible course of action than to execute a complete U-turn, and the whole crisis was only resolved by rolling back the increases to the minimum wage. Those workers who managed to hold on to their jobs in the end received a modest increase of about $40 per month.

It was true that workers' wages had lagged behind the rate of inflation for almost 20 years and, according to one report from the Labour Ministry to parliament, the minimum wage had in fact decreased by about 40 per cent in real terms, and this needed adjustment. Ahmadinejad's heart might have been in the right place on this issue but to increase the minimum wage by about 50 per cent in one swoop at a time of economic downturn was more than the industrial sector could take. Observers could once again see an incredible streak of naivety in the fundamentalist president.

Parliament was hardly enthusiastic about the crown jewel of Ahmadinejad's wealth distribution policies: the Imam Reza Love Fund. The government submitted a bill to parliament requesting the establishment of the fund using 30 per cent of Iran's foreign exchange reserves. This would entail exchanging just under $8 billion into rials on the market and then depositing the money into the fund. MPs found the figures alarming. They calculated that the project could mean an increase in the annual rate of inflation of about 20 per cent. Parliament made several structural alterations to the fund as proposed in the bill and even went so far as to change the name, fearing that criticism of the fund would be an insult to the Imam Reza.

But this was unacceptable to Ahmadinejad and he decided to go ahead with his original plan by circumventing parliament, using his prerogative to amalgamate a number of dormant funds already set up by previous governments to establish his Imam Reza Love Fund. The main source of the fund was to be the savings made by various government departments against their annual budgets. These budget surpluses would be deposited with the Imam Reza Love Fund directly and lost to the departments themselves.

A year after coming to power, the fund was inaugurated. The president again declared that its main focus was to help young people pay for their weddings in the first year. The plan was that as the fund gradually increased year on year, it would be able to do more and would ultimately assist in finding jobs and giving housing loans to newly wedded couples. It is rather difficult to assess the success or otherwise of the fund. Apart from anecdotal accounts of people receiving assistance, there are no hard facts detailing the amount of money accumulated or distributed by the fund, nor have figures been published relating to how many individuals have been helped.

Even though his social and economic reforms met with only limited success at the start of his presidency, Ahmadinejad had managed to bring slight improvements and a sense of optimism to Iran's poor, at least in the short term. He had also won himself the reputation of being the champion of Iran's poor and needy. And this was something that was hardly likely to harm him at the ballot box in the future.

Purges at the top

Everyone was aware that the arrival of Ahmadinejad was going to mean fundamental changes to the personnel running Iran. Everyone expected the change to be rapid and drastic but they were perhaps not quite prepared for the president's revolutionary fervour to translate into a series of purges. When Ahmadinejad's new Supreme National Security Council (SNSC) staff took over, they moved in before the previous team – the appointees of President Khatami – had had time even to clear their desks. The new regime was a broom sweeping away the perceived corruption of the previous administration. Moreover the SNSC was Iran's most important foreign policy body, with particular responsibility for the nation's nuclear strategy. Ahmadinejad wanted to demonstrate that some very significant changes were going to take place in this area and that these would start at the very top of the tree. Several top officials were removed from the SNSC and were treated as little more than traitors by the incoming president's men. Safes were broken into, computer hard-drives confiscated and telephones tapped. In due course, the new SNSC staff even arrested the spokesman of the Council, Hussein Mussavian, and accused him of spying. Mussavian had been Iran's ambassador to Germany for many years and was tipped to be the foreign minister if Rafsanjani came to power again. Many saw his arrest as an attempt to undermine the credibility of Rafsanjani as a national leader. Ahmadinejad had also described Khatami's national security team as weak, made up of pathetic individuals who had slowed down Iran's progress in its quest for nuclear know-how. It was no secret that Ahmadinejad fiercely rejected their suspension of the uranium enrichment programme.

Ahmadinejad was putting Iran on the offensive in the confrontation with the West; any diplomats versed in the old orthodoxy of sweet-talking their foreign counterparts had to go. Iran was going to demand its rights from now on and needed a new team to bring new authority to its foreign policy. More than 40 ambassadors were summarily called back to Tehran – the biggest shake-up of the Foreign Service since the 1979 Revolution. After the first revolution, the Iranian Foreign Service had been purged extensively. The strategy was to favour committed Islamists over seasoned diplomats. Understandably, this did Iran considerable damage on the world stage as it suffered from the lack of trained and high-calibre diplomats who spoke English and were familiar with international affairs. Now even those that had been trained on the job over the years were put aside in one go, leaving Iran unrepresented in much of the world – a situation that dragged on for many months. Those who were recalled included

Iran's ambassadors to London, Paris and Berlin. Even more worrying was that this withdrawal of ambassadors and the purge of the Foreign Service took place just as Ahmadinejad's pronouncements on the nuclear programme had put Iran in the dock in the court of world opinion.

Ahmadinejad intended to lever Iran's trade relations so as to coerce other states into supporting its aggressive international diplomacy and, in particular, its pursuit of nuclear capability. This approach was based on a massive overestimation of Iran's importance and potency. The president believed his country to be strong enough to call the shots in talks and thought that he could railroad members of the international community into backing Iran. 'We spend 30 billion dollars on imports, and this represents an immense means of pressure in negotiations. It is we who should impose our conditions on them and not them on us, and if they do not accept our conditions, it's simple – we won't buy anything from them,' he said in a campaign broadcast. This stance was quickly tested and discarded when South Korea and India were among 22 countries that voted against Iran in a crucial vote in the IAEA demanding that Iran suspend its enrichment programme immediately. Rumours spread quickly that Iran had put on hold its economic and trade relations with the two countries. The Foreign Ministry denied any such decision officially but Iranian businessmen insisted that they were unable to open letters of credit for imports from South Korea. South Korea was a major trading partner of Iran and supplied the Islamic Republic with a considerable proportion of its durable goods. Conversely, South Korea was also the fourth largest importer of Iranian oil. And India was even more vital to Iran's economic survival, not least because it was to be a major importer of Iranian natural gas through a new pipeline that would pass through Pakistan. This was a $7 billion project intended to break the crippling US sanctions on Iran's gas exports. Sanctions against India and South Korea would have been an act of madness tantamount to economic suicide. Ahmadinejad's leveraging policy was poorly thought through and the sanctions were swiftly lifted.

The purges were by no means limited to the foreign-policy bodies. They stretched across every area of government. Domestically, Ahmadinejad replaced the governors of every single one of Iran's 30 provinces. He was also keen to purge those who held economic power and thus replaced the governors and deputies of all the state banks. Civil servants and non-political officials in every Iranian ministry fell underneath the axe of his Third Revolution. But the domestic purge was slower: Ahmadinejad simply lacked sufficient manpower to fill all the key posts immediately and so was having to prioritize his person-nel shifts. This practical difficulty actually helped the president, as it gave the impression that these reappointments were rather more considered and thoughtful than they actually were.

Building a new economy on the ruins of the old

Ahmadinejad wanted to remodel the economy to bring about social justice. His spokesman, Gholam Hussein Elham, spoke of the need to destroy the economic foundations of the country – foundations that previous governments had put in place. 'We must destroy these foundations and start from scratch. And this will take time,' Elham announced.[17] Ahmadinejad himself spoke of 'a fundamental reform' in the economy, in which 'business would become unsafe for profiteers'.[18] Ahmadinejad's concept of the new economic order was essentially a quasi-socialist command model that should help the government to distribute wealth or, more likely, poverty more equitably.

Not surprisingly, Ahmadinejad's election victory found expres-sion in a 7 per cent devaluation of the Tehran stock exchange. This would eventually worsen to 20 per cent, reflecting concerns that Ahmadinejad had no deep understanding of the market and was tainted by an outsider's mistrust of high finance. A few days before his final victory in the second round of the elections, the future presi-dent told national television that trading on the exchange was akin to gambling, and this was something Islam did not allow. 'Because of the sort of activities that take place there, [trading] is like gambling. We have to put an end to all that,' he said to the amazement of many observers.[19] However, after months of a depressed stock exchange riddled with doubts about its future under a fundamentalist regime, the president gave a speech in which he implied that his enemies had made up the quote, despite the fact that it had been broadcast on television. But the usually fiery candidate's lukewarm support for the market proved too little too late to stop the crash. His economic advi-sor made things worse when he denounced the crash as a conspiracy against Ahmadinejad. 'The fluctuations in the stock market are in effect the aftershocks of the earthquake caused by the huge march of the people. Those who are behind these fluctuations should join the people,' said Mohammad Khoshchehreh, hours after Ahmadinejad had been declared the winner of the presidential race.[20]

The Tehran stock exchange's performance went from bad to worse. Under new, young and inexperienced management, the TSE index steadily declined. In two years, Iran had changed from being one of the top emerging markets in the world to one of the top ten worst-performing markets. There were many factors at play in this collapse, but the government's suspicious attitude towards the capital market, coupled with the chronic inexperience of the new management of the TSE, did much harm, particularly when set in the context of Iran's aggressive foreign policy and ongoing nuclear dispute. There were rumours that the president might soon act on the issue with characteristic simplicity. Unable to stop the rot, Ahmadinejad was reported as telling his cabinet that if he could execute two or three people in the market, the issue of the stock exchange would be solved forever.[21]

The chaos in the stock market also had its consequences for other sectors of the economy. Many who withdrew their investments in stocks and shares now went into the property market, where prices began to increase sharply. House prices and rents went up by 30 per cent within a few months of Ahmadinejad coming to power.[22] In two years, some property values had more than doubled. This was a huge financial burden on the low-income Iranians who rented their accommodation. The very people whom Ahmadinejad was attempting to help were being hit hardest by his administration's economic inexperience.

The falling TSE index also made a mockery of the privatization plans that had been set out in the government's long-term development plan. The centrepiece of its social justice programme was the distribution of Justice Shares (Sahame-e-Edalat), according to which 40 per cent of the shares in government-owned factories earmarked for privatization would be distributed among lower-income groups at discretionary rates and paid for in instalments. Four billion shares were to be sold to 5 million people in lower-income groups. They were offered directly to those eligible and not to the stock exchange, where prices were falling. The envisaged privatization was designed to make lower-income groups stake-holders in state-owned industries – a policy that had been tested and shown to fail in socialist economies.

The economy as a whole took a huge battering under Ahmadinejad. One example was a sudden and huge increase in duties on imports of mobile-phone sets from 4 to 60 per cent. It was a decision that stunned many, and the logic behind it remains a mystery. Ostensibly, large import duties would serve to encourage local industry. But Iran had no mobile-phone industry at the time. The idea was that Iran should set up one in due course. Such lack of preparation and joined-up thinking was breathtaking. Of course, there were a lucky few who had already imported a huge number of phone sets and therefore made a killing in the market, as they were able to double their prices overnight and still remain competitive thanks to the government decision. Even when a mobile-phone assembly line was set up a year later, it could only manage 20,000 units compared to an annual market demand of nearly 6 million.[23]

The government's interventionist policies meant that the free market economy that had been gradually encouraged under presidents Rafsanjani and Khatami after the Iran–Iraq War was in danger of being replaced by a command economy in which the government played a major role in regulating the market. Many on the left might argue that this was ideologically no bad thing, but Ahmadinejad's administration exhibited terrible managerial ineptitude and economic naivety.

As part of his series of purges, the president replaced all the top management of the banks, whom he accused of only providing loans to well-connected clients at the expense of the lower-income groups. In Ahmadinejad's view, the banks' job was to provide financial assistance to the less-well-off members of society and to do so at discretionary rates with government help. According to Ahmadinejad, the high interest rates of banks only benefited those who already had deposits in the banks, and therefore some defining action had to be taken to shift the benefit to lower-income groups. Ahmadinejad's answer was to order the banks, both government-owned and private, to lower their interest rates to 12 per cent. This was lower than the official rate of inflation, which was just over 15 per cent, and much lower than the real rate, which was alleged to be more than 23 per cent.[24] He made the decision while he was on an official visit to Belarus and without consulting even his closest advisors. He simply phoned his office to dictate his wish. By doing so he circumvented the Money and Credit Council, whose job it was to approve the rate in consultation with the banks, and his own hand-picked economics minister and the governor of the Central Bank. A government spokesman told journalists that the decision to cut interest rates had been taken to help people of different strata benefit from banking facilities and to increase competition between all banks. It immediately put the banks on the verge of bankruptcy as it was technically impossible to operate profitably with an interest rate below the rate of inflation. As expected, it was not long before the governor of the Central Bank resigned.

Once again, observers might have been baffled by the president's devil-may-care approach to economic stability, but Ahmadinejad believed he had an ace up his sleeve – Iran's huge windfall from the sudden increase in the price of oil. Iran's income from exports of oil had almost doubled to about $50 billion in the year ending 20 March 2006, and was close to $60 billion the following year.[25] As with so many of his policies, Ahmadinejad's thinking on the economy was simple: provided he had a high oil income, he could ride the occasional problem. And in very simple terms, he was correct in his assumption. The oil income enabled Ahmadinejad to go on populist spending sprees. If a province needed new roads, it would come from the oil income. If a town needed a new sports hall or a new factory, it would come from the oil income. Even his beloved Imam Reza Love Fund would be financed out of the oil revenue. Few could fault Ahmadinejad's intentions when it came to redistribution of wealth and support for the low-income members of Iranian society. Even his detractors and enemies would have to concede that he was sincere and focused in his anti-poverty measures. But unfortunately, he had not even a basic grasp of economics. The spending spree, which meant the direct injection of oil money into the economy, had a huge inflationary impact. Prices of basic goods were already rising faster than before, forcing many Iranians to tighten their belts in order to make ends meet. But Ahmadinejad was oblivious to the danger, or at least did not seem to be overly concerned.

A year into his presidency, concerns were widespread enough for 50 professors of economics to write a joint letter to Ahmadinejad warning him that his policies could spell disaster. They warned that

Iran's economic growth could come to a halt and plunge the country into recessionary inflation. They cautioned that the golden opportunity provided by the increase in the price of oil could be lost forever. Perhaps more disturbing was the fact that the professors felt the need to teach Ahmadinejad a lesson in economics: 'Economics, like any other science, is the result of the accumulation of human knowledge, and scientific achievements of economics are used for the advance and prosperity of human societies. For this reason, economics can and must be used in drawing up the government's economic policies,' the letter said.[26] But they were wasting their energies. The populist, religious fundamentalist at the helm was characterized by his disregard for science and intellectualism. Two years into the presidency, the economists wrote a second letter highlighting the dire state of the economy. According to the figures taken from Iran's central bank, in his first year Ahmadinejad had withdrawn $35.3 billion from the oil reserve fund. In his second year he had withdrawn $43 billion. These massive drains on the resources came despite his explicit long-term development plan in which his government was only supposed to take out $15.2 billion and $15.6 billion respectively in these two years. In effect, Ahmadinejad had spent $78.3 billion in the first two years of his presidency. All he had to show for it was a rise in inflation from 13 to 17 per cent and expectations that it would rise further. And yet across the nation, his little pet projects were gradually springing into life. The economists were desperate and begged the government to stop the worsening crisis.[27]

To Ahmadinejad, the economists' pleas were not advice: they were a challenge and had to be met head on and defeated. The president's response was to portray economists as a number-crunching elite bereft of human compassion. On several occasions Ahmadinejad declared his hatred for economics. 'I pray to God that I will never know about economics,' he said on one occasion.[28] On another occasion, he said he detested economics because it did not help the people. He saw himself as actively doing things in the real world to alleviate genuine suffering and hardship. For him, this was more important than kowtowing to the false gods of economics and the market. If it came to a choice between helping his people – such as by immediately providing a village with drinking water through direct government funding – or tending to the dictates of the economists, Ahmadinejad claimed that he was firmly for the people. 'Immediately these people say our decisions raise people's expectations and that they are not in accordance with the science of economics. If your economics does not help meeting the rightful demands of the people, then we hate your economics!' he said.[29] As with many critical policy issues, the president transformed the debate into an adversarial face-off. It was no longer a question of how to successfully manage Iran's economy. It was now a simple fight: people vs. economists. The president went further, with his spokesman claiming that the 50 professors had written their letters with a political motive – to undermine the government.

The rise in the price of basic foods, as well as huge increases in rents, brought Ahmadinejad under a lot of pressure. These were becoming facts of life in Iran and something that the president could not simply wish away. The newspapers were full of stories about the price rises. For a period, tomatoes became a celebrated delicacy, with their price rising to $3 a kilo. Yet even facts were malleable for the president. When MPs in parliament complained about the soaring prices, Ahmadinejad disputed the fact that prices had increased as much as was claimed. He suggested, half jokingly, that people should go to the corner shop near his old house where fruit and vegetables were offered at reasonable prices. But when journalists visited his neighbourhood they found that none of Ahmadinejad's family had shopped there for months and that the people there were just as desperate as anywhere else.[30] The owner of the shop around the corner from Ahmadinejad's old home said he was thinking about changing jobs: 'There's no stability. My situation and that of many others was better before Ahmadinejad. When he won I was happy because he didn't dress like a mullah and wore humble clothes, but he is no different. If he had solved youth unemployment, people would have been happy.'[31]

Here was a turning point for the populist president. His policies were not solving daily problems but creating new ones. And this began to undermine his popularity with the public and within the establishment. Even his erstwhile supporters among the ultra-conservative religious leaders in Qom criticized the government and called on Ahmadinejad to help relieve some of the pressure on ordinary people. After months of denying that there had been increases in rents and the prices of basic goods, Ahmadinejad finally conceded that indeed there was a problem. But characteristically he blamed the previous government. 'The rise in prices has its roots in the economy and in the politics of the country that this government has inherited,' he told his cabinet.[32] This churlish buck-passing was not going to sway the Iranian populace. Many ordinary people who had voted for him now turned against him. Ahmadinejad's hyperbolic statement that he would bring Iranian oil money to people's dinner tables, was repeatedly used by ordinary people and the reformist newspapers to show the folly of his words and deeds. As might be expected, Ahmadinejad now denied having said any such thing, but the transcript of his speech to members of parliament a few days before the elections was posted on the Internet by an Islamist website for all to see.[33] In the face of such incontrovertible evidence, the president could not deny his words. 'This is like bringing oil money to the dinner tables of the people,' he had specifically said. Few were now convinced.[34] Some critics of Ahmadinejad quipped that he had taken Iranian oil money to the dinner tables of the Chinese, as imports from China had increased dramatically.[35] Fearing for their jobs because of the government's wage-increase policies, a group of workers wrote to Ahmadinejad saying they did not want the oil money; they just wanted to be able to keep their jobs which had provided a meagre meal for their dinner tables.[36]

Petrol rationing

What should have been a wake-up call for Ahmadinejad came on the night of 27 June 2007, when angry motorists up and down the country attacked petrol stations after the government suddenly announced petrol rationing.

At 9.30 pm, at the end of the evening news bulletin on national television, Iran, OPEC's second largest oil producer, announced that petrol rationing would start from midnight. Although there had been a good deal of debate about this, few expected the government to go ahead with the controversial plan, and fewer had any inkling about when it was going to come into effect. Even the police had not been forewarned that trouble might ensue.

And there was trouble. Dozens of petrol stations in Tehran and other parts of the country were set alight by angry motorists who had rushed to fill up before the deadline, only to find the pumps dry. Several people were killed in the fires, and demonstrators shouting obscenities against Ahmadinejad ransacked and looted banks and government supermarkets.

Outside the stations that still had petrol, queues of cars a few kilometres long formed, blocking traffic in many streets of the capital and other big cities. In the absence of security forces on the streets, the situation could easily have descended into an uprising. But luckily for the government, it soon cooled as dawn broke. It was, however, the worst unrest Iran had seen for many years.

Ever since the Revolution, Iran had ignored its growing need for refined oil, and by 2006 its refineries – short of spare parts and becoming run down – could only supply about half of its needs. The rest had to be imported at market rates and sold domestically at heavily subsidized prices. Cheap fuel had led to conspicuous consumption that was costing the country close to $5 billion a year. A poor public transport system had encouraged car ownership, which in turn led to monumental traffic jams in Tehran and elsewhere, causing choking pollution and costing many lives. Successive governments agreed that something had to be done, but there was no quick fix. The country needed more oil refineries and better public transport. The subsidies had to be gradually removed to discourage over-consumption while keeping rising prices in check. All this needed a well-thought-out plan that would have to be implemented over several years. But Iran in the summer of 2007 was not a place for far-sighted and comprehensive policies. Ahmadinejad favoured 'revolutionary decisions' – he had little patience for long-term plans. Initially he was not convinced that petrol rationing would be a sensible solution, but he was forced to implement it when parliament passed a bill making it mandatory.

Once the decision had been made, Ahmadinejad did not hold back. The rationing was done by means of charge cards given to motorists which were credited automatically with an allowance of 100 litres a month – about half of what the average driver needed in the capital. Taxis, vans and government cars, however, were given different allowances, but still woefully small. The result was a major shock to the system. Overnight, Tehran's roads, normally blocked with traffic, turned into quiet, serene thoroughfares as the rationing forced many people – including some whose livelihoods depended on their cars – to stay at home. Reports came in of produce left rotting in the ground because of lack of transport. Fire stations said they could operate only for another couple of weeks. Inter-city travel came to a halt, with tourist and road-service industries suddenly facing ruin. Prices rose sharply as trucks, vans and taxis put up their prices by 25–30 per cent. A black market for petrol saw prices rocket from a subsidized ten cents a litre to more or less international prices – four or five dollars a litre. Some taxi drivers found that they could sell their petrol ration on the black market, stay at home, and still make about as much money as they would working.

Overnight the government had created huge anomalies and no one knew where they would lead. In the cities at least, few had a kind word for Ahmadinejad. And fewer still could understand the logic of it all. It was clear that the government could not reduce reliance on imported fuel overnight without major disruption to the workings of Iranian society. And given that it was earning record revenues from its oil exports, it was hard to argue that Iran was short of money to pay for fuel. The speaker of parliament, Gholam-Ali Haddad-Adel, was the first official to link the decision to the government's fears of a possible US blockade of Iranian ports – something that could seriously choke imports. But even this did not seem logical. If one were threatened with murder, would one commit suicide in anticipation?

The only thing that cushioned the impact a little was the introduction of a four-month allowance for motorists. This led to a gradual return to normal levels of consumption – and traffic – and served only to postpone the decline of the country's economy.

Ahmadinejad, who uncharacteristically had kept quiet on the issue for some days, seriously misread public sentiment by saying that soon Iran would be able to *export* fuel. Furthermore a joke which had been sent anonymously on SMS to millions of mobile phones had the president saying 'those who cannot use their cars anymore should get rides on the millions of donkeys that voted for me'. The authorities suspended SMS for several hours until the message had been expunged.

A wake-up call had come and gone, but the president was fast asleep. A few weeks later the government tabled a bill to authorize parliament to spend the savings made from the fuel rationing on social projects. Parliament threw out the bill, with one senior member describing it as a ridiculous propaganda stunt.

If fuel rationing was a banana skin under Ahmadinejad's feet, he didn't slip. But it was clear that his standing had been dealt a major blow, judging by the anger among many ordinary Iranians at what they saw as government incompetence. The long-term consequences of the affair have yet to become apparent.

The Second Cultural Revolution

After 32 years as a professor of international relations at Tehran University, Ahmad Saiee's teaching career came to an abrupt end in the summer of 2006. In fact, he heard demands for his reinstatement even before he learnt that he had been fired. 'One morning at the university, I was walking back to my office from a class when I heard a group of students demonstrating outside the department and chanting my name, among others,' he said. 'When I went closer, I heard they were calling for my reinstatement.' Saiee had picked up his mail from his pigeonhole earlier in the day but had not opened it. When he rushed back to his office, he found the letter from the personnel department that told him what the students already knew. 'The letter said I had been given "the honour of retirement",' Saiee said at his home.

Saiee was one of 40 professors at Tehran University who unexpectedly began mandatory retirement that summer. Altogether, some 200 university professors across the country had been given retirement notices. Their forced retirement led to fears of another Cultural Revolution. 'We believe the forced retirements are part of a political move by the government to remove independent-minded lecturers and replace them with those they can lean on,' said Vahid Abedini, a student activist and a member of the university's reformist Islamic Student Association.[37] Purges of professors did not stop there. More were given their marching orders as Ahmadinejad and the hardliners consolidated their grip on the universities.

Ahmadinejad wanted an Islamic education system that would exclude all other influences. 'Islam,' he said, 'provides us with a comprehensive education system which we must introduce to the world.' And he made it clear that he had little regard for professors who had been educated abroad: 'Now a gentleman goes to the West for 25, 26 years, limits his thought to some materialist topic like psychology and acquires a little bit of experience by taking four classes – and for us to use that experience is definitely to take a step back. We must revert to the treasures of Islamic knowledge, which is unending and our only hope for salvation.'

Soon after the 1979 Revolution, the pro-Khomeini Islamists took over the universities and closed them down for more than two years under the pretext of a Cultural Revolution. What took place was a massive purge of university professors and students with left or liberal sympathies. Intellectual freedom was dealt a severe blow and was only just recovering in 2005 when Ahmadinejad stormed into power.

As a student, 27 years earlier, the president had helped close down his own university in support of the Cultural Revolution. Now he was keen to finish a job he believed had been left incomplete. He wanted to build a truly Islamic society in which there was no room for the liberal thought of Islamic reformists. Ahmadinejad, in common with many other hardliners in Iran, despised any talk about the compatibility of Islam and democracy. Ahmadinejad himself did not believe in democracy. In interview after interview he would argue against the idea that the 1979 Revolution was a revolution for democracy. It was, in his view, a revolution purely for Islam.

A year into his presidency, he spoke more openly at Tehran University about what he wanted to see in the universities. Speaking to a select group of Islamist students, Ahmadinejad invited them to rise up against secular and liberal influences in their universities. 'Today our students must raise their voices in front of the president and ask why a secular professor is allowed to give a low mark to a student just because the student does not share his thoughts,' he told them. 'Today our students must raise their voices against liberal and liberal economic thoughts.'[38] Ahmadinejad and his mentor, Ayatollah Mohammad Taqi Mesbah-Yazdi, wanted to Islamicize the atmosphere in the universities as well as the social sciences that were taught in them. Ahmadinejad shared the view of the ultra-conservatives among the religious leaders in Qom who had always looked on universities with a good deal of suspicion. They believed that since their establishment more than 100 years ago, higher-education institutions had operated as insidious vehicles for secular and liberal thought that pushed Islam to the margins.

Now, although 27 years had passed since the Islamic Revolution, the universities remained a hotbed of political opposition. They had survived several rounds of purges of the left, liberal and secular influences conducted under the guise of the Cultural Revolution. For the conservatives, a new push was needed to stop the universities from becoming a breeding ground for liberalism and secularism again. And, in Ahmadinejad, the hardliners had someone who was most certainly committed to just such a push. The president began Iran's second Cultural Revolution at Tehran University – the oldest and one of the most prestigious universities in Iran. First, he appointed a clergyman as chancellor, Ayatollah Abbas Ali Amid Zanjani – the first ever cleric to become chancellor of an Iranian university. Predictably, this appointment was met with student protests but these were stonewalled. Ahmadinejad decided that he needed to move slowly against the universities, which still commanded considerable respect as the political conscience of the nation.

A few months after the controversial appointment of Zanjani, Ahmadinejad gave a speech to another university in Tehran, the Amir Kabir University. At Amir Kabir, the students noisily rejected him as a dictator and a fascist. Although the auditorium had been filled with student members of the Basij militia from many universities, dozens of Amir Kabir students managed to get in. Time and again, they drowned out the voice of Ahmadinejad with their shouts of 'dictator' and 'fascist'. Ahmadinejad tried to make the best of the situation by raising his own voice and appearing calm and unfazed. But the students simply raised the temperature. Rising from their seats, they held his posters upside down – a strong mark of disrespect – and some even set fire to them. Others threw firecrackers at the stage, but the president's security men remained calm. The Amir Kabir protest was taking place at the same time as the notorious Holocaust-denial conference, and the students took the opportunity to express their disgust, with placards clearly branding the president a friend of neo-Nazis.

The Amir Kabir demonstration might only have comprised several dozen students but it was a significant event and the first public protest against Ahmadinejad since his taking office nearly 18 months earlier. The students believed that they had sent a strong message to

the president: do not mess with the universities. With cheeky bold-
ness, Ahmadinejad even tried to represent the protest as a proud testa-
ment to the political and personal freedoms of Iran, claiming in his
weblog that the sight of 'a small group who against a massive majority dared to insult the president in full freedom' made him proud
that the Islamic Revolution had brought such freedoms to the nation.
Ahmadinejad went further and promised that the students would not
be persecuted for what they had done. But it was a hollow promise.
Reprisals would come but only after the furore had died down and
would be conducted through indirect channels. Many of the students
were later harassed, beaten, jailed and expelled from the university. A
few were sent on military service.

In fact, the Amir Kabir protest gave the hardliners the opportunity
to launch their second Cultural Revolution in earnest. And now they
had the ideal academic establishment at which to begin it. All that
was needed was a pretext. One day at Amir Kabir, a rumour spread
as swiftly and as dangerously as a forest fire. Across the campus it was
whispered that four student publications had launched a coordinated
attack on Islam through a series of insulting articles. No one had yet
seen these articles but that quickly became an irrelevance. All that
was needed was the initial spark. There was nothing the editors could
do. Masses of students were already mobilized against them. Their
cries that the publications were fake and that they had no intention of
insulting Islam went unheard. Within a short period of time, the Basij
students had laid siege to the campus and were calling for a second
Cultural Revolution to purify their houses of learning. Basij members
from other universities in the capital and across Iran flocked to Amir
Kabir and hundreds of Basij students held vigils outside the university
gates. For several days, this tense stand-off was maintained until the
authorities arrested all the editors. But the second cultural uprising
did not happen. The events remained localized. The Basij were given
the tacit support of the Supreme Leader, who summoned the leaders of
the protest against the editors and told them that the future was theirs
for the taking. Many onlookers thought that it needed only another
similar spark to bring about a fundamentalist purge of the universities and academic establishments similar to the Cultural Revolution
of 1979–80. And in the current political climate, such a spark seemed
inevitable.

Andy Warhol, Anna Karenina and martyrdom

A single bulb produced a dim light in the dark basement of the Museum of Modern Arts in central Tehran. Keys in hand, a suspicious museum official reluctantly led the way to an iron grill door at the end of a narrow corridor. The clunk of the large key in the keyhole opened a door on to a dark interior where yet another door stood tightly shut. When finally this second door was opened and the lights were switched on, a large air-conditioned room with row upon row of sliding wall racks revealed itself. Unceremoniously the official pulled out the first rack to reveal several paintings that had been hung on it. The one on the left looked familiar – a landscape. 'It's a Monet,' said the official excitedly. Another rack revealed several other paintings, including a couple of renditions of a portrait of Mick Jagger by Andy Warhol.

The vaults are home to a collection of hundreds of paintings and sculptures from world-famous artists – the biggest collection of Western art outside Europe and the United States. The paintings have been kept in the vaults and well away from the Iranian public for 28 years. They include paintings by Renoir, Monet, Picasso, Pissarro, Magritte, Pollock, Francis Bacon, Toulouse-Lautrec, Salvador Dali and Andy Warhol – an amazing distillation of the finest talents in European and American art of the last two centuries. The history of this buried treasure is straightforward and tragic. Empress Farah had put the collection together in the last years of the Shah's reign. But to Islamists, who overthrew the monarchy, these paintings and sculptures were decadent manifestations of Western culture. They could not be reconciled with the revolutionary movement and had to be banished to the basement vaults.

Under moderate President Khatami and his Iranian *glasnost*, a few of the paintings that were not regarded as risqué were brought up for display for short periods. By a quirk of timetabling, the largest exhibition of European art in the history of the Islamic Republic took place soon after Ahmadinejad's election victory. His new ministers were still coming to terms with their appointments and certainly had no time to prevent the exhibition from taking place. Under Khatami, the atmosphere had been sufficiently relaxed for the Ministry of Culture and Islamic Guidance to agree, through the persuasive arguments of the then head of the museum, Alireza Sami-Azar, to allow a public viewing of this collection of twentieth-century art. But under Ahmadinejad, Sami-Azar's days were numbered. The president had a strict Islamic revolutionary opinion of art. Its key purpose was to glorify martyrdom in a jihad – a function highly unlikely to be fulfilled by the surrealist fantasies of Dali or the existential anxiety of Magritte. 'We want art that is on the offensive. Art on the offensive exalts and defends the noble principles, and attacks principles that are corrupt, vulgar, ungodly and inhuman,' the president told state television. He asked: 'Is there art that is more beautiful, more divine, and more eternal than the art of martyrdom? A nation with martyrdom knows no captivity.' [39]

Somehow, Ahmadinejad thought that art could play a role in his new revolution and could help export Shiite Muslim values across the globe. First, Iranian art had to be entirely Islamicized if it was to become a footsoldier in militant Islam's attempt to conquer the world. In fact, his view of the role of art was not so different from Stalin's insistence on didactic socialist realism in the new culture of the USSR. 'A sincere man or artist must always be critical of the status quo. Protesting the status quo is the expression of a spirit that seeks enlightenment ... arts must be the soft but effective voice against injustice.' [40]

But, of course, the only status quo that it was permitted to challenge was the reformist, secular one. The president was hardly likely to countenance any artistic attacks on his new regime. Iranian artists were obviously dismayed. The artistic climate since 1979 had been severely repressive, but Khatami had been the first president to attempt to encourage artists rather than to simply control them. No one believed that this enlightened approach would be maintained under Ahmadinejad. 'We are in very grave danger of reverting back to the post-revolutionary days, when only those artists who were deemed as expressing so-called Islamic values were displayed,' said Sami-Azar, speaking soon after his resignation as the head of the museum and barely a few months into the presidency of Ahmadinejad. 'In those days artists who had flourished under previous regimes were persecuted. Culturally it was the dark ages for Iran.' [41]

These fears were not unfounded. And Ahmadinejad soon actively set out to change the country's culture and to reappropriate it as a vehicle for the communication and realization of his ideal Islamic society.

He appointed himself head of a body called the Cultural Revolution Council and then moved to ban 'Western and vulgar' music from state television.[42] This was an immediate echo of the early days of the Revolution when Ayatollah Khomeini banned singing and singers altogether – a practice the Taliban followed in Afghanistan a decade and a half later. This meant that only classical music was acceptable in post-revolutionary Iran. Music had crept back gradually as the revolutionary fervour faded, and over the years state radio and television had begun gradually to use some Iranian male singers and, on rare occasions, a Western rock or pop piece in their programmes.

On taking office, Ahmadinejad appointed an ultra-hardliner, Saffar Harandi, as his Minister of Culture. This was a clear indication to the artistic community that the years of relative freedom and tolerance were at an end. A former Revolutionary Guard commander with a history in the security services, Harandi's job was to bring the arts and the media back in line with a strict revolutionary interpretation of the laws of Islam. In keeping with the early rulings of Khomeini, Harandi said he would support classical music that promoted spiritualism.[43] However, it was soon clear that promoting music was not exactly top of the government's agenda. The already infrequent concerts of classical Persian and Western music became more rare, with the Ministry refusing to grant concerts public-performance licences. Classical music was driven abroad. Although still on the government payroll and officially condoned, the Iran National Symphony Orchestra hardly ever performed in its home country and, with nothing else to do, would often travel abroad to give concerts. Musicians of all different traditions were performing at small private parties to earn a living, as public concerts became ever rarer and more restrictive. Popular music, which had managed to surface during the late 1990s and the early part of the twenty-first century, was forced back underground. But the digital revolution that had done so much to threaten the music industry of the West was the only thing that kept pop music alive in Iran. Young pop and rock bands took to recording their music at home and publishing them on CDs, which were then distributed privately by their friends and fans.

Restrictions on book publishing became so comprehensive that they drove many publishers into bankruptcy. Very little would now get through without an official examination and at least some amendments. The Ministry of Culture and Islamic Guidance increased the number of its censors to cope with the volume of work to be censored. Writers and publishers told tales of Kafka-esque unseen censors, known only by their numbers. At any moment faceless censor 101 could swoop down and block a piece of writing. Ahmadinejad even increased the remit of the censors. Not only were they given powers over every new piece of writing in Iran, but previously approved books, which had been printed many times over, were now to be reassessed. 'Dostoevsky needs permission,' read the headline of one newspaper. A group of hardline members of parliament, supporters of Ahmadinejad, joined the attack on books by producing a very critical report on the performance of the Ministry of Culture under President Khatami. The report said that hundreds of books that were contrary to Islamic morality were published in Khatami's eight-year reign. Tolstoy's *Anna Karenina* was lambasted for having 'spread the culture of drinking, normalized relationships between unmarried couples, undermined spiritual values, removed the stigma attached to sin, propagated vulgarity, promoted unethical traditions and glorified the aristocracy'. Time and again, authors – new and old, domestic and foreign – were rejected by the censors with bland and vague expressions, such as 'worthless', 'lacking content' or 'inappropriate'. Classics of world literature and potential new gems of Iranian writing were dismissed by these overstretched, under-educated religious bureaucrats for their 'incompatibility with the norms in our society'. Iranian literary culture was being squashed on the basis that it was 'contrary to national culture'.[44]

Censorship became so widespread that a large group of writers and intellectuals wrote an open letter to the people of Iran warning of a huge social and cultural crisis. The former Culture Minister under President Khatami complained to his successor that even his own book had not been given a licence to be published.

Cinema and theatre did not fare much better. Many of the films produced and directed by world-renowned Iranian directors did not receive permission to be screened. Two years into Ahmadinejad's presidency, the Film Makers Production and Distribution Council protested that Iranian cinema was 'going through its worst crisis since the Revolution'.[45] Ahmadinejad had appointed the filmmaker Javad Shamaghdari, who had produced his election campaign videos, as his art and cinema advisor. Shamaghdari's job was to advise the Ministry of Culture on film and cinema censorship. He brought to the job an only too apparent political bias and made his mark by almost immediately banning a film that had contained a few lines of dialogue critical of the president. In interviews, Shamaghdari would talk about a holy light that surrounded the president and which could only be seen by those who were spiritually close to him.

Fame and success did not place directors or their films beyond the reach of the censors. Internationally acclaimed Iranian director Darius Mehrjui's film *Ali Santuri* was to face problems. Objections centred mainly on scenes in which a character speaks of the rumours that Iran's Supreme Leader, Ayatollah Khamenei, had once been a keen player of the tar – a three-stringed instrument. This was something that the authorities felt undermined the pious image of the Leader.[46] Given the richness and quality of Iranian film over the previous decade and the fact that Iranian cinema had been universally acclaimed as making a real contribution to the world of the arts, this undermining of one achievement in which Iranians could take a real pride was nothing but inept.

The theatre was even less capable of surviving the bureaucratic and artistic shackles of the censors. The Play Writers and Critics Society also protested against government policies and censorship, which it said had brought Iranian theatre to 'the verge of death'. In a letter entitled 'A Requiem for Theatre', playwrights and critics said that 'censorship at different stages of script approval, pre-performance and even during performance has dealt such a terrible blow to artistic creativity that staging a decent play is now just a distant dream'.[47]

Censorship was not to be limited to the arts, however. News reporting was to come under considerable political scrutiny, and censorship was imposed on the media via the Supreme National Security Council that Ahmadinejad headed. As Iran came under increasing sanctions for continuing its uranium enrichment activities, the SNSC adopted a new method of censorship. A senior official of the council would phone newspaper editors to warn them about reporting on the economic consequences of the sanctions. As time went on, this became a commonplace occurrence, with the council actually writing directives demanding self-censorship on the part of the news media on a range of issues.

Iranians were familiar with self-censorship, which had become a part of life for the media since the Revolution, and even earlier. But even by post-revolutionary standards, the self-imposed wall of silence in the Iranian media under Ahmadinejad was shocking. As international sanctions increased and the country lurched towards war, Iranian newspapers, even the reformist ones, avoided reporting on the issues. Even if the subject was broached, nothing but the official line would ever be voiced. The newspapers would limit themselves to announcing the news of the sanctions and writing editorials defending Iran's right to uranium enrichment. The media blackout plunged many Iranians into an ignorance which was doubly perilous, as it was an ignorance the existence of which they were also ignorant. Few knew how close to the wind they were sailing. Few heard the international condemnation or the desperate attempts by European powers at reconciliation. As knowledge is empowering, so ignorance is debilitating. Ahmadinejad was able to bend public opinion to his will and claim the Iranian people's full support for Iran's quest for nuclear technology.

Harandi regularly threatened reformist newspapers, describing them as 'the footsoldiers of the enemies' and promising to deal with them. The *Iran* newspaper, which had been physically taken over by the government as its own mouthpiece, spelled out the attitude of the government towards the media in an editorial. 'The policy of the government in dealing with mass media is based on patience, kindness and civility. However, this policy is not unlimited and the government's patience is not infinite. The mass media, considering the fact that they belong to political groups and they are seeking ways to take power, should respect the people's rights.'[48] The government quickly banned the biggest reformist newspaper, *Shargh* (East), after an uncaptioned cartoon depicted a chess board on which a knight faced a donkey with a halo around its head. The government media supervisory board later said that the donkey was an obvious depiction of Ahmadinejad, an admission that itself was difficult to make without some loss of face. The managing editor of the paper, Mohammad Atrianfar, said the paper was paying the price for criticizing the government of Ahmadinejad. A year later, the judiciary lifted the ban on *Shargh*, but the paper had been taught an important lesson: speaking out only brought pain. *Shargh* was later banned again. Under Ahmadinejad, journalists complained that there was less access to government officials. Press conferences became rare, and when they did happen, foreign journalists were frequently not invited. The reformist ILNA news agency was banned from ever attending the president's press conferences, and was later forced to close down before it reappeared with a new editor. Less than two years in office Ahmadinejad was seeing a conspiracy behind every headline that criticized him.

But reality is resilient and Iranian journalism was not slow in retreating to the wilder terrain of the Internet. Even in the more open and relaxed years of Rafsanjani and Khatami, Internet filtering was rife and repressive. Under Ahmadinejad, Iran could lay claim to be a world leader in the field. From the word go, the conservative establishment of Iran feared and hated the Internet. Here was an ungovernable, anarchic, international, multi-vocal stream of information and opinion. And it was instantly deliverable into any home with a telephone line and a computer. It was obviously to become an instrument of political dissent and, like a many-headed hydra, it had an almost limitless capacity to regenerate. Filtering was adopted almost at once and has increased exponentially to hold back the lawless realm of cyberspace. At the time of writing, the authorities had added the BBC's Persian language news website BBCPersian.com, YouTube, the Apple music store iTunes, the online encyclopaedia Wikipedia.com and a host of Iranian political sites, including even the conservative Islamic website Baztab to the list of filtered sites. By the summer of 2006, a year after Ahmadinejad came to power, the number of blocked sites had exceeded 10 million. The filtering of the BBC Persian website was a particularly hard blow to Iranian Internet users, as it had become the most reliable and objective source of news for non-English speakers. Almost every opposition website and all Persian-language news sites originating outside Iran were filtered.

Filtering of sites is a rudimentary form of censorship. Blocks to certain sites can be placed at a country's gateway to the international network and similarly local Internet service providers (ISPs) can filter sites that their customers can access. Iranian ISPs gave undertakings to comply with the official recommendations on filtered sites in order to be allowed to operate.

The extent of the filtering is remarkable. 'On average 1,000 sites are added to the filtered sites every month, as required by various government offices,' said Ismaeil Radkani, the general director of the Management and Technical Support of the Internet Network.[49] But 90 per cent of these proscribed sites are home to pornographic material. That political dissent and secular culture should be lumped together with pornography is a telling indication of the Iranian conservative mindset. And Radkani confirmed that it was about the blocking of legitimate news sites and political or social pages that his office predominately received complaints.

This increasingly pervasive filtering led 13 reformist members of parliament to write to Ahmadinejad demanding an end to the practice. The 13 deputies, all close to the reformist camp, said that filtering certain websites, particularly scientific publications, was contrary to the constitution and laws of the country. They contested that 'immoral' sites could legally be banned.[50] Publicly the president appears as a moderate advocate for the Internet, and the reformists were possibly hoping to capitalize on Ahmadinejad's endorsements of the world wide web as a research tool, having gone on the record as saying that both his children and his wife used the Internet and that he would not curtail its use. 'My phone bills are enormous because my children are constantly online,' he once said.

The age of broadband Internet and the increasingly cyber-savvy nature of Internet users makes filtering a futile exercise. Apart from the basic flaws and failures of any filtering system, there are currently no means of blocking sites that cannot be circumvented by determined users with a little computer know-how. In its war on awareness, the Iranian government has had to limit the public's access to ADSL (broadband) connections. Newspapers carried a leaked government directive to ISPs ordering them to limit the provision of ADSL services to registered companies. The directive also ordered ISPs to offer services to individuals only at speeds of 128 kilobits per seconds (KBps) or below. Few people understood the logic of this directive, other than that it would make it more time consuming to download films and music. But it spoke of the authorities' concern.

The trouble with women

Only days before the FIFA World Cup finals began in Germany in June 2006, Ahmadinejad thought he had spotted an idea that could dramatically increase his popularity with Iranian women. When he took office, many feared that the subtle progress on women's rights under Khatami would be rolled back. Ahmadinejad's views on women had not encouraged many. Prior to his election, he had expressed the opinion that women could be 'helpful' in some arenas but that the predominant role of women was motherhood and the 'provision of love and affection'.[51] His track record was not particularly ambiguous. On becoming mayor of Tehran, he had sacked the only female district mayor in the capital. When he became president, he appointed an all-male cabinet. But it was precisely this perception problem that now worried Ahmadinejad. Obviously he did not want women in his cabinet but he did want them to vote for him. It was this desperation that was to lead the president into making his largest domestic policy mistake so far.

Soon after the Islamic Revolution, Iranian women saw their rights curtailed. Today they enjoy far fewer rights than men, and family law is stacked against them. They cannot have guardianship of their children after divorce, the right to which rests almost exclusively with men. Women are not able to leave the country without the permission of their husbands or their fathers, and in the courts and in the laws governing inheritance they count as one-half of a man. It genuinely is the case under Iranian law that two women witnesses are needed when a single male would do. Many jobs and positions are denied them, including becoming judges or running for president. Most famously of all, they have to wear clothes that cannot provoke arousal in men. In practice this means covering their hair, and wearing top-to-toe loose clothes to hide their body shapes and legs. In Sharia Law, the laws governing arousal seem to make no provision for the wonders of human imagination and fantasy.

Women are also banned from attending sporting events because religious leaders believe that women must not look at the bodies of men – especially if they are half naked in their sports gear. For a time, Iranian television stopped showing sport on television altogether because of this very problem. However, if there was ever one personal liberty that modern man was willing to die for it would be his inalienable right to watch football on television, and the sheer force of public opinion, even among Islamists who in their heads were aware of the firm theological injunctions against it, forced the authorities to resume televising football matches. The decision was given the Sharia stamp of approval by arguing that the players were so far from the camera and their images so small on the TV screens that women were unlikely to be aroused.

Ahead of the World Cup, football was very much on the minds of the Iranians, as Iran had qualified for the finals. And women wanted to watch football. A film by the well-known Iranian director Jafar Panahi, entitled *Offside*, had highlighted the problem. In his film he told the story of several girls who disguise themselves as boys to attend a World Cup qualifier in Tehran's main stadium. For his part, Ahmadinejad had been a keen football player. Although he did not explicitly state this, his love of the game must surely have gone some way to allaying his fears about the morality of the sport. The president believed that he could deliver a win-win situation by allowing women limited access to stadiums. Women would be able to watch live sporting events and he would boost his popular appeal in a demographic that had thus far eluded him. After a year of international fame and notoriety, Ahmadinejad was sufficiently emboldened to tackle the gender taboo. He issued a directive ordering the head of the national sports organization to devise a plan to allow women to attend football matches in stadiums by 'allocating the best section of the terraces to women'.[52] By being away from men, the women could also be shielded from the filthy language male spectators used to cheer or jeer players.

But Ahmadinejad soon found himself in deep trouble with the religious establishment in the holy city of Qom where a number of ayatollahs immediately condemned and rebuked the directive. Even Ahmadinejad's own mentor, Ayatollah Mesbah-Yazdi, sent a message to the president urging him to revoke his directive immediately. Another ayatollah issued a statement categorically rejecting the presence of women in stadiums. He explained, 'the Islamic Sharia does not allow women to look at men's bodies even if they do not get pleasure from it or get aroused by it'. A third ayatollah issued a fatwa rejecting 'the mixing of men and women who are strangers to one another, and other activities that are injurious to the chastity of women and which undermine the Islamic character of society'.[53]

When Shamaghdari, Ahmadinejad's filmmaker friend, advisor and acolyte, criticized the opposition to Ahmadinejad's directive as 'an enemy plot' against the country, the religious leaders in Qom saw red. They regarded themselves as above petty political mud-slinging and believed that Islam and the constitution placed them beyond this kind of attack from a mere political appointee. Ahmadinejad soon revoked his directive but was careful to place the blame at the door of the religious leaders.

Without managing to win new support from Iran's women, the president had succeeded only in weakening his relationship with the clerical hierarchy of Qom. In their eyes, he had shown his true colours. For all his zeal and piety, Ahmadinejad was ultimately a secular politician. He was a layman, not a cleric, and not in a position to take on the clergy in areas they considered to be their exclusive domain. It would take many months before they received Ahmadinejad again. Even then, they refrained from declaring their full support for him. With his fingers badly burnt, Ahmadinejad decided to avoid the gender issue as too contentious and complex to manipulate to his political advantage.

The president became so wary of engaging with women's issues that he kept his distance, even when it threatened to undermine his government's authority. At the start of 2007, a group of women had been peacefully demonstrating on a square in central Tehran, singing women's rights songs to draw attention to the inequalities of the Islamic law. As they sat, they collected signatures for a petition to repeal some of the more notorious and restrictive of the anti-women laws. Suddenly, and without any warning, they were descended upon by policemen and brutally beaten with batons and sprayed in their faces with pepper gas. It was a straightforward and unprovoked assault. Ahmadinejad, still smarting from his dreadful miscalculation over the sporting directive, decided to keep quiet. What made the problem worse was that, to give legitimacy to their actions, the police had arrested several of the women they had beaten. When the trial came around in April 2007, 30 more women demonstrated outside the courthouse, only to be arrested and jailed in the infamous Evin Prison. Again, Ahmadinejad and his government kept their silence and in doing so sent out the message: the government will not intervene on gender issues again.

As spring gave way to summer in 2007, the Islamists in the police and judiciary prepared for their seasonal crackdown on women whom they believed ignored the Islamic dress code by revealing too much hair from under their loose headscarves, or by wearing tight clothes. The idea was that the police would caution offenders, with dedicated patrols set up to enforce the code. The lack of condemnation of their heavy-handed tactics from central government made the police even more enthusiastic in their brutality. Within a short period of time, the whole campaign became very ugly, even by the standards of the hardline Islamists. Many women were arrested and taken to police stations; some were beaten up in public. Videos turned up on the Internet of scenes shot on mobile phones of women covered in blood after being beaten by the police. Behind closed doors, many Iranians were horrified by the fierce oppression that was being unilaterally conducted by the police. Even Iran's hardline top judge, Ayatollah Mahmoud Hashemi Shahrudi, felt that the police had overstepped the mark in their use of force. And still there was no word from the central government. Ahmadinejad's spokesman, Elham, would only comment that the government refused to interfere in the world of the judiciary. This comment rang somewhat false given Shahrudi's own condemnation of the police. Iranians were growing increasingly baffled. If the judiciary was not driving the campaign against women and if the president and his central executive were not taking responsibility, then who exactly was behind it? A terrible realization began to spread that in a state built on force and control, the police themselves had decided to assume the combined role of legislature, executive and judiciary and had meted out summary justice.

The normally verbose Ahmadinejad maintained his silence until it became politically impossible. 'Our enemies want to lead a number of people of inappropriate appearance on to the streets and provoke a crackdown, so that they can broadcast that in Iran the young people are dealt with harshly. And with this they hope to bring despair and depression to our young people.'[54] With one simple statement, the president had reneged on his campaign pledge that his government would not support a crackdown on women. His political caution had gone head to head with his populist leanings, and had prevailed.

An Islamic baby boom

Ahmadinejad had yet another surprise for the Iranian public. As inflation drove prices higher and higher, as the mishandling of the economy and the disastrous minimum wage led to a spike in unemployment, as the oil funds were squandered on vote-winning demonstrative generosity and the whole nation danced closer and closer to a crippling recession, the president proposed the abandonment of Iran's successful population-control programme in favour of more children.

'I am against saying that two children is enough. Our country has a lot of capacity. It has the capacity for many more children to grow in it. It even has the capacity for 120 million people,' he said to the amazement of the many observers. Iran had tried population growth before in the early 1980s when Ayatollah Khomeini, faced with a particularly bloody war of attrition with Iraq, advocated more children. The price of this policy is being exacted on present-day Iran. Some two-thirds of the 70 million Iranian population is aged under 30. The demand for the creation of millions of jobs as these people enter the job market is a nightmare facing successive governments.

But with his simplistic tribal outlook and gleeful refusal to understand essential economic principles, Ahmadinejad saw a huge population as a source of strength. To him the large populations in China and India had turned these nations into the new superpowers. He also saw a large population as a deterrent against the aggressive designs of the enemies of Islam. Like so many things he found distasteful, Ahmadinejad had decided that birth control was nothing but an imperialist conspiracy. 'It's the Westerners who advocate few children. This is their problem, because their population growth is negative. Understandably, they are concerned. They fear our population might grow bigger than theirs. That is why they want to export their problem to other countries.' [55]

Until late 2006, Iran had one of the world's most successful population-control policies. It had succeeded in bringing down the rate of population growth from 3.2 per cent in the 1980s to 1.2. Under successive presidents, both moderate and conservative, the consensus had been to limit the population to save the economy and the country. With one bravado speech, Ahmadinejad had thrown nearly 20 years of government policy out the window on the basis of his own personal instincts. Even the conservative Islamists could not bring themselves to support a decision which was nothing other than foolish. One ultra-conservative woman member of parliament said the president had been joking and was expressing only a personal opinion.[56] The reformists saw this as another sign of erratic behaviour from Ahmadinejad. 'The statement of the president is stupefying,' said the reformist newspaper *Etemad-e-Melli*. It said that two decades of work to bring the population explosion under control was in danger of being undone. 'It seems the president is constantly trying to grab the headlines with his strange statements,' mused the paper's editorial. 'It is the people of Iran who have to pay the heavy cost of his controversial and often non-scientific statements.'[57]

Ahmadinejad's Third Revolution was supposed to be a reaffirmation of the discipline and ideological purity of the 1979 Revolution. But as policies such as these show, he was heading the country to the brink.

CHAPTER 8

FRIENDS IN HIGH PLACES

*Our government today is the most popular government in Iran since the
Constitutional Revolution one hundred years ago.*[1]

Friends and masters to keep

Ahmadinejad, holding the green leather-bound folder containing his
credentials under his arm, bowed and kissed the hand of Supreme
Leader Ayatollah Khamenei. The occasion was the swearing-in ceremony at the start of his term in office as the sixth president of Iran
since the 1979 Islamic Revolution.

In the Iranian system of government the Supreme Leader is the *de
facto* head of state with extra-constitutional powers, while the president is the top executive power. The hand-kissing raised eyebrows in
Iran. Some thought Ahmadinejad had belittled the position of the
president of the country. They pointed out that in the early days of
the Revolution, when the highly respected Mehdi Bazargan, a non-
cleric, was appointed as the first prime minister of revolutionary Iran,
he did not kiss the hand of Ayatollah Khomeini, the man who had
appointed him. Others argued that the president's gesture was nothing
other than a harmless display of Ahmadinejad's personal esteem for
a senior cleric. Either way it suggested how the relationship between
the two leaders would develop – a relationship between a master and
a servant.

While Ahmadinejad was aware that he might not have been
Ayatollah Khamenei's first choice, he still was part of the leader's
long-espoused desire for a uniformly hardline system of government.
Now all centres of powers and powerful positions were occupied by

hardliners, who could now pursue their goal of a puritanical and revolutionary Islamic state.

With more than 17 million votes behind him and with the hardline Supreme Leader supporting him, Ahmadinejad was in a strong position. This had not been the position of his predecessor, Khatami, who, despite winning 20.5 million votes, was paralysed in government because of the hardliners' almost daily assaults on him throughout his two terms of office. Ahmadinejad also had powerful friends in the Revolutionary Guard and the Basij militia. When, after a year in office, his popularity began to wane and many began to voice serious misgivings about his management of the country, Ahmadinejad stood firm and unrepentant. He knew that with friends in high places, his opponents were no threat to him.

One of Ahmadinejad's first tasks as president was to reward his friends for their support. In the first months of taking office his government awarded the Revolutionary Guard and the companies affiliated to it no less than $10 billion in contracts, bypassing the requirement that all government contracts should be put out to public tender. The contracts included the building of a 900km gas pipeline, the development of two offshore gas fields and the construction of two lines of Tehran's metro system.[2] The government's justification for circumventing the tender process was that they were in a hurry to get the work done. These hefty awards helped further unite the Guard commanders – some of whom were still not sure about Ahmadinejad – behind the new president.

The Supreme Leader

Wearing a black turban and robe, a long white beard and over-sized spectacles, Iran's Supreme Leader, Ayatollah Ali Khamenei, sat sternly on a single chair that had been placed in the middle of the slightly raised platform. He was facing an audience of top government officials sitting on the floor of the mosque on a plain carpet. Ahmadinejad and the leaders of the two other branches of the government – the speaker of parliament and the head of the judiciary – sat on the floor of the platform on the left. On the right sat the outgoing President Khatami and the leaders of three other constitutional bodies.

The ceremony was held at the mosque adjacent to the heavily

guarded residence of the Supreme Leader. According to the constitution, he had to sign the decree formalizing the election of the president of the republic. Throughout the country it was assumed that Ahmadinejad was the choice of the Supreme Leader. This seemed the only plausible explanation for his surprise victory. But when the Ayatollah rose to his feet and read out his decree it became clear that he was wary of Ahmadinejad – a man he did not know very well, and who could, conceivably, prove to be a problem.

'It goes without saying that the votes of the people as well as my order of appointment will remain effective so far as he [Ahmadinejad] remains committed to the path he has [publicly] chosen, which is the path of Islam and the ideals of the Islamic government as well as the defence of the rights of the people and resisting the oppressors and aggressors,' the Supreme Leader said in his decree. But he couched his doubts about Ahmadinejad in words of praise. He spoke of the Iranian nation having chosen a 'knowledgeable revolutionary' and a 'competent and experienced manager'. 'His clear and sincere statement about his commitment to serve and to fight poverty and corruption, and his laudable dedication to Islam and the ideals of the Revolution as well as his humility and simple lifestyle, drew the people's attention and votes, and ultimately put the heavy responsibility of the presidency on his shoulders,' continued the decree.[3]

Without a doubt, the decree also reflected Khamenei's pleasure at the fact that after eight years of unconstructive antagonism with a reformist president, he could now look forward to the executive branch being in the hands of a fellow conservative and Islamic hardliner. When, at the end of the ceremony, Ahmadinejad proceeded to kiss his hand, Ayatollah Khamenei could be sure that the elections had gone his way – all the way. Like Ahmadinejad, Khamenei is an Islamic hardliner. He also has strong views on many issues, including relations with the US, Israel and the Holocaust. His views on Western democracy leave little room for interpretation: 'The bitter and venomous taste of Western liberal democracy, which the United States has hypocritically been trying to portray through its propaganda as a healing remedy, has hurt the body and soul of the Islamic Ummah [community] and burned the hearts of Muslims.' Like Ahmadinejad, Ayatollah Khamenei had developed increasingly hardline views, particularly since a clerical body chose him – the least objectionable candidate – as the Supreme Leader immediately after the death of Ayatollah Khomeini in June 1989.

The system of government in Iran is based on the concept of Velayat-e-Faghih, or 'the Rule of the Jurisprudent'. This thesis was the brainchild of Khomeini, who had developed the concept while still a young clergyman. With the removal of the monarchy and the success of the Islamic Revolution, Khomeini used Velayat-e-Faghih to fill the constitutional void, establishing the rule of the clergymen. Under this system, the Supreme Leader is Vali-e-Faghih, the Supreme Jurisprudent leader, whose legitimacy is bestowed on him by God as the result of his own religious learning. The Supreme Jurisprudent or Leader is commander-in-chief of the armed forces and has the power to appoint and dismiss the country's top officials, declare war and peace and set out the country's strategic policies. He has direct control over the Intelligence Ministry, the judiciary, and the national broadcast network.

Before the Revolution, as a junior cleric, Khamenei was a student of Ayatollah Khomeini. Like all future revolutionaries, he had spent time in the Shah's jails for his opposition activities. During the early days of the Islamic Revolution he was a confidant of Khomeini's. A brilliant orator with a penetrating voice, he was chosen by Khomeini as the Friday prayer imam of Tehran and was twice elected president in the 1980s. The years of the Iran–Iraq War saw him spending much time in the green camouflage uniforms of the Revolutionary Guard, organizing the resistance at the front. While on the front line, he forged close relations with Guard and Basij commanders who saw him as one of their own. The war hardened his attitudes, particularly when he saw Western powers ganging up against Iran and supporting Iraq's Saddam Hussein by supplying him with weapons and intelligence. He also witnessed the Western powers turning a blind eye to Saddam's use of chemical weapons against Iranian civilians. At first hand, the future Supreme Leader saw that most of those who fought and died at the fronts were poor villagers rather than the middle-class urban dwellers of Tehran and other cities.

But he was still a relatively junior Islamic clergyman – a hojatoleslam, not an ayatollah – when an assembly of top religious leaders elected him as Supreme Leader on the back of his political rather than religious credentials. His not-quite-adequate religious and scholarly credentials led to a crisis of confidence in him particularly among the ever scheming religious leaders in the holy city of Qom. This crisis undermined his authority and he needed to bring the religious estab-lishment into line in order to consolidate his position. He had to make ayatollahs in Qom respect him as a religious leader as well as a political one. This proved an uphill struggle and took him many years to achieve. During the same period he had to deal with the reformists who wanted Iran to move towards an Islamic democracy – a concept that was wholly alien to the conservative religious leaders in Qom. Ayatollah Khamenei had to choose between the competing centres of power in Tehran and Qom. Decisively, he chose Qom. Whether this was a cynical decision to shore up his credibility as both a religious and political leader or an indication of his true political leanings is up for debate. But his choice made him unpopular outside the tradition-alist and hardline circles. As a consequence, the years of Rafsanjani and Khatami had been difficult and divisive, with the religious ortho-dox in perpetual tension with the executive.

With Ahmadinejad's election, Khamenei's hardline supporters had taken control of the last remaining independent centre of power, the executive branch. For the Ayatollah, this was the culmination of 18 years of effort to consolidate his power. He now controlled all levers of power in Iran including the three branches of government, the Revolutionary Guard and the Basij as well as having influence over most of the religious leaders in Qom.

For the moment it seemed that Khamenei and Ahmadinejad needed each other to varying degrees. Neither would rock the boat if he could help it. For Ahmadinejad this meant that he enjoyed the support of the most powerful figure in Iran. This support had already proved useful but was to be even more important as his presidency progressed and his tendency to court controversy became apparent. On many occasions when Ahmadinejad was under domestic pressure, Khamenei rose to his defence. One angry riposte at Ahmadinejad's critics or one statement in support of Ahmadinejad would silence criticism for weeks.

When Ahmadinejad invited a barrage of internal and international criticism over his remarks about Israel and the Holocaust, the Supreme Leader was silent. This was seen as a sign of support for Ahmadinejad. When, contrary to Iran's policy, Ahmadinejad threatened to reconsider Iran's membership of the nuclear Non-Proliferation Treaty, the Supreme Leader said that Ahmadinejad was speaking the minds of the people.[4] Yet again, when Ahmadinejad was under fire at home for high prices and the mismanagement of the economy, Khamenei lauded his 'economic achievements'.[5] When he made remarks which patently undermined Iran's nuclear diplomacy, Khamenei did not condemn his president but praised him for setting out the agenda in Iran's dealing with the outside world.[6] Just as Ahmadinejad was criticized in the newspapers for almost his every action, Khamenei attacked the newspapers for blowing these problems out of proportion.[7] In his support for Ahmadinejad, Khamenei went so far as to describe his government as the best in modern times. 'Our government today is the most popular government in Iran since the Constitutional Revolution one hundred years ago,' he said in a speech,[8] referring to the turmoil of 1907 when royal autocracy was – at least briefly – reined in as Iran attempted a political system based on constitutional rule.

But while Khamenei's support freed Ahmadinejad from the fear of his critics at home, the Supreme Leader was in danger of losing his own credibility by allowing himself to be identified with Ahmadinejad's excesses. And this was not the only problem. Over many years, Ayatollah Khamenei had consolidated his grip on power by adopting hardline policies and appealing to the most extreme sections of Iran's polity. Now, Ahmadinejad seemed to be preempting him. Often it was the president who would take pole position, particularly on contentious and delicate foreign policy issues. On several occasions observers noticed that Khamenei simply repeated the words of Ahmadinejad. The Supreme Leader was actually in danger of becoming a follower. This could lead to a bigger constitutional crisis – something that frightened all the governing clergy. A popular layman zealot could eventually pull the rug from under Iran's clerical leaders and force them back to the mosques.

A year into Ahmadinejad's presidency Ayatollah Khamenei set up a foreign relations council to supervise foreign policy initiatives and decisions. This was seen as an attempt to curtail Ahmadinejad's destructive influence on the country's relations with the outside world. But with Ahmadinejad continuing to hold forth on foreign policy issues, and even refusing to see the head of the council, former Foreign Minister Kamal Kharrazi, the council never found a role for itself and quietly disbanded. The challenge for Ayatollah Khamenei was to keep Ahmadinejad under control. But equally Ahmadinejad had to watch his step. It would not do to lose Khamenei's favour just as quickly and as naturally as he had won it.

The Guardian Council

At one of his weekly press briefings, a journalist asked government spokesman Gholam Hussein Elham whether it was true that Ahmadinejad had married into the family of the ultra-conservative Ayatollah Ahmad Jannati, the powerful head of the constitutional watchdog, the Guardian Council. 'So far as I know, Ayatollah Jannati has neither a daughter nor a sister the president could have married!' came the reply.[9]

The question was not as odd as might first appear. It is one of the characteristics of the Islamic regime in Iran that many of its top leaders and officials are related to each other, perhaps distantly, through marriage. But the journalist's question also reflected the general opinion that Ahmadinejad was very closely associated with Ayatollah Jannati. What had led to this perception was the relentless support Ayatollah Jannati gave to Ahmadinejad after his election, and the favouritism that the Guardian Council displayed towards the mayor of Tehran in the run-up to the election.

Ayatollah Jannati is a highly political, ultra-conservative clergyman. He is also reputed to be close to the Islamic vigilante group Ansar-e-Hezbollah, with which Ahmadinejad was also associated. Over the years the Guardian Council under the stewardship of Ayatollah Jannati has become a powerful and yet highly controversial body, repeatedly intervening politically to block reforms and reformists. Its original function in the constitution was to make sure that legislation passed in parliament conformed with Islamic tenets. It is also the state body whose job it is to interpret the constitution. Most importantly, it has the task of overseeing elections. It is made up of six senior clergymen who are appointed by the Supreme Leader, and six lawyers who are appointed on the recommendation of the judiciary.

In the parliamentary elections of 2004, the Council disqualified thousands of reformist candidates on the grounds that they lacked proper Islamic credentials. It thus engineered a coup in favour of the hardliners who swept the parliamentary seats. In the 2005 presidential elections, it did not allow anyone from outside the hardline Islamic establishment to stand, disqualifying many hopefuls, again because of their insufficient Islamic credentials. It later allowed two Islamic reformists to run but not before the Supreme Leader intervened. Khamenei had acted because he was concerned about the possibility of a boycott of the elections by the reformists – something that would have undermined the legitimacy of the poll and potentially sparked a constitutional crisis.

During the two terms of the presidency of the modernizing president Khatami, the Guardian Council was a major obstacle to his programme of reform. In this period, when reformists enjoyed a majority in parliament, the Council repeatedly threw out parliamentary legislation of which the hardliners did not approve. They frequently used the excuse that the legislation violated the tenets of Islam, but to many this was an obvious falsehood. The Council thus effectively rendered the reformist-dominated legislature impotent, which served to demonstrate that over the years the Guardian Council had become an important instrument of control in the hands of the Islamic hardliners and ultra-conservatives.

President Ahmadinejad enjoyed the support of this all-powerful body, thanks to Ayatollah Jannati, who had been the secretary of the Council since its inception soon after the 1979 Revolution. The two met during the early 1990s when Ahmadinejad was still active in the Ramazan HQ of the Revolutionary Guard in the west of the country. The Ramazan HQ was involved in some operations outside Iran, including an excursion into Bosnia during the Balkans war. Ayatollah Jannati was at the time in charge of coordinating all of Iran's activities in Bosnia in support of the country's Muslims. He was responsible for dispatching men and weapons in the last two years of the war. Later, Ayatollah Jannati put Ahmadinejad on the payroll of the Guardian Council as an inspector of the Council. This brought Ahmadinejad close to Gholam Hussein Elham, the spokesman of the Council, who later became his government spokesman.

Days after Ahmadinejad was elected, a hugely excited Ayatollah Jannati took the unprecedented step of taking all 12 members of the Council to see the president personally to congratulate him. 'You have the Council's full support,' he told Ahmadinejad.[10] There was complete mutual admiration. Ahmadinejad told the Council that they were 'a powerful dam resisting the pressure of those who want to expropriate the rights of the people'. Earlier in the run-up to the elections, the Council approved the candidacy of Ahmadinejad in spite of the objections of the Intelligence Ministry.[11] The ministry had sent the Council a file detailing Ahmadinejad's oil-swap arrangement to fund the election of Islamic hardliners in 1996 when he was the governor of Ardabil province. The Guardian Council announced that it had looked into the episode and had found no truth in the allegations.[12]

When Ahmadinejad wrote his letter to President Bush, Ayatollah Jannati waxed lyrical. 'The letter is spectacular, and when I say it is an inspiration from God, I really mean it,' Jannati said. 'This man is truly a brave, God-fearing and powerful figure ... who could have dared writing such a letter to the president of the United States?'[13] Describing the letter as divinely inspired was ridiculous in the eyes of many, including the former speaker of parliament, Mehdi Karroubi, who wrote an open letter to Jannati criticizing him for exaggeration and accusing him of demeaning the whole nation.[14] Jannati's reply was revealing in that it also provided a window into his thinking about Ahmadinejad. He told the Friday prayer congregation in Tehran that by 'divine' he had meant the sort of inspiration that ordinary souls sometimes get, 'like, at the time of earthquakes, the people whose time has not arrived might suddenly get an urge to go on a trip and stay alive just because they were not at home at the time of the quake'. But he also had this to say about Ahmadinejad: 'Mr Ahmadinejad is what he says he is, a servant. He says he is a servant and wants to serve. Whenever there is a need, of course we caution him.'[15]

Mesbah-Yazdi and Ahmadinejad

Another key supporter of Ahmadinejad is his controversial mentor, Ayatollah Mohammad Taqi Mesbah-Yazdi. With his position in the heart of the religious establishment in Qom, and with his disciples in key posts throughout the country, Mesbah-Yazdi is an important source of strength for Ahmadinejad.

In the summer of 2007, the president visited Mesbah-Yazdi in Qom and spoke at the graduation ceremony of his institute. He praised the

Ayatollah and hinted that he might even bring him into the cabinet. It transpired that during the visit to Qom, Ahmadinejad had been unable to see other top religious figures, which indicated that they were still angry at his aborted directive to allow women spectators into football stadiums. The president's speech in Qom at Mesbah-Yazdi's institute indicated that he still believed Mesbah-Yazdi could provide him with an important foothold in Qom, the bastion of the conservative religious establishment in Iran.

Reformist newspapers splashed the picture of the two on their front pages, describing their relationship as that of 'a mentor and a disciple'. Certainly Ayatollah Mesbah-Yazdi had done all he could to help support Ahmadinejad in the elections. And after his victory, Ahmadinejad visited Mesbah-Yazdi's institute to thank him and his students for their help. During the meeting, Mesbah-Yazdi told him he and his aides did not expect any pay-off. President-elect Ahmadinejad assured them that he intended to use 'all resources' open to him in his administration to express his gratitude.[16] And as it turned out, once in government Ahmadinejad did pay Mesbah-Yazdi back. He chose many of his aides and ministers from among the Ayatollah's disciples. Ahmadinejad appointed Sagha Biria, one of the clerical students of Mesbah-Yazdi, as his liaison with the clergy. Biria is on record as suggesting that Ahmadinejad will one day rule the world.

No matter how he might provoke the international community, isolate Iran, offend the electorate, ruin the economy or clash with the clerics of Qom, provided he retains the support of Jannati, Mesbah-Yazdi, Khamenei and the Revolutionary Guard, Ahmadinejad will be untouchable.

EPILOGUE

IN A MAKE-BELIEVE WORLD

I had been invited to speak at Columbia University. But events followed one after the other in a way that I believe God had designed, so as to show that all the materialist, evil, greedy non-believers had ganged up against the great decent and innocent people of Iran and the humanitarian message of Islam.[1]

Late in the evening on Friday 28 September 2007 the top leaders of the country gathered at Tehran's Mehrabad airport to greet President Ahmadinejad on his return from a controversial visit to New York where he had attended the 62nd UN General Assembly.

Ayatollah Khamenei's representative had shown up, as had the speaker of parliament, the head of the judiciary and the top commanders of the Revolutionary Guard. Ahmadinejad's erstwhile supporter, Ayatollah Jannati, had joined them too. All were there to show a united front behind the president, who was claiming that his visit had been a complete success – a spectacular victory. At the top there were fears that Ahmadinejad might come under heavy criticism inside the country where many were unhappy with the way the president and the nation had been insulted during the visit. One reformist opponent of Ahmadinejad told the newspapers that if either of the moderate former presidents, Rafsanjani or Khatami, had visited New York, neither they nor the country would have been slighted.

At Mehrabad airport, Ahmadinejad met every one of the top leaders who had come to greet him with an emotional embrace like a victorious warrior who had just returned from a difficult and bloody battle. He spoke of his success in putting on a display for the whole world to see 'the real face of the great nation of Iran'. He spoke of his experience at Columbia University, arguably his most difficult moment in New York: 'I had been invited to speak at Columbia

University. But events followed one after the other in a way that I believe God had designed, so as to show that all the materialist, evil, greedy non-believers had ganged up against the great decent and innocent people of Iran and the humanitarian message of Islam,' he told reporters at the airport.

A few days earlier in New York, Ahmadinejad had faced a storm of criticism. One American newspaper splashed the front page with the banner headline 'THE EVIL HAS LANDED'. He had been refused a visit to Ground Zero, where hundreds of Americans had died during the terrorist attacks on the city on 11 September 2001. At Columbia University, where he was to speak and respond to questions, the president of the university, Lee Bollinger, made an introductory speech in which he repeatedly insulted Ahmadinejad, describing him as 'undereducated' and 'exhibiting all the signs of a petty and cruel dictator' – saying this to his face in front of a large audience of students and TV cameras. Bollinger had more insults up his sleeve, before he finished with the sentence, 'I feel all the weight of the modern civilized world yearning to express revulsion at what you stand for.'

Taken by surprise, Ahmadinejad nevertheless had kept his composure, only briefly criticizing Bollinger for his personal insults, saying that his remarks went against the tradition in universities whereby students are encouraged to listen and are left to make their own judgements. Undaunted, Ahmadinejad had gone on to deliver his set speech.

The incident was deemed damaging enough that state radio and television and many newspapers in Iran did not report the robust words of the president of Columbia University and so many people back home were unaware of what had been said.

The reception Ahmadinejad received in New York showed just how far he had outraged sensibilities abroad, and in particular in the US. (In fact when, in the question and answer session, he denied that homosexuality existed in Iran, some in the audience went beyond outrage to laughter.) By his statements on the Holocaust, by threatening Israel and by his undiplomatic language, Ahmadinejad had crossed many of the red lines of international politics. In the West, Iran under Ahmadinejad had gained a reputation as a major threat to world peace and security.

Yet Ahmadinejad showed no signs of a rethink even after his visit to the US, where he saw for himself the extent of the feeling there against Iran. On his return, he even stepped up his attacks on Israel, repeating a call for the Jews there to be relocated to Canada or Alaska.

Increasingly Ahmadinejad and his supporters seemed to be living in a world of make-believe, oblivious to the dangers facing their country. In this fantasy world the New York visit was a victory. Iran under Ahmadinejad is going from strength to strength. It has isolated all its enemies, putting them on the defensive. Iran's economy is flourishing with a respectable growth rate, attracting unprecedented levels of foreign investment. It is Iran that is imposing sanctions on unfriendly countries. Iran is already sitting at the high table of nuclear powers. In this make-believe world, people all around the globe are with him – the world is 'Ahmadinejadized', as he once put it.

And Ahmadinejad and his supporters frequently show signs that they believe their own rhetoric. Diplomats observe that in their meetings with Iranian officials and leaders, the hosts regularly show a disconnection with reality, in particular when they speak of Iran's development and its position vis-à-vis the rest of the world. Many Iranian leaders and top officials do not speak English, hardly travel outside the country and consequently lack first-hand knowledge of Iran's relative position in the world. When Ahmadinejad visited several west African countries on an official tour, he returned to Tehran to declare excitedly that the continent had many resources Iran could use.

Furthermore, to defend themselves against accusations of mismanagement, hardline supporters of Ahmadinejad increasingly took to fantastical glorification of the president – something that had been hitherto reserved for the late Ayatollah Khomeini.

A group of the families of martyrs of the Iran–Iraq War bestowed on Ahmadinejad an award for 'having bravely defended the revolution on the international stage, especially for his speech at Columbia University'. Weeks earlier one of Ahmadinejad's aides in all earnestness described him as 'a latter-day Socrates'. He claimed that Ahmadinejad had developed a Socratic-style polemical politics that had put the world's powers on the defensive by taunting them to respond. He said, 'Ahmadinejad's letter to the latter-day pharaoh,

President Bush, his letter to the German chancellor Angela Merkel and his call for live debates were a confirmation of the Socratic methodology Ahmadinejad had employed.' But even this level of elevation of Ahmadinejad is not enough for some of his more devoted fans, one of whom wrote that comparing Ahmadinejad to Socrates was an injustice to Ahmadinejad. The writer claimed that Socrates occasionally added sophistry to his polemics, while no one could doubt the sincerity of Ahmadinejad. All this came at a time when, at the start of the president's third year in power, his supporters were portraying the results of two years of mismanagement as signs of the monumental success of an extraordinary leader. Earlier, the man who originally compared Ahmadinejad to Socrates announced that the president's office had formed a 'committee to publish the thoughts and works of President Ahmadinejad' – an announcement that was met with a good deal of scepticism in Tehran even among Islamic hardliners. A few asked what the president had written to merit such a committee except for his university PhD thesis on 'Cold Asphalt'.

The make-believe world of Ahmadinejad and his supporters is particularly worrying to many Iranians because their country is under threat of military strikes from the US and Israel. Israel carried out a spectacular attack on a nuclear facility in Syria – not unlike the one against Iraq's Osirak nuclear reactor in 1981 – that sent the clear message to Iran that its nuclear facilities could also come under attack. Western countries are almost unanimous on the need to impose tougher sanctions against Iran. President Bush has warned that Iran would be raising the risk of a World War III if it comes to possess nuclear weapons. There are almost daily speculations in the international media detailing how the US is preparing for pinpoint strikes against targets in Iran.

Even some hardliners have begun to show concerns about the direction in which Ahmadinejad is taking the country. While they support Iran's quest for nuclear know-how, some are wondering whether, with patience, Iran could eventually arrive at what it wants without having to go to war.

So far, the Supreme Leader has supported Ahmadinejad's policies against the doubters. The first sign of dissent at the top of the hardline establishment came on 27 September 2007 when Ayatollah Khamenei replaced the top commander of the Revolutionary Guard, Brigadier

General Yahya Rahim Safavi, just as a new round of speculation began about the possibility of US strikes against Iran. Although Safavi had been a hawk and a trusted lieutenant of Ayatollah Khamenei, of late he had privately been urging caution while sounding bellicose in public. It seemed that Khamenei did not regard Safavi as hardline enough in the circumstances. A few weeks later Safavi made a speech in which he publicly cautioned politicians to take the threats of a US war on Iran seriously – a caution directed mainly at Ahmadinejad but also at Khamenei. The change at the top of the Revolutionary Guard indicated that some among the militarists who had previously backed Ahmadinejad to the hilt were now in two minds. The commanders know that their men and equipment are no match for the sort of aerial fire power the US might use against targets in Iran. But the change of the commander of the Revolutionary Guard also showed that Khameini still supported Ahmadinejad's confrontational approach. The president's make-believe world was left undisturbed.

The second sign came less than a month later on 20 October 2007 with the resignation of Iran's chief nuclear negotiator, Ali Larijani, and his replacement with a hardline cohort of Ahmadinejad, Saeed Jalili. Larijani had taken over more than two years earlier as the secretary of the all-powerful Supreme National Security Council. A hardliner appointed by Ahmadinejad, Larijani had criticized his predecessor Hassan Rohani for being allegedly weak in his dealings with the outside world over Iran's nuclear programme. But Larijani found himself to be a relative moderate compared to Ahmadinejad, whose bellicose statements routinely undermined him as he pursued negotiations with the Europeans and others. In office Larijani had gradually become a moderating influence, but his efforts came to naught. Ahmadinejad did not want to hear about negotiations – he wanted Iran's nuclear file closed. To Ahmadinejad there was nothing to talk about, and he routinely criticized 'those who constantly want to go off on their own and negotiate'. Larijani's resignation came soon after Russian president Vladimir Putin's visit to Tehran. During the visit Putin met with Ayatollah Khamenei and put forward what Larijani said was a new proposal on the nuclear issue. Khamenei said that Iran was considering this proposal, but Ahmadinejad swiftly contradicted this, saying that there had been no new proposals. It later became clear that in Tehran Putin had called on Khamenei to stop nuclear enrichment activities in return for peaceful nuclear cooperation with Russia and other world powers as well as the IAEA. Larijani saw this as at least worth considering, but Ahmadinejad dismissed the proposal out of hand. To Larijani, flatly rejecting a proposal from a power that Iran badly needed to keep on its side was symptomatic of Ahmadinejad's reckless temperament.

With a nod from the Supreme Leader, Ahmadinejad replaced Larijani with a hardliner in his camp, Saeed Jalili. A veteran of the Iran-Iraq War in which he lost a leg, Jalili was, according to diplomats, an 'unreconstructed' revolutionary, an ideological hardliner. Jalili frequently lectures Foreign Ministry diplomats that Islamic Iran has a responsibility to defend the oppressed anywhere in the world. He has spoken of inviting Cuba's Marxist leader, Fidel Castro, to Iran, and suggesting to Che Guevara's son that the Islamic Revolution could be replicated in Latin America.

The change showed that Ayatollah Khamenei, who accepted the resignation, had effectively taken Ahmadinejad's side again. Ahmadinejad and the hardliners had won the day. If some in Iran were hoping that common sense would prevail in the corridors of power, these developments did not inspire optimism.

Ahmadinejad's defiant posturing on the nuclear issue has led some in Tehran to believe that he and the militarists may in fact actually relish a US attack on Iran, thinking that it could rally support for the regime.

Ahmadinejad believes that those who have faith in God cannot be defeated. In his worldview God has entrusted him with a divine mission. His belief that a divine halo engulfed him during his first ever speech at the UN General Assembly is indicative of this mindset. His belief that the Missing Imam, the Mahdi, will return soon has provided him with the reason with which to reject the existing order inside Iran and abroad.

And to those around Ahmadinejad, he knows best - he is the miracle of the third millennium. To them, Ahmadinejad is capable of wonders that are often hidden from mortals. Ahmadinejad is on a mission to change the world and not just Iran, and he is ready for a battle, if need be.

NOTES

Chapter 1. From the Desert to the Palace

1. Personal notes from Ahmadinejad's weblog. http://www.ahmadinejad. ir.
2. Interview with the author, March 2007.
3. Interview with the author, April 2007.
4. In 1961 Mohammad Reza Shah Pahlavi decreed that ownership of agricultural land should be vested in the peasants who farmed it, thus initiating a campaign of redistribution.
5. Interview with the author, April 2007.
6. Reuters, 23 June 2005.
7. Interview with the author, March 2007.
8. Interview with the author, April 2007.
9. Baztab, 2 May 2007. http://www.baztab.com/news/65982.php.
10. Interview with the author, April 2007.
11. Interview with the author, April 2007.
12. Interview with the author, April 2007.
13. Interview with a top reformist politician who did not wish to be named.
14. 'I was with Khamenei ... ', Roozonline, 5 July 2005.
15. The MKO was an armed student organization which had been active and enormously influential in the 1979 Revolution. However, because of their perceived cult-like characteristics, combined with a formidable military capacity, they were seen as a threat by the new clerical establishment. Within two years of the Revolution, the MKO and Khomeini

had severely fallen out, and the MKO ended up in exile as the most fervent opponents of the regime.

16. 'Exclusive: Photo Shows Iran's Ahmadinejad as Hostage-Taker of US Diplomats', *Iran Focus*, 29 June 2005.

17. Mark Bowden, *The Guests of the Ayatollah*, p 615.

18. 'U.S. Pursuing Reports That Link Iranian to Embassy Seizure in '79', *New York Times*, 1 July 2005.

19. *Shargh* (newspaper), 4 July 2005.

20. 'U.S. Pursuing Reports That Link Iranian to Embassy Seizure in '79', *New York Times*, 1 July 2005.

21. CNN, 17 September 2005.

22. Bowden, *Guests of the Ayatollah: The First Battle in the West's War with Militant Islam* (Atlantic Books, 2006), p 10.

23. *Shargh* (newspaper), 3 November 2004.

24. *Yalesarat*, no. 223, 30 April 2003.

25. Roozonline, 3 November 2006.

26. A close friend of Ahmadinejad in an interview with the author, summer 2007.

27. Interview with the author, summer 2007.

28. Interview with the author, summer 2007.

29. Interview with the author, summer 2007.

30. T. Christian Miller, 'Iraqi Election Catapults Critic of U.S. to Power', *Los Angeles Times*, 14 February 2005.

31. Sources interviewed by the author.

32. Interview with Abbas Khodadi, his student. http://shivathespy. blogspot.com/2005/09/professor-ahmadinejad.html.

33. Najmeh Bozorgmen, *FT* interview with the author.

34. Fatemeh Rajabi, *Ahmadinejad: The Miracle of the Third Millennium* (Nashr-e-Danesh Amouz), p 68.

35. 'Iran's Unique Elections', by Jim Muir, BBC, 24 February 2000. http://news.bbc.co.uk/1/hi/world/middle_east/654135.stm.

36. *Ibid.*

37. A close associate of Ahmadinejad in interview with the author.

38. Iran Va Jahan, 2 October 2002, press review. http://www.iranvajahan.

net/cgi-bin/printarticle.pl?l=fa&y=1381&m=7&d=10&a=18.

39. Jalal Yaghoubi, 'Ahmadinejad and the Abadgaran', 19 December 2005. See website of the Union of the Republicans of Iran.

40. Abadgaran, Statement of 28 April 2005. http://www.abadgaran.ir/ farsi/index.php?id=12&tx_ttnews%5Btt_news%5D=36&tx_ttnews% 5BbackPid%5D=1&cHash=99b1538c7f.

41. Fars News Agency, 3 May 2003.

42. Behnam Majidzadeh in Roozonline, 19 October 2005.

43. His cousin, in interview with the author.

44. ISNA, 6 February 2004.

45. Aftab News, 15 October 2006. http://www.aftabnews.ir/vdccieq2bsqip. html.

46. Baztab, 13 April 2007.

47. Saeed Leilaz in interview with the author.

48. Baztab, 11 October 2006.

49. ISNA, 29 April 2005.

50. ISNA, 13 May 2005.

Chapter 2. Ahmadinejad for President

1. Ahmadinejad speaking to his supporters during the presidential campaign, June 2005. Ansar-e-Hezbollah, quoted by Persian news website Gooya. http://mag.gooya.com/president84/archives/031478. php.

2. *Shargh* (newspaper), 5 April 2006. http://www.inroozha.com/ news/002673.php.

3. Rajabi, *Ahmadinejad: The Miracle of the Third Millennium*, p 185.

4. *Ibid.*, p 121.

5. *Kayhan* (newspaper), 15 June 2005.

6. Entekhab, 9 June 2005. http://www.entekhab.ir/display/?ID=2401.

7. ISNA, 6 May 2005.

8. ILNA, 13 June 2005. Rajabi, *Ahmadinejad: The Miracle of the Third Millennium*, p 217.

9. Fars News Agency, 21 June 2005.

10. 'Bush Says Iranian People Deserve Genuinely Democratic System', 16

June. http://london.usembassy.gov/iran12.html.

11. Off-the-record interviews with the author.

12. http://mag.gooya.com/president84/archives/031478.php.

13. Gooya News, 11 May 2005. http://mag.gooya.com/president84/archives/028600.php.

14. Aftab News, 21 June 2005. http://www.aftab.ir/news/2005/jun/21/c1c1119350486.php.

15. Fars News Agency, 22 June 2005.

16. Baztab, 19 June 2005.

17. Baztab, 19 June 2005. Agence France-Presse quoted by Sharif News, 20 June 2005.

18. ISNA, 20 June 2005.

19. Letter of Moin's supporters to Ayatollah Khamenei, 20 June 2005. http://mag.gooya.com/president84/archives/031508.php.

20. Agence France-Presse, 30 May 2005.

21. Two sources who did not want to be named speaking to the author.

22. Sharif News, 8 May 2005.

23. Bill Samii, 'Goods Smuggling Highlights Economic Problems in Iran', Radio Free Europe/Radio Liberty's Radio Farda, 7 January 2005. http://www.payvand.com/news/05/jan/1056.html.

24. ISNA, 14 June 2005.

25. Gooya News, quoting Mehr News Agency, 13 June 2005.

26. Gooya News, 18 June 2005.

27. Baztab, 12 June 2005.

28. Gooya News, quoting ILNA, 20 June 2005. http://mag.gooya.com/president84/archives/031506.php.

29. The statement of the Islamic Iran Participation Front, 19 June 2005. http://mag.gooya.com/president84/archives/031420.php.

30. Associated Press, 21 June 2005.

31. ISNA, 24 June 2005.

32. ISNA, 26 June 2005.

33. Ali Akbar Hashemi Rafsanjani, ISNA, 25 June 2005.

34. *Guardian*, 26 June 2005.

35. Interview with the author.

36. 'Iran: A New Paradigm and New Math', Radio Free Europe/Radio Liberty, 26 June 2005. http://www.rferl.org/featuresarticle/2005/06/db1b7a87-c90b-4647-991b-49c00607a718.html.

37. Rajabi, *Ahmadinejad: The Miracle of the Third Millennium*, pp 285, 288.

Chapter 3. Apocalypse Now

1.   Ahmadinejad speaking in Kermanshah, Mehr News Agency, 19 December 2006.

2.   Aftab News, 6 November 2005, quoted by Hussein Bastani, Roozonline: 'Ahmadinejad in Touch with the 12th Imam'.

3.   Ahmadinejad press conference, Tehran, 31 December 2005. http://www.president.ir/fa/view.php?ArtID=2592.

4.   Fars News Agency, 11 November 2005.

5.   *Etemad Meli* (newspaper), 4 May 2007.

6.   Fars News Agency, 9 May 2007.

7.   Baztab, 27 November 2005. http://www.baztab.com/news/31076.php.

8.   Official website of the Jamkaran Mosque. http://www.jamkaran.info/fa/mosque/tarikhcheh/tarikhcheh.aspx.

9.   Scot Peterson, 'True Believers Dial Messiah Hotline in Iran: Energized by President's Beliefs, End-of-Timers Redouble Their Outreach, *Christian Science Monitor*, 4 January 2006.

10. *Jomhuri Islami*, 11 October 2006.

11. *Jomhuri Islami*, 13 September 2006.

12. Interview with Abdulkarim Soroush, Homa TV, 9 March 2006. http://www.drsoroush.com/Persian/Interviews/P-INT-13841218-HomaTV.html.

13. *Resalat* (newspaper), 29 March.

14. ILNA, 16 August 2003. http://akhbar.gooya.com/politics/archives/014798.php.

15. Baztab, 12 October 2005.

16. Ayatollah Mesbah-Yazdi's weekly publication, *Parto Sokhan*, no. 283 (2005).

17. Baztab, 27 December 2005.

18. Gooya News, 12 October 2004. http://akhbar.gooya.com/politics/

archives/017329.php.

19. Shahram Ragizadeh, 'A Review of the Serial Murders of Kerman',
     Gooya News, 14 October 2003. http://akhbar.gooya.com/politics/
     archives/000367.php.

20. Rohshangari.net, 3 July 2005. http://www.roshangari.net/as/ds.cgi?art
     =20050703092826.html.

21. Nazila Fathi, 'Iran Exonerates Six Who Killed in Islam's Name', New
     York Times, 19 April 2007.

22. Interview with the author.

23. 'Never in Iran's History Has Philosophy Been So Political: An Interview
     with Abdulkarim Soroush', by Maryam Kashani, January 2006. http://
     www.drsoroush.com/English.

24. Ibid..

25. Ibid.

Chapter 4. Iran's Nuclear Quest

1.   Ahmadinejad's election campaign speech, June 2005, in Nezamud-
     din Mousavi, The Ninth Presidential Elections (The Centre for National
     Documents of the Islamic Revolution), p 538.

2.   'Iranian Leader Says Nuke Program Like Train Without Brakes'. http://
     www.farsnews.net/newstext.php?nn=8512060238.

3.   Report by the Directory General, 11 March 2007. http://www.iaea.
     org/Publications/Documents/Board/2007/gov2007-08.pdf.

4.   Mohammad Sahimi, 'Iran's Nuclear Program. Part I. Its History'.
     http://www.payvand.com/news/03/oct/1015.html.

5.   'Reported Past Arguments Don't Square with Current Iran Policy',
     Washington Post, 26 March 2005. http://www.washingtonpost.com/wp-
     dyn/articles/A3983-2005Mar26.html.

6.   John K. Cooley, 'More Fingers on Nuclear Trigger?', Christian Science
     Monitor, 25 June 1974, quoted in Nuclear Threat Initiative, 'Iran Chro-
     nology'. http://www.nti.org/e_research/profiles/Iran/1825.html.

7.   Chris Quillen, 'Iranian Nuclear Weapons Policy, Past, Present and
     Possible Future'. http://meria.idc.ac.il/journal/2002/issue2/jv6n2a2.
     html. Mohammad Sahimi, 'Iran's Nuclear Program. Part I. Its History'.

http://www.payvand.com/news/03/oct/1015.html.

8. *Nucleonics Week*, 12 January 1978, pp 2–3, quoted in Daniel Poneman, *Nuclear Power in the Developing World* (London: George Allen & Unwin, 1982), p 88. http://www.nti.org/e_research/profiles/1825_1826.html.

9. 'Iran in Brief: Cost of Cancellation of Bushehr Nuclear Project', BBC Summary of World Broadcasts, 13 August 1979.

10. Nuclear Threat Initiative, 'Iran Chronology'. http://www.nti.org/e_research/profiles/Iran/1825.html.

11. Michael Rubin, 'Iran's Burgeoning WMD Programs'. http://www.meib.org/articles/0203_irn1.htm.

12. Frances Harrison, 'Iran Mulled Nuclear Bomb in 1988'. http://news.bbc.co.uk/1/hi/world/middle_east/5392584.stm, http://www.baztab.com/news/49451.php.

13. 'Rafsanjani Addresses Foreign Diplomats: Nuclear Weapons Are Against Iranian Ideology', BBC, 11 February 1995. http://www.nti.org/e_research/profiles/Iran/1825_6245.html.

14. 'Rafsanjani Says Mideast Nuclear Conflict Possible', Agence France-Presse, 14 December 2001, quoted by NTI.

15. Nuclear Threat Initiative, 'Iran Chronology'. http://www.nti.org/e_research/profiles/Iran/1825.html.

16. ISNA, 9 February 2003. http://www.isna.ir/Main/NewsView.aspx?ID=News-198694.

17. Leonard S. Spector, 'Secret Quest for the Bomb', *YaleGlobal*, 16 May 2003.

18. 'Iran Agrees to Suspend Uranium Enrichment', 15 November 2004. http://edition.cnn.com/2004/WORLD/meast/11/14/iran.nuclear.

19. 'Ahmadinejad Meets Members of Parliament', ILNA, 20 June 2005.

20. Mousavi, *The Ninth Presidential Elections*, p 538.

21. http://www.isna.ir/Main/NewsView.aspx?ID=News-567096.

22. ISNA, 8 October 2005. http://www.isna.ir/Main/NewsView.aspx?ID=News-567148.

23. Baztab, 15 November. 2004 http://www.baztab.com/news/18154.php.

24. Full text of President Ahmadinejad's speech at General Assembly, IRNA, 17 September 2005.

25. 'Iran May Share Nuclear Know-How', CNN, 15 September 2005. http://edition.cnn.com/2005/WORLD/meast/09/15/iran.nuclear/index.html.

26. 'Iran Offers to Share Nuclear Technology', Associated Press, 16 December 2006, Tehran.

27. 'Iran Offers to Share Nuclear Technology', Associated Press, 25 April 2006, Sudan.

28. Jason Burke, 'Meet the West's Worst Nightmare', Observer, 15 January 2006.

29. http://www.isna.ir/Main/NewsView.aspx?ID=News-585315.

30. http://www.un.org/News/Press/docs/2006/sc8928.doc.htm.

31. 'Iran to Defy Sanctions by Expanding Enrichment', Agence France-Presse, 24 December 2006. http://www.france24.com/france24Public/en/archives/news/middle-east/20061224-Iran-Nuclear-.html.

32. 'Iran Warns West of Historic Slap over Nuclear Drive', Agence France-Presse, 2 January 2007. http://www.spacewar.com/reports/Iran_Warns_West_Of_Historic_Slap_Over_Nuclear_Drive_999.html.

33. http://www.jonge-khabar.com/news/articlekhabar.php?id=21995.

34. 'Ahmadinejad on 16-Year-Old Nuclear Scientist', YouTube, added 20 February 2007.

35. 'Iran Warns West of Historic Slap over Nuclear Drive', Agence France-Presse, 2 January 2007. http://www.spacewar.com/reports/Iran_Warns_West_Of_Historic_Slap_Over_Nuclear_Drive_999.html.

36. 'Ahmadinejad: Iran Open to Talks', CNN, 11 May 2006. http://edition.cnn.com/2006/WORLD/asiapcf/05/11/indonesia.iran/index.html.

37. 'Iran Rules Out Backing Down', Agence France-Presse, 14 March 2006. http://www.iiss.org.uk/whats-new/iiss-in-the-press/press-coverage-2006/march-2006/iran-rules-out-backing-down.

38. Aftab News, 21 February 2007. http://www.aftabnews.ir/prtirvaw.t1ayp2.attax1zcdcbbnc.t.html.

39. Ahmad Zeidabadi, 'Atom and Nothing Else', Roozonline, 28 February 2007.

40. 'Iran Hits Milestone in Nuclear Technology', Associated Press, 11 April 2006. http://www.breitbart.com/article.php?id=D8GTUL906&show_

article=1.

41. *Kayhan* (newpaper), 12 April 2005. http://www.kayhannews. ir/850123/2.htm.

42. Report of the Director Geneal of the IAEA, 'Implementation of the NPT Safeguards Agreement in the Islamic Republic of Iran'. http:// www.iaea.org/Publications/Documents/Board/2006/gov2006-27.pdf.

43. George Jahn, 'IAEA Head: Iran Attack "Act of Madness"', Associated Press, 14 June 2007. http://news.yahoo.com/s/ap/20070614/ap_on_ re_eu/iran_nuclear_1.

44. *Ibid.*

45. *Ibid..*

46. Rob Broomby, 'Nuclear Watchdog's Attack Warning', BBC News, 6 June 2007. http://news.bbc.co.uk/1/hi/programmes/nuclear_detectives/6707457.stm.

47. Agence France-Presse, 16 June 2007. http://news.yahoo.com/ afp/20070616/pl_afp/usirannucleardiplomacy2_070616170825.

Chapter 5. Ahmadinejad vs. the World

1. President Ahmadinejad speaking at a press conference in Tehran, 24 April 2006.

2. 'Rafsanjani Says Mideast Nuclear Conflict Possible', Agence France-Presse, 14 December 2001, quoted in Nuclear Threat Initiative, 'Iran Chronology'. http://www.nti.org/e_research/profiles/Iran/1825_ 1878.html.

3. Speech, 17 January 2001, the Iranian Leader's website. http://www. leader.ir/langs/FA/index.php?p=news&id=839.

4. Speech at Intifada Conference, ISNA, 24 April 2001. http://www.isna. ir/Main/NewsView.aspx?ID=News-39454.

5. 'Iran Leader's Comments Attacked', BBC News, 27 October 2005. http://news.bbc.co.uk/1/hi/world/middle_east/4378948.stm.

6. *Jerusalem Post*, 8 May 2008. http://www.jpost.com/servlet/Satellite?cid =1145961301962&pagename=JPost/JPArticle/Printer.

7. BBC, 28 October 2005. http://newsvote.bbc.co.uk/mpapps/pagetools/ print/news.bbc.co.uk/2/hi/middle_east/4384264.stm.

8. *Kayhan*, 30 October 2005.
9. Agence France-Presse, 8 December 2005. http://www.breitbart.com/article.php?id=051208164944.y49anqze&show_article=1.
10. Associated Press, 10 December 2005: 'Saudis Fumining'. http://archive.newsmax.com/archives/articles/2005/12/9/164807.shtml.
11. Associated Press, 14 December 2005: 'Iran President: Holocaust a Myth'. http://www.cbsnews.com/stories/2005/12/14/world/main1124255.shtml.
12. Iranian Jewish MP, Moris Motamed, speaking on Radio Farda, 11 February 2006. http://www.radiofarda.com/Article/2006/02/11/20060211153017750.html.
13. Mosharekat Front statement, 12 December 2005. http://jomhouri.com/a/06ann/004937.php.
14. Michael A. Hoffman, 'Mahmoud Ahmadinejad: Prophet and Satirist'. http://www.revisionisthistory.org/revisionist17.html.
15. BBCPersian.com, 14 December 2006. http;//www.bbc.co.uk/persian/iran/story/2006/12/061214_mf_holocaust.shtml.
16. Ahmadinejad, press conference, 24 April 2005. http://www.president.ir/farsi/ahmadinejad/interviews/inter85/pdf/mosahebeh-850204.pdf.
17. 'Iran as Bad as Nazis', Times Online, 5 February 2006. http://www.timesonline.co.uk/tol/news/world/article727156.ece.
18. ISNA, 22 July 2006.

Chapter 6. A Wolf and a Sheep: US–Iran Relations

1. Ahmadinejad speaking in Kerman, 5 May 2007. See Baztab website, 'We Will Speak to Anyone Except Israel'.
2. Reuters, 21 February 1998.
3. Reuters, 2 February 1998.
4. Reuters, 18 February 1998.
5. Transcript of interview with Iranian president Mohammad Khatami, 7 January 1998. edition.cnn.com http://edition.cnn.com/WORLD/9801/07/iran/interview.html.
6. Associated Press, 18 June 1998.
7. *The Poison of Reform, Abdullah Nouri's Defence in the Special Court of the*

Clergy (Tarh-e-Now Publishers, 2000), p 117.

8. Azadeh Moaveni, *Lipstick Jihad: A Memoir of Growing Up Iranian in America and American in Iran* (Public Affairs, February 2005).

9. Agence France-Presse, 6 April 1999. http://www.iranian.com/News/2000/April/ershad.html.

10. Reuters, 16 January 1998.

11. Ahmadinejad's acquaintances in interviews with the author.

12. http://www.president.ir/fa/president/outlooks/si-kh-mb/siasat12.htm.

13. 'The New York Trip', the President's website. http://www.president.ir/fa/president/outlooks/si-kh-mb/siasat12.htm.

14. Highly placed source in private conversation with the author.

15. Private conversations with the author.

16. Highly placed source in private conversation with the author.

17. IRNA, 8 May 2006.

18. *New York Times*, 9 May 2006. http://www.iht.com/articles/2006/05/09/news/iran.php.

19. *Ibid.*

20. Letter of Karroubi to Jannati, ISNA, 16 May 2006.

21. CBC News, 29 August 2006. http://www.cbc.ca/world/story/2006/08/29/iran-uranium.html.

22. Baztab, 11 January 2007.

23. President's Address to the Nation, the White House website. http://www.whitehouse.gov/news/releases/2007/01/20070110-7.html.

24. Robin Wright, *Washington Post*, 12 January 2007. http://www.washington-post.com/wp-dyn/content/article/2007/01/11/AR2007011100427.html.

25. *Ibid.*

26. *Ibid.*

27. Patrick Cockburn, *Independent*, 3 April 2007. http://news.independent.co.uk/world/middle_east/article2414760.ece. *Washington Post*, 14 April 2007.

28. Baztab, 24 January 2007.

29. Baztab, 20 January 2007.

30. Aftab News, 2 March 2007.

31. For the full text of the interview, see Baztab, 24 January 2007.
32. Mohammed Abbas, aboard USS *John C. Stennis*, Reuters, 23 May 2007.
33. *Ibid.*
34. Ahmadinejad; 'We Will Speak to Anyone Except Israel', Baztab, 5 May 2007.
35. Fars News Agency, 9 May 2007.
36. Nasser Karimi, 'Iran Leader Takes Hard Line in Backing Talks with US', Associated Press, 17 May 2007. http://www.boston.com/news/world/articles/2007/05/17/iran_leader_takes_hard_line_in_backing_talks_with_us.
37. www.president.ir, 5 June 2007.

Chapter 7. Iran in Turmoil

1. Presidential campaign speech, IRNA, 9 June 2005.
2. ISNA, 2 July 2005.
3. IRNA, 9 June 2005.
4. ISNA, 2 July 2007.
5. Fred Halliday, 'Iran's Revolutionary Spasm, Open Democracy'. http://www.opendemocracy.net/content/articles/PDF/2642.pdf.
6. Gooya News, quoting Ansar News, 17 May 2005.
7. *Ibid.*
8. Roozonline, 24 April 2007.
9. 'Ahmadinejad Decision Leads to Riots', Roozonline, 24 April 2007.
10. Najmeh Bozorgmehr, 'Iran President Takes Message to People', *Financial Times*, 23 April 2007. http://search.ft.com/ftArticle?queryText=On+the+road+with+Iran%E2%80%9A%C3%84%C3%B4s+populist+president&y=8&aje=true&x=10&id=070423000117.
11. Baztab, the full text of the challenging interview of France 2 with Ahmadinejad, 23 March 2007, http://www.baztab.com/news/63403.php.
12. ISNA, 3 August 2005.
13. http://www.iranmania.com/News/ArticleView/Default.asp?NewsCode=39251&NewsKind=Current%20Affairs.

14. Emruz.Info, 8 March 2007. http://emruz.info/ShowItem. aspx?ID=5865&p=1.

15. http://www.president.ir/fa/view.php?ArtID=671.

16. 'Ortega's Visit: This is Most Amazing', 10 June 2007. http://www. roozonline.com/archives/2007/06/005111.php.

17. 'We Will Rebuild from Scratch', *Hambastegi* (newspaper), 7 June 2007.

18. Fars News Agency, 15 June 2007. http://www.farsnews.net/newstext. php?nn=8603250157.

19. Aftab News, 20 June 2005.

20. BBCPersian.com, 25 June 2005. http://www.bbc.co.uk/persian/business/story/2005/06/printable/050625_ra-ahmadi-stock.shtml.

21. Roshangari, 30 October 2005, quoting Roozonline http://www. roshangari.net/as/ds.cgi?art=20051030083511.html.

22. Jamshid Amuzegar, 'The Ahmadinejad Era: Preparing for the Apocalypse', *Journal of International Affairs*, Spring/Summer 2007.

23. Member of Parliamentary Commission on Industry, speaking to *Hambasteghi* (newspaper), 14 June 2007.

24. 'Banking System Awaiting a Second Tsunami', Aftab News, 25 May 2007. http://www.aftabnews.ir/vdcayun496n6i.html.

25. 'Iran Forecasts 60 Billion Dollars Oil Income', Agence France-Presse, 25 June 2006.

26. 'Open Letter of Economists to the President', Economic News Agency, 2 July 2006.

27. *Kargozaran* (newspaper), 12 June 2007.

28. Jahangir Amuzegar, 'The Ahmadinejad Era: Preparing for the Apocalypse', *Journal of International Affairs*, spring/summer 2007.

29. 'I Know What They Are Angry About!', Aftab News, 5 March 2006.

30. Robert Tait, *Observer*, 28 January 2007.

31. *Ibid.*

32. Fars News Agency, 10 January 2007.

33. 'Questions and Answers with Members of Parliament: 'I Will Cut the Hands of the Power and Oil Mafia', Baztab, 20 June 2005.

34. IRNA, 26 January 2007.

35. 'Oil Money on the Dinner Table of the Chinese and Europeans', ILNA,

26 January 2007.

36. 'We Do Not Want Oil Money', Aftab News, 3 March 2007.

37. Interview with the author.

38. ISNA, 5 September 2006.

39. Iranian Channel One, 25 July 2005, quoted by the Middle East Media Research Institute (MEMRI).

40. President's website. www.president.ir, farsi section: viewpoints, arts and artists.

41. Lillian Swift, 'Iran is on the Brink of a Dark Age', Daily Telegraph, 19 November 2005. http://www.telegraph.co.uk/news/main.jhtml?xml=/news/2005/11/20/wiran120.xml&sSheet=/news/2005/11/20/ixnewstop.html.

42. 'Iran's President Bans All Western Music', Associated Press, 19 December 2005.

43. BBCPersian.com, 19 Janauary 2006.

44. 'When All the 180 Books of a Publisher Get Rejected', Roozonline, 7 May 2004.

45. 'Protests against Censorship in Cinema and Theater, Roozonline, 7 May 2007.

46. Reza Jahani, 'Ahmadinejad Team Control Iranian Cinema', Roozonline, 22 May 2007.

47. 'Protests against Censorship in Cinema and Theater, Roozonline, 7 May 2007.

48. BBC Monitoring quotes from Iranian press, 7 June 2007.

49. Internet technology site www.citna.ir, 11 September 2006. http://www.citna.ir/435.html.

50. 'Reporters without Borders', 20 December 2005. http://www.rsf.org/article.php3?id_article=15956.

51. 'Ahmadinejad Meets Parliamentarians', ILNA, 20 June 2005.

52. Baztab, 24 April 2006.

53. Baztab, 25 April 2006.

54. BBCPersian.com, 27 April 2007. http://www.bbc.co.uk/persian/iran/story/2007/04/printable/070427_mf_ahmadinejad.shtml.

55. 'Two Children Are Not Enough', Baztab, 23 October 2006.

56.   Fatemeh Rahbar, Baztab, 30 October 2006.

57.   'Not So Fast Mr President', *Etemad-e-Melli* (editorial), 23 October 2006.

Chapter 8. Friends in High Places

1.   Ayatollah Ali Khamenei's speech to supporters of the Islamic Revolution, 4 June 2006. http://www.leader.ir/langs/FA/index. php?p=bayan&id=3140.

2.   Behruz Khlique, 'The Position of the Guards and the Clergy in the Power Structure'. http://www.falsafeh.com/sepah_khaligh.htm.

3.   http://www.isna.ir/Main/NewsView.aspx?ID=News-563781   08-03-2005.

4.   Baztab, 3 February 2006. http://www.baztab.com/news/34849.php.

5.   http://www.kayhannews.ir/850822/3.htm.

6.   *Kayhan* (newspaper), 13 November 2006. http://www.kayhannews. ir/850822/3.htm.

7.   Baztab, 12 November 2006.

8.   Leader's speech, 4 June 2006. http://www.leader.ir/langs/FA/index. php?p=bayan&id=3140

9.   Baztab, 2 July 2005.

10.   ISNA, 29 June 2005.

11.   SharifNews.ir, 1 June 2005.

12.   *Ibid*.

13.   IRNA, 12 May 2006.

14.   'Karroubi's Letter to Jannati', ISNA, 16 May 2006.

15.   ISNA, 9 June 2007.

16.   Qabas: The Imam Khomeini Education and Research Institute. http:// www.qabas.org/farsi/index.htm.

Epilogue. In a Make-Believe World

1.   Ahmadinejad speaking to journalists in Tehran on his return from a visit to New York to attend the 62nd UN General Assembly, 28 September 2007.

INDEX